To Melissa —
Thanks for the support.
Enjoy every step of the
journey. — *Erin*

broken bits

and

GLITTER

Erika Worth

a memoir

ERIKA WORTH

ROAR Voices

AUTHOR NOTE :

All of the stories in this book are true. Some people and conversations are composites. Some names have been changed.

Published by Roar Voices LLC :

1701 Broadway #340

Vancouver, WA 98663

http://www.roarvoices.com

Cover art by Scott Clarke

Author photography by Irina Negrean Photography

Edited by Kristen Corrects

ISBN: 978-0-9998138-0-5 (print)

ISBN: 978-0-9998138-1-2 (eBook)

Libary of Congress Catalog Number : 2018900341

First Edition: January 2018

Printed in the United States of America

for Momma
with my undying love

and for anyone who feels too broken to breathe
this is for you

CONTENTS

preface

I've been telling my stories in recovery and performance circles for thirty years. What it was like. What happened. What it's like now. Those are safe environments where we speak freely about embarrassing, awful things we've done, then laugh (and cry) about them. It's how we heal. We uncover, discover, and discard shame, secrets, and mistakes and replace them with courage and hope.

Because of this experience, I (hysterically) assumed writing this book would take no more than a few months. These stories are ancient history. I'd done the work decades ago. The wounds are healed. How hard could this be?

Four years later, my skin is tissue-paper thin. I'm either laughing hysterically, weeping (which might be hormonal), or waxing poetic about days gone by. But I finished the thing I swore I could not do. And that's something.

I would be remiss if I didn't say in big bold letters **TRIGGER WARNING**. Some of these stories are extremely graphic. They are not told to traumatize the reader. I can only tell my story one way—messy, raw, vulnerable, fierce. The broken bits are only part of my story, and I tell them from the other side of healing. I'm still alive, and that is nothing short of a miracle.

This is my journey through shame: inheriting it, acting out in it, processing it, and releasing it. These stories are my way of hanging lanterns in shadowy halls for anyone still going through it. *Do not give up.*

I am privileged to be a woman in the middle of my life. Not everyone makes it here. I honor the generations of women who came before me who were stifled and silenced, who nobly fought for the rights I have today, and for the ones who suffered in silence. Thank you. To the generations of young women behind me, the future is yours. I am in awe of your possibility.

Somewhere in between, I've had the good fortune of having my worst fears realized. Only through survival have I realized nothing can break me. There is a grace and dignity that comes from perspective, from seeing the interconnectedness of the events of my life—each one necessary for the next.

This has been one hell of a ride so far. Welcome to my journey.

Lastly, I could not possibly tell my story without music. It has been the constant backdrop of my life. It's how I first learned there were other people in the world who felt like me, and that I wasn't alone. Music is attached to every memory, so each chapter title is a song which sets the mood for that time and place. There's a playlist on Spotify if you're interested.

we are fine

I'm obsessed with an old photograph of my mother. She's eighteen or nineteen, a beautiful young hippie in the late '60s. Her flaxen hair hangs down the front of her brown vest. She's wearing brown bellbottoms and leather sandals. She sits in the driver's seat of a van and stares off at something in the distance I can't see. I like to imagine in that moment she felt hopeful. Happy.

I show Momma the picture and ask her what she wanted from life as a young woman.

"To be free," she says.

"Free? Free from what?"

"Free from my mother." Her voice cracks with pain, and her eyes glaze over. She drifts away from the moment.

I didn't mean to push a pain button. Her emotional landmines are hard to avoid. "No, Momma. What about before?" I gently rub her back and try to lighten the mood. "What did you dream of being when you were a little girl?"

"There was no before," she whispers. "The only dream I ever had was to get away from my mother."

At sixty-nine years old, Momma is still haunted by the wounds from her mother, a woman who didn't want her, who never once wrapped her arms around her daughter and told her she loved her. Years of scathing criticism and emotional abandonment grew like cancerous tumors onto Momma's belief about herself.

I know there's nothing I can say or do to heal her. The dull throb of my own inheritance from my mother tightens in my belly, but I don't want my truth to hurt her, so I stay silent.

In our family, we don't pass down heirloom quilts or boxes of family recipes. Our legacy is the annihilation of our daughters. Thick emotional scars twist deep beneath our skin.

Momma looks at the photograph and almost smiles. "I was so beautiful then, but I never felt it. *She* always told me how fat and ugly I was. Even when I was a little girl."

I go to hug her, but stop myself. As much as we love each other, we can wound without warning. When a storm settles over one of us, the other knows to keep her distance. "Momma, you're still beautiful."

She runs her fingers through her thinning hair. "No. I'm not. I'll never be beautiful again. I'm practically bald. My eyelids sag so much I can hardly see. My nose has a big ball on the end. My neck hangs like a turkey." She pinches the flesh of her neck between her fingers. "Look at this skin..."

This laundry list of Momma's physical shortcomings is the remnant of my grandmother's vanity. She taught us a woman's only value is in her perfection. At my grandmother's funeral, the minister asked if anyone wanted to share fond memories. One by one, acquaintances remarked on her beauty and how she always kept an immaculate home. They neglected to mention that two of her four children and most of her friends weren't in attendance. Those who truly knew my grandmother knew she was human poison wrapped in a beautiful cocoon. The family who showed up remained silent in the front row, except for Momma, who was beside herself with grief.

"...and a tummy tuck and lipo," she continues.

"Oh, Momma. You're being silly."

"When are you going to get rich so I can have plastic surgery?"

"If I'm ever a bajillionaire, you'll have so much work done I won't even recognize you. Some blonde stranger resembling Joan Rivers will knock on the door and claim to be my mother."

She laughs, and the sadness spell is broken. "I won't knock on your door. I'll be in Scotland chasing men in kilts," she says.

"Sam Heughan had better be careful." I wink.

The mention of Sam Heughan tinges my mother's cheeks a rosy pink and she giggles like a schoolgirl.

"So when is your book going to be finished?"

She's asked me this question no less than 382 times. I could do without the daily reminder that I haven't finished. I take a deep breath and smile. "I'm working on it, Momma. It's a process."

"Why aren't you done yet? You're only forty-seven. How much is there to talk about?"

The words are innocent enough, but her tone stings. The closer I get to finishing it, the louder my self-doubt rages. I don't need any extra negativity, as I have an ample supply of my own. "You should write a book sometime. See how easy it is." I quip.

"I still don't see why you have to write a *memoir*. Why don't you work on that other story? The science fiction one."

She doesn't say it, but I know she's afraid. I am too. I have always been her protector, and the keeper of secrets. But silence has never healed our wounds.

"You know I'm not doing this to hurt you, right?" *You're going to be sad and afraid no matter what I do.* "I love you more than any other human in the world."

"I just don't see why you have to talk about all this stuff. It's ancient history. Aren't you afraid of what people will think?"

"A little, but I need to do this, even if it terrifies me. Partly because it terrifies me."

"You never seem afraid. You do all sorts of things *I* never could. You stand on stage in front of people. *I* could never do that. You can go up and talk to people. *I* was always too shy. You run your own business. *I always worked at jobs I hated, because I had to make money to raise you."*

"This isn't about you. And just because I do things doesn't mean I'm not terrified. I just refuse to let fear own me. I don't want to die with regrets about choices I was too scared to make."

Kaboom. I hit another one.

She crosses her arms in front of her and stares out the window, sadness frosts over the icy pools of her eyes. "I've made so many mistakes. I never should have moved us to California. We should have stayed in Virginia. Your life would have been so different. I've always been such a failure."

"Geez, Mom, I wasn't talking about you, or your choices. I was talking about me. Look at me."

She continues to stare out the window.

"I have a spectacular life. I don't regret anything from the past, including moving to California. I have a one-hundred percent survival rate of everything that's ever happened. None of it killed me. I'm so grateful for all of it, including the pain."

She clenches onto her sadness and refuses to let go.

I soften my tone. "Maybe I went through all of that crap to do exactly what I'm doing now, to be useful in some unique way. Maybe this is why I'm here."

"Everything could have been so different. I never had a chance with a mother like her." She absently chews on the end of her fingernail.

I am thirty years sober. As a private investigator, I keep people safe. As the creator of ROAR, I strive to empower women and girls. I want to raise women's voices to heal us, to cast spotlights on shadowy corners, to break cycles of abuse and silence. The irony that I can't reach my own mother is not lost on me.

She makes me want to pull my hair out sometimes, but she is also one of my greatest teachers. I am who I am in part *because* she is my mother. She had no voice of her own, so I learned to roar. She had no self-worth to give me, so I've spent my entire life seeking it, trying to infuse value into others around me.

"Momma, she's gone now, and you still have plenty of years left in you."

"I'll be dead soon enough."

"Ugh. Don't say that. You're sixty-nine, not a hundred. We'll be driving each other crazy for years to come."

"You'll put me in a home. I'll end up alone, with Alzheimer's just like *her.*"

She is no longer my sun, moon, and stars, the woman who abandoned me, the woman I want to war with, or a distant stranger. Today, she is my heart, and whatever time we have left is precious. The thought of being in this world without her shreds me. Intimately acquainted with death, I have no idea how I will survive hers.

I give her a bear hug and pepper her temple with kisses. "Never gonna happen, Momma. I'll hire a bevy of half-naked Scotsmen in kilts to feed you grapes and rub your feet. Promise."

She laughs, and the world is right again.

the hurting

From the passenger seat of my best friend's Hyundai, I try to shake off my depression as we head to a party in Venice.

"Hey. Where are you?" asks Stacey. She snaps her fingers in front of my face.

"I'm here. Just devastated you're abandoning me."

"Like, oh my gawd, Erika. I just graduated from high school. It's not like I'm moving to another country."

"You might as well be. How am I going to survive without you?"

"I'm only going to Pierce College. We just won't ditch class together anymore. And it's your senior year. Believe me, it'll fly by."

"Whatever. It's a major bummer and it won't be the same without you." I flick the class of 1987 tassel that hangs from her rear view mirror, then look out the window to inspect people in other cars on the 405.

A middle-aged, balding man driving a sedan picks his nose. His wife hands a tissue over her shoulder to a young boy in the back seat. An ancient, wrinkled woman grips her steering wheel, her hands firmly at ten and two. On top of her head is a tuft of hair that looks like a dollop of lavender whipped cream. She's so tiny, she can barely see over the steering wheel of her vintage Mercedes. A handsome man driving a black BMW talks on a car phone. His gold watch and tan skin glisten in the sun. Two blonde teenage girls in a Volkswagen convertible seat dance to music.

"Do you ever think about other people? What their lives are like?" I ask.

"Um, not really. You think way too much. Can you check the directions and make sure we're going the right way?"

I grab the paper with Stacey's scribble on it and guide us to the party. I get out and stand next to her gold Hyundai, trying to see my reflection in the glass of the passenger window. "Hey Stacey, do I look okay?" I adjust the shoulder pads of my black, V-neck T-shirt, center my wide black belt, then pull up my black-stretch mini skirt, making it even shorter.

"Here, let me see."

I turn to face her, and she inspects me from my intensely teased and abused hair to the toes of my cherry-red stiletto pumps.

"Like, oh my God, you look totally rad. How about me?"

She's wearing an American flag T-shirt, denim miniskirt, and red sandals. "Our Founding Fathers would be very proud of you, but your bangs could use a little oomph." I reach into my oversized purse, pull out my can of Aqua Net White, and spritz and shape her bangs a bit. I decide to douse my hair in a fresh cloud for good measure, put the can back in my purse, and pull out a cigarette. "Like, you *totally* look like a crimped goddess. John Taylor would marry you if he saw you right now." I light my cigarette, careful to keep the flame away from my sky-high mane.

"Oh my God, I fucking love you. Happy fourth of July. Let's go get fucked up."

"Awesome." I carefully navigate my heels around the cracks in the jagged Venice sidewalk. "Whose party is this again?"

"I don't know. Some girl named Fiona that Erin knows. It's a bunch of older people in their twenties. She promised there would be a ton of free booze." Stacey looks at the scrap of paper with the address on it, then squints at the 1940s bungalow we're standing in front of. "This is it."

We walk up the driveway and through the side gate, following the party noises coming from the back of the house. About forty people are standing around in the back yard, beer bottles and red Solo cups in hand. Echo and the Bunnymen blare out of the speaker propped in one of the windows facing the yard. My heels sink into the grass.

"Geez, Stacey, I'm going to kill myself walking here."

"Let's go inside and find Erin."

"And alcohol," I chime in.

I wobble behind her as she heads to the cooler by the back-door stairs. She grabs one Corona, I grab two, then we head into the kitchen. A handful of guys are deep in conversation about *Full Metal Jacket*. We walk past them and continue to the living room, where we find a space to stand in front of a big picture window. X's *Los Angeles* starts to blare through the house.

"Oh my God, I love this song." I down the first Corona, then take a few gulps of the second to try to still my nerves. Sobriety always makes me uncomfortable. "Do you see Erin?"

"Not yet, but she definitely said she was coming." Stacey sniffs the air like a bloodhound. "I wonder who's got weed."

I take a drag on my cigarette and bob my head frenetically to the music in true punk-rock/Valley Girl fashion. I look around the room and see him watching me. He doesn't flinch or look away, just stares at me. I look around to see who else he could be looking at, but there are just a few guys next to us and a couple in the corner. Trying my best to look casual, I turn back toward his direction. He's still laser-focused on me. "Like, oh my God, Stacey, I could just, like, totally *die* right now. Look at that guy," I whisper, then chug more of my beer.

Stacey stretches her five-foot-ten frame even taller, looks over my head, and asks loudly, "What guy? Where? Who?" She looks around the room, squinting, because she can't see a thing without her glasses.

"Shhh. What are you trying to do, give me a heart attack? He's behind me. Bandana. Intense eyes."

She looks over my head, squints a little more, then her eyes widen. "Oh my God, Erika. He's *hawt*. And he's staring right at you."

"Oh my God. I'm, like, wigging out to the absolute max. There's probably something on my ass. Can you see if—"

"Shhh." Stacey plasters her biggest princess smile across her face, and talks through her teeth like a ventriloquist. "He's walking over here. Smile."

I'm fairly certain my face now matches my shoes, and before I can dart to the bathroom to hide, he's standing to my left. He doesn't look at Stacey, just stares right at me. I'm lost in the magnetic, steely eyes of Mr. Beautiful. He looks like Mickey Rourke and Billy Idol's love child. Six feet tall, shirtless, tan, wearing long Dickies shorts and combat boots. A red bandana covers his head. I don't think I've ever seen a more bitchin' dude in my entire life, and the way he looks at me is like he sees my soul. I guzzle down the rest of my Corona.

"Hey, beautiful. I'm Patrick."

I'm so lost in staring at him, it takes me a second to realize he's actually speaking to me.

Stacey chimes in. "Hey, Patrick. I'm Stacey. This is Erika."

He moves an inch closer to me, and I can smell the Coppertone on his bronzed skin. "Hmm. Erika. Beautiful name for a beautiful girl."

Be cool, Erika. Be cool. "Thanks. Hi. I mean, hey. Nice to meet you." I try to pretend like talking to drop-dead-gorgeous men every day is no big deal.

He lights two Marlboros and hands me one. The romantic gesture makes me swoon. He's better than Nicolas Cage in *Valley Girl.*

"I was just going to get another drink. You two want anything?" he asks.

"I'll take another Corona. And do you know where can I get some weed?" asks Stacey.

Patrick reaches into his cigarette box and hands Stacey a joint. *Wow. Handsome and generous. He's fucking Prince Charming.*

"And for you, beautiful?" He runs his fingers down my back and electricity shoots through me.

"Oh, I'll have whatever you're having."

"Can you handle whiskey?" He moves his hand slowly up my back, then wraps a crispy tendril of my hair gently around his finger. He brushes my left cheek with the back of his fingers and moves closer to me. I can feel the warmth of his skin.

Breathe, Erika. Just breathe. I swear I'm going to melt into a puddle, but my skeleton miraculously remains intact and I fidget and try to stay balanced on my stilettos. I clear my throat, then respond, "I can handle whatever you've got." My face flushes, but I don't care.

"Good girl." He squeezes my hand before walking back through the kitchen.

"Jesus Christ, Erika. I thought I was going to need a fire extinguisher to put you two out. Talk about chemistry!"

"So I wasn't just imagining all of that?"

"Um, no. That was super intense. He didn't even see me. Can I borrow your lighter? Mine's not working."

I distractedly hand her my Bic, lost in a fantasy of my future relationship with Patrick. Him kissing and making sweet love to me. Us holding hands. Him loving me. Stacey lights the joint, inhales, and hands it to me. I shake my head no and light up another cigarette instead.

"There you bitches are. Where have you been?"

I turn to see Erin grinning at us.

Stacey exhales and we're surrounded in a plume of smoke. "We've been looking for you. And Erika's picked herself up a new boyfriend in the span of about five minutes. Or a hot fuck at the very least."

"He is not just a fuck!" I protest. "He's a fucking dreamboat."

"Who is he? Point him out to me." Erin grabs the joint from Stacey and scans the room.

"He went outside to get us drinks. His name is Patrick. Pretty fucking intense from what I saw. He never took his eyes off Erika."

"Patrick? Oh shit. Is he wearing a bandana? No shirt?" asks Erin, taking another huge toke off the joint.

"Quit bogarting." Stacey snatches it back from Erin.

"Yeah, that's him. Why? Do you know him?" If there's dirt on my fantasy boyfriend, I want to hear it.

She leans in closer to us and lowers her voice. "That's Fiona's ex, and according to her, he's *psycho*. He used to live in here with her, but when they broke up he moved into the back house. He made a side deal with the landlord, so there's no way she can get him out."

Already feeling defensive of my new crush, I chime in. "He doesn't seem psycho at all. He seems really sweet, actually. Different."

"Oh, fuck, she's sprung already. Typical Erika," chides Erin.

"Oh, bite me. That is so not true. And Fiona's probably bitter he doesn't want her anymore. Patrick is rad."

Suddenly, I feel his warmth behind me and his breath on my neck. "So, I'm rad, huh?"

How I don't pass out on the spot is beyond me. I clear my throat. "Um, yeah. So far, I mean...well, yeah."

Patrick hands Stacey her beer and me a red cup half-full of whiskey, then winks at me while he drinks out of his cup. I take a few gulps to calm my nerves.

"Well, well, well. Hello, Patrick." Erin is smiling, but there's bitchiness in her saccharine sweetness.

A flicker of iciness flashes in his eyes, but vanishes so quickly I must have imagined it. "Hey, Erin. I thought you were joining the Army?"

"I am. I go in next week. This is my last weekend of freedom, so I figured I'd go out with a bang."

"I did my time. Good luck." He turns his attention back to me, and he's all warmth and intensity again. "Come with me. I want to show you something." He grabs my hand and leads me away from the girls.

I look back at them with a shit-eating grin and wiggle my fingers at them. "Bye, ladies."

"Don't do anything I wouldn't do," Stacey yells behind me as I'm pulled away.

He guides me through the party to his studio guesthouse at the back of the property. His place is meticulous. Cozy. Dark hardwood floors. To the left is a small table and two chairs, behind which is a small kitchenette with a fridge and small stove. Straight ahead is a queen-size bed, the sight of which gives me goosebumps. The wall to the right of the bed is a long closet, and to the right of the front door is the bathroom.

"Wow. Cool pad."

"Thanks, beautiful." He closes the front door behind me, then gently pushes me back against it. I drop my purse to the floor and kick my shoes off. He braces his right hand against the wall near my head. His left hand strokes my cheek, his thumb traces my lips. Taking the red cup out of my hand, he holds it up to my lips. "Drink," he commands. I do, and the whiskey burns its way down my throat, adding to the warm fire in my belly. "More."

I grin at him. "You have no idea who you're dealing with." I guzzle the contents until my cup is empty.

His eyes widen and he chuckles. "Whoa. I'm fucking impressed. You weren't kidding."

"There are certain things I never kid about."

"Fuck, Erika. You really are my kind of girl."

Jesus. Is this really happening? I stare into his eyes, trying to mask my need, and wait for him to fulfill my fantasy. He doesn't disappoint. Leaning down, he brushes his lips against mine ever so gently. Gratitude washes over me and I want to cry. I suddenly feel wanted. Unbroken.

His kisses grow more intense. His tongue probes my mouth, searching for ownership. I give it to him willingly. His lips move across my cheek. He nibbles on my ear, then sucks on and bites my neck. The sensation is the perfect combination of pleasure and pain. Every nerve in my body sings.

"Wrap your legs around me," he orders.

I don't hesitate, and as he lifts me up, I wrap my limbs around him. He carries me to the bed and lies back on it. I'm now on top, straddling him. I can't look away.

"My God, Erika, look at you, and those eyes. You're a fucking angel." He secures a hand on each hip. "Except for all the hairspray and makeup. You don't need that shit."

Damn. Where did he come from?

He undoes the belt around my waist and tosses it on the floor. "Take off your shirt. Slowly."

Turns out a big cup of whiskey mixed with one part fear, three parts lust, and a dash of excitement is the perfect recipe for an intoxication cocktail. Seeing myself through his eyes, I feel beautiful. I want to make him as happy as he's making me, so I start to pull my T-shirt off—slowly, as instructed.

He drinks me in, scanning my eyes, then his gaze moves slowly down my face, my neck, then to my chest. Even though he's not touching me, I can feel him on my skin. I'm infected. He sits up and buries his face in my cleavage, smothers my face with more kisses. Clenching his fist in the back of my hair, he pulls my head back, exposing the other side of my neck to his teeth and tongue. Without taking my bra off, he pulls down the black lace fabric, exposing my nipples, which he sucks and nibbles on painfully. He shifts his cannibalistic desire from my nipples to the flesh surrounding them. The sensation is otherworldly, and I close my eyes, drunk and lost and found all at the same time. Resistance and propriety are abandoned, and I moan loudly.

"Erika, look at me."

My eyes snap open and I stare at him. Normally, I hide and play games with men, safely hidden away in plain sight. But Patrick *sees* me, and it feels like destiny. I search his eyes for some indication of what he wants next.

"See these?" He drags his finger across the fresh hickeys emerging across the skin on my chest.

Holy shit. I didn't realize that's what he was doing. Oh my God. If Mom sees this I'm going to be—

"These are mine. Understand?" He cups a hand around each

breast.

Oh fuck. He was marking his territory. He wants me to be his. A man's hands are my weakness, and his are sculpted perfection. Strong with thick fingers. Veins like rivulets mark the tops of them, and they fit perfectly around my breasts. Some invisible cord connects us, breathes new life into me. Dad doesn't want me. Mom hates me. No one else matters. Only Patrick. This makes no sense, but it's right, I just know it.

"Did you hear me?" he asks, sinking his fingers into my ivory flesh.

I whisper my response to him, "Yes."

"Yes, what?"

Usually sarcastic and witty or loaded and shut down, I've never been the submissive type. Control is a precious commodity, one I've fought my whole life to keep. I could respond with some clever quip, but I don't want to. I *want* to be his, to belong to something other than my loneliness and damage. I place my hands over his. "These are yours." I'm not just saying what he wants to hear. I mean every word.

"Good girl." He rewards me with a gentle kiss.

He shifts us around so he's now lying on top of me, his elbows braced on either side of my head. The full weight of him pressed against me is exquisite.

"Wrap your legs back around me."

I do exactly as I'm told. My skirt has risen and, since I'm not wearing underwear, his shorts are now the only barrier between us. With intense pressure, he gyrates his torso between my legs. Aching to feel him inside of me, I respond in kind, raising my hips to match his rhythm. Through his shorts, I feel how much he wants me. I groan and wrap my legs tighter around him, pulling him closer to me.

"I'm going to make long, slow love to you, and fill up every inch of you," he whispers in my ear, "but not yet." In a flash, he's up off the bed and adjusting himself in his shorts, which now have a huge wet spot on them.

I gasp. He might as well have just poured an ice-cold bucket of water all over me. *What just happened? Why doesn't he want me? What did I do wrong?*

"Listen, angel, don't look so sad. Can you spend the night?"

Trying to catch my breath and speak proves challenging. "Um, fer sure. Mom already thinks I'm staying at Stacey's. But I don't have a car. Can you take me back to the valley tomorrow?"

"A valley girl, huh?"

I roll my eyes at him. "Like, I just live there. I'm totally not like them."

"Like, really?" He imitates my accent.

"Okay. Maybe the accent. But I'm not like them. I'm not like anyone."

"No, doll, you're not. Of course I can take you back. I don't have to be at work until Monday."

I roll over on my left side and prop my head up on my hand. "So, what do you do, anyway?" I suddenly realize I know nothing about him except that I'm willing to surrender to him completely.

"I was in the Army for a while. Been in a few bands. Now I work as a telemarketer. You?"

Shit, this might be the end before we've even begun. Um, actually, I'm still in high school. I start my senior year this fall."

"What school?"

"Alemany?"

"Never heard of it."

"It's a private Catholic school in the north end of the valley."

He lies next to me, leaning on his right side facing me. "Does that mean you wear those little plaid skirts?" he asks and bites his lower lip.

"Ha. Yeah. I always feel like a dork in those skirts. It amazes me men find them attractive."

"I think you would be hot in anything. Or nothing." He leans over and kisses me. "Where did a Catholic school girl learn to kiss like that?"

"I'm not actually Catholic, and that's all you," I coo back at him.

"How old did you say you are?"

"Seventeen...and a half." I search his reaction for rejection, but he doesn't flinch. "How old are you?"

"Twenty-two. I'll be twenty-three in December."

"So my age doesn't bother you?"

"Baby girl, nothing about you bothers me." He brushes his fingers against my cheek again.

I swear no gesture has ever felt as sweet.

"So, you live at home with your parents?" He rests his hand on my hip while we talk.

"Just my mom, actually."

"Where's your dad?"

Here we go. I look away from him, focus down at our feet, uneasy about telling him the truth.

He puts his hand under my chin and looks right into my soul again. "There's nothing you can't tell me, Erika."

Don't tell him the truth. He'll throw you away if you do. Just lie. "I've never actually met my dad. I don't know anything about him, except for some pictures I found a couple of years ago. Before that, I didn't even know what he looked like. My mom won't talk about him, except when she's pissed at me. Then she tells me I'm just like him, but I never know what she means and she never explains."

The moment the words come out of my mouth, I feel stupid and pathetic. I'm afraid to look at him. He doesn't say anything, just wraps his arms around me, and I bury my cheek against his warm chest, breathing in the smell of him. His was the absolute perfect response. *I could get used to this.*

"So, your mom never married?"

"Once, right before I turned one. It didn't work out so well. He fucked with their money then took off, leaving her with a shitload of bills. I remember them coming and taking our furniture. It takes two years to get a divorce in Virginia, and he kept racking up debts. Mom was broke for a while, so I went to live with my grandparents in Pennsylvania until she could get back on her feet. Then she met her boyfriend, George, which is how we ended up in L.A."

"And what happened with him?"

I try to put on my tough-girl act. I think about what lie I can tell him, or whether I should give him a blowjob to distract him from the question. The last thing I want to tell him is the truth.

"Erika, where are you right now?"

I look at him and I don't feel like I could hide anything from him, even if I wanted to. I take a deep breath. "I was eleven when we moved in with him. Within a year, he started...he..." The tears come and I'm powerless to stop them.

"Aw, babe, it's okay. I'm here now. I'll look out for you. No motherfucker will ever mess with you while I'm around."

He kisses the tears streaming down my cheeks. Kisses my eyelids. The tip of my nose. Sweetly kisses my lips, and I fall head-over-heels in hopeless gratitude with him.

"Fuck, Patrick, where did you come from?"

"Santa Monica," he says, smiling. "Come on. Let's go get some grub."

"God, I must look like a fucking wreck." I'm suddenly self-conscious about my makeup, my near-nakedness, and how vulnerable I've just been with him.

"You look fucking beautiful, but you can freshen up in there." He points to the bathroom door.

I grab my purse, enter his bathroom, and inspect my face in the mirror. *Not too bad, considering.* I wipe the Maybelline mascara smeared underneath my lower lashes and down my cheeks, try to remove the red smear of what used to be my lipstick off the general area around my mouth. I search my purse for my makeup bag to reapply a fresh layer, but then remember what Patrick said about not needing too much makeup. I decide to go without it.

Patrick comes in and stands behind me, looks at our reflection in the mirror. He rests his chin on the top of my head and wraps his arms around my chest. "We look good together."

I smile sweetly at him, feeling like the weight of the world has been lifted from my shoulders. "That we do."

I freshen up, put my shirt back on, and we walk back out to the party hand-in hand. "You like barbecue?' he asks.

"Sure."

"Let's eat."

And just like that, we are a twosome. We walk around the party, where he introduces me to his friends. Fiona shoots me looks occasionally, but I ignore her. As his friends talk about work, shows, surfing, and whatever else Venice people in their twenties talk about, I get lost in my lust fog and whiskey haze. Patrick drapes his arm over my shoulder and runs his fingers up my back. His constant touch feels precious. Intimate.

We make our way back inside the house, where I see the girls.

"There you are. I wondered what had happened to you two," says Stacey as she eyes us suspiciously.

Patrick crooks his arm around my neck and kisses my cheek. "I was showing her my record collection."

Stacey looks back and forth between us. "Uh huh. I *bet*. That must be some record collection."

"Hey, Patrick. Where's the bathroom in here?"

"Down that hall. Don't be gone long." He kisses me and points the way.

"I've gotta pee too," chimes in Stacey.

"Me, three," says Erin.

The three of us find the bathroom miraculously unoccupied. We're no sooner crammed inside when Stacey says, "Spill it. What the fuck did you guys do?"

I put on my innocent face and start to pee. "Nothing. We just kissed and talked. I swear!"

"Well, if you just kissed, why is your shirt on inside out?" asks Erin.

I look down on my side, and sure enough, there's a tag sticking out from the seam. "Geez, how many people have seen my shirt like this? Okay, so we kissed and my shirt *may* have fallen off, but that's it. Swear."

"How was the kissing?" asks Stacey.

"Oh my God, Stace! I thought I was going to pass out. It was fucking perfect."

Erin rolls her eyes at me. "Look, Erika, I know you're a smitten kitten, but watch out for this guy. Fiona says he's dangerous," Erin warns, with actual finger wagging. "And hurry up. I have to pee."

I flush, stand up, then move to the sink to wash my hands. Erin sits.

"Erika, what the fuck is on your neck?" asks Stacey, moving my hair aside.

I look in the mirror at my neck and see the biggest hickey I've ever had in my life. I'm proud when I think about Patrick marking me to make me his. I pull my hair forward and turn to face both of them. "Look guys, I'm not some stupid kid. And you know I've seen my share of shit. I can handle myself, okay? Erin, you're going into the Army. Stace, you've got Tony, and you're starting college soon. What the fuck do I have, besides no car and living in a shitty condo in Van Nuys with a mother who can't stand me? Maybe this is my shot to be happy."

Erin balks. "Erika, you barely know the fucking guy. You sound like a total airhead. Next, you'll be saying you're in love."

I bristle like a porcupine, and the daily rage I try to suppress surges. "Do you have any idea what it feels like to be grateful to have a man's arms around you? To fuck some guy, any guy, just for the five sweet minutes afterward when you can pretend someone actually cares about you? I'm damaged goods, guys, and you both know it. I fuck guys who buy me alcohol and supply me with drugs. Hardly the same thing."

Always the peacekeeper, Stacey jumps in. "Erika, calm down. Erin didn't mean anything by what she said. She's just concerned. If this guy makes you happy, that's awesome. We support you. We love you."

Tears of anger well up and threaten to further wreck my Maybelline. "Can't I just have one fucking thing that's sweet and mine, just *once* in my goddamn life?"

"Of course you can, Erika. Don't cry. Here." Stacey hands me a strip of toilet paper. "Wipe your eyes before you get black all over your face."

Erin stands up and flushes, then moves to the sink. Stacey takes her turn to pee.

Erin takes the tissue and dabs my face. "Geez, Erika. What was I supposed to do? Not tell you?"

"No." I sniffle.

"But if he hurts you, I'll fucking kill him," says Erin. "And I'll have a gun, so I can really do it."

After a pause, all three of us burst into laughter, breaking the tension.

Erin continues. "I really wasn't trying to upset you. We're just looking out for you."

"I know, Erin. And I'm sorry I freaked out on you. I've just been so bummed lately. Sometimes I'm not sure how much more I can handle."

"Jesus, Erika. Don't talk like that." Stacey looks concerned.

She doesn't know how my brain works. That I think about suicide every day. That I have nightmares. I don't talk about any of it. I smile, make people laugh, fuck guys for good drugs, share the wealth, and pray that no one catches on to what's really going on with me.

I wipe the last remnants of tears from under my eyes and smile at them reassuringly. "Jesus, I'm fine. I'm probably PMSing." I stick my fingers in my hair to puff it up more. "Someone give me a cigarette. I want to get back to Patrick. Oh! Stace, that reminds me. I'm spending the night here. Cover for me in case Mom calls? He'll take me home tomorrow. If she calls, just tell her I'm swimming or in the shower or whatever."

She stands up, flushes, then washes her hands. "Of course. And if he does turn out to be a major jerk, you call me and I'll come get you."

"He's not a jerk, you guys. He's...he's awesome, and honest. I can't explain it, and I don't know what happened with him and Fiona, but I'm telling you, he's a good guy."

There's a knock on the door, and Patrick's muffled voice from the other side. "Did you guys fall in?"

"No, we're coming right out," I say in a cheery voice. I whisper to the girls, "Be nice. Especially you." I point an accusatory finger at Erin.

I open the bathroom door and see a concerned Patrick standing in front of me.

"Everything okay, babe?" He searches my face, then the girls'.

"Totally. We were just peeing and talking. You know how girls are."

"Girl talk. Yay," he says with sarcasm.

The party winds down, the girls leave, and we're finally alone. After several whiskey shots, a pack of cigarettes, and a million more kisses, I feel no pain. I lie on the bed and watch the blades of the ceiling fan, or the room, spin. I can't tell which.

Patrick stands by the bed and pulls me up next to him. He unbuckles my belt and drops it to the floor. Then he lifts my shirt up over my head. His fingertips trace down my arms, across the fresh bruises on my breasts, then across my back, where he unhooks my bra. One by one, he gently pulls the straps down off each arm. Then he places his fingers between my skin and skirt, slowly cinching it down until it drops to my ankles.

I am now naked, both physically and emotionally. Insecure, I clutch my hands under my chin, covering my breasts.

"Don't cover yourself in front of me, Erika." He kisses each hand, then places one over the erection in his shorts. "This is what seeing you does to me."

He unbuckles his belt, and his boxers and shorts drop to the ground. Was a more beautiful man ever created? I drink in the lean, chiseled statue standing before me: strong chest, ripped abdomen, narrow waist, muscular arms. *And those hands*. And the largest dick I've ever seen. There is not an ounce of self-consciousness or insecurity in him. He is the epitome of raw masculinity, and I have a visceral reaction just being near him.

I trace my fingertips across his chest, down his stomach. Before I go any lower, he drops to his knees in front of me and buries his face between my legs. I grip his shoulders and try to steady myself as his deft tongue brings me to the brink of climax. Once again, he stops abruptly and stands up.

"Oh, my sweet Erika. Not yet," he commands.

He takes my hand and leads me into the shower. When the water is warm enough, he steps in first, then pulls me in and positions me under the showerhead facing away from him. The water scalds my skin, washing away my sins and sorrow. I close my eyes and lean my face into the stream of water. Patrick massages my scalp, and I realize he's washing my hair. The simple, sweet gesture stuns me. No man has ever been so tender. I start to turn around to face him.

"No. Stay where you are."

When he finishes washing my hair, I rinse. Sudsy water cascades down my skin. He conditions my hair, and again I rinse. He turns me around to face him. "Close your eyes."

He washes my face, then slowly washes my breasts, stomach, and between my legs. He turns me around, washes and massages my back and buttocks.

This is what it's supposed to feel like, Erika. This is what love is.

When he's done, I turn around and reach for the soap to return the favor.

"No, angel. This is for you. You don't have to do anything."

Like a voyeur, I watch his glorious hands spread lather around his physique. I have never envied soap until now, and I have never wanted anyone more than I want him.

When the shower is done, we step out and he wraps a huge bath towel around me, pats me dry, then gently blots water from my hair. With a fresh towel, he dries himself, rubbing it vigorously across his scalp.

Naked and clean, he takes me back to the bed and makes love to me. My life is even better than *Sixteen Candles.*

I went to bed a schoolgirl, albeit a tarnished one, but wake up a woman with a killer hangover. Patrick, his arms wrapped around me, is sleeping peacefully and gently snoring in my ear. *So, this is what it feels like to be grown-up.* I wrap my fingers around his arm and nestle in closer to him.

"Good morning, angel," he says softly into my neck, and pushes his erection against my buttocks.

I'm proud I have that effect on him, and smile to myself. "Good morning, yourself."

"It's about to be a very good morning." He rolls me over onto my back and kisses me.

We make love off-and-on all morning, stopping only when we need to forage for food. I dress in my miniskirt, T-shirt, and heels.

"Um, no. You're not wearing that," he says.

I look down at my clothes. "Huh? What's wrong with what I'm wearing?"

He reaches into his closet and tosses me a pair of 501s. "Wear these instead."

High on kisses and multiple orgasms, I do as he says and put his jeans on. I roll up the cuffs at the bottom, then slip into my heels.

He grabs my ass in his jeans and kisses me hard. "Much better. Now let's eat."

We eat at a neighborhood diner, make googly eyes at each other over pancakes. It feels like all the other people have fallen off the face of the planet and there's only the two of us. I kick off my heels under the table and pull a move from *Flashdance*, run my bare foot up his thigh and gently press against his groin.

"Don't start something you can't finish, angel," he warns in a gentle tone.

"Oh, I intend to finish everything I start." I wink at him.

"Do you have to go home? Can you stay the week?"

His words are salve to my weary soul. He wants me. He barely knows me and he wants me to stay. "I'd have to go home first, get some clothes and stuff. I can tell my mom the girls and I are camping at the beach... You really want me to stay?"

He takes my hand and kisses the back of my fingers. "Yes."

I sigh. Has there ever been a guy radder than Patrick?

Later in the afternoon, he drives me to the Valley. He waits in his car while I go upstairs to deal with Mom.

"Hey, Mom." I burst through the front door.

Mom eyes me suspiciously from the kitchen. "What are you so happy about?"

Not even the emotional canyon between us can bum me out today. "Nothing. It's summer and gorgeous outside. Can't I be happy?"

"Sure you can, it's just been awhile."

"Stacey and the girls want to go camping this week before Erin goes into the Army. Can I go?"

"Where are you going and when will you be back?" she asks, not taking her eyes off her cooking.

"Leo Carrillo, and next weekend."

"Yeah. Whatever. Just don't do anything stupid and get into trouble."

"We won't." I dash into my room, throw a bunch of black clothes into a duffel bag, and head back out the front door. "Bye."

Twenty-four hours after meeting, I unofficially move in with my punk-rock boyfriend. Once we get back to his place, I call Stacey and tell her the plan. From there, I immerse myself in life with Patrick.

At night, we listen to X, The Stooges, and the Flamin' Groovies while we get loaded on alcohol, cocaine, and our mutual lust for each other. In the morning, he kisses and fucks me awake. Then he jumps in the shower while I cook breakfast.

"Stay pretty, and don't step outside of this house," he commands before he leaves for work. "I don't want anyone coming after what's mine."

I roll my eyes at him. "As if. That's, like, totally impossible. I'll be right here when you get back. I miss you already," I wrap my arms around his neck and kiss him long and sweet. My own father couldn't be bothered to even find me, and all Patrick wants is for me to be close and safe.

I jump in the shower to wash away last night's sins and this morning's hangover. I dress in one of his white T-shirts and boxers, then fold the laundry and do the dishes. Domesticity reminds me of my grandmother, but I like being the little woman for him, anticipating his needs.

Our new routine fits me like a latex body glove. When I'm done with chores, I watch *General Hospital* and *Oprah* reruns, listen to my Walkman, read Anaïs Nin and Tom Robbins, and think about Patrick.

He feasts on my senses between sex and sleep, seasoned with vodka and Marlboro reds. He consumes every part of me, and it's as if I exist only to experience him: to hear the timber of his voice, to taste him, to smell his skin, to feast on every inch of him, and to feel his fullness inside me.

The week goes by too quickly. On Sunday, I call Stacey to check in. Patrick sits next to me on the bed, kissing my shoulder while I make the call.

"Hey Stace."

"Oh my God, Erika. There you are. Your mom called an hour ago. I didn't know how to get a hold of you. Are you still with him?"

"Yep. Did she ask you about camping?"

"You've been there all week? And yeah, I told her we just got back and that you and Erin went to grab food."

"Yep. Thanks for covering." I cover the mouthpiece of the phone and whisper to Patrick, "Can I give her your number, just in case Mom tries to get ahold of me?"

"Yes, but tell her it's only for emergencies. I don't want her tying up my line."

After I give Stacey the number, she starts probing. "So, how's it going?"

Patrick watches me intently. It's weird talking to her with him staring at me. I smile into the phone. "Great, Stace, but I've gotta call Mom."

"But everything's cool? And when are you coming home? I wanna hang out. It's summer."

Guilt tickles my conscience for ditching my best friend in the whole world for a guy. Patrick mouths *hang up* and makes the motion with his thumb and pinkie to put the receiver down.

"Soon, Stace. Promise. I've really gotta go now. Love you."

He takes the phone out of my hands. I hear her voice in the receiver, "Love you, too—" before he places it back on the cradle.

Patrick pulls me down onto the mattress and pins my arms above my head. "I didn't think she'd ever shut up."

I feel a pang of defensiveness for my friend, but then his mouth is on mine, and he's on top of me, pushing my thoughts out, injecting me with him and only him.

"You can't go," he says, as he put his fingers between my legs.

"Patrick. That's not fair."

"Who says I play fair?"

I call Mom and make another bullshit excuse, tell her I'm with Kathy this time. She grants me another week of freedom and happiness.

My second week with Patrick scurries by as quickly as the first. When I'm depressed and miserable, time leeches by, slowly sucking moments of my life away. Now that I'm finally happy, I blink and it's over. While Patrick runs to the store for smokes and refreshments, I take a shot of vodka and call Mom.

"Hey, Mom. Can I stay at Kathy's for another few days?"

"Listen, missy, I don't know what the hell you're doing, but you need to get your ass back here tonight. You've been gone for two weeks. What the hell are you doing that you can't come home?"

Shit. "We're just hanging out, swimming, playing pool. What is there to do at home? It's summer."

"Well, I'm sure Kathy's parents don't appreciate you being there all the time. Come home."

"But Mom—"

"Don't 'but Mom' me. You're not eighteen for another six months. After that, you can do whatever the hell you want. Until then, get your ass home tonight or you're grounded."

Jesus. Why does she have to be a bitch, like, all the time? "Okay, okay. Take a fucking chill pill. I'll be home in a bit." I hang up, then take another shot to try to quell the dread that's moved into the pit of my stomach. I look around the studio apartment. This place has become my refuge, his body my home. The thought of leaving kills me.

Patrick walks in, cigarette hanging out of his mouth, carrying a paper bag in his left arm. He's so beautiful it hurts, wearing a white wife-beater and faded Levi 501s, his dark hair spiked to perfection. He reaches into the bag and retrieves a bottle of Jack Daniels, vodka, a six-pack of Guinness, and a carton of Marlboros. He places all of them on the counter, then lifts me up next to his purchases. He takes each of my ankles in his hands and wraps my legs around him.

"I was thinking we could go see *RoboCop* tonight. Oh, and *Lost Boys* opens next weekend. Looks cool."

I lean my forehead against his, trying to figure out the easiest way to tell him my bad news. I take his face in my hands and kiss his lips gently.

"Babe, is that a yes to *RoboCop?*"

I'm lost in the pools of blue concrete staring back at me. "I have to go home tonight."

"Come on. Just tell her you're hanging with Stacey again, or Kathy, or whoever."

"It won't work this time. She's super pissed. I have to go back, at least for a day or two." I slide down to the floor and wrap my arms around his back, rest my cheek against his chest, and breathe him in. "And then I'll come right back. Promise."

"Don't. Go." He braces his arms against the counter on either side of me, then leans into me. There's intensity in his eyes I've only seen in brief flashes. He's now directing it at me full-force, and the effect is hypnotic.

"Babe, you know I don't want to leave you, but I have to—"

"You don't have to do anything but stay here. Don't I take good care of you?" he asks, wounded.

"Oh my God, of *course* you do, Patrick. How could you even think that? This isn't about you at all. It's my mom. I've been gone for two weeks. She's starting to get suspicious—"

He silences my words with kisses. "Fuck her. Stay with me."

He's not listening to me, and I can't breathe. "Patrick, no. I'm go—"

The back of his hand slams against my cheek, leaving it red hot. My mouth hangs open in shock. Like an earthquake or a car accident, I never saw it coming. For a second, and only one tiny second, I want to yell at him, to hit and kick and punch him for hurting me—but his face. The veins at his temples bulge like angry worms. His fists are balled tight, poised on either side of his body, ready to strike again.

My brain crackles with confusion. I know it's not right to hit a girl, not even a girl like me, but I can't move. I stand motionless, tears streaming down my cheeks, rooted to this spot and to this man. *Where is my sweet Patrick?*

"You're mine. Don't you fucking understand that? I don't want you to go home. I don't want you hanging out with other guys. I don't want you to leave me."

I try to comprehend what he wants from me. What he needs. Our broken pieces fit together seamlessly, and I finally get how much I mean to him. So much I make him crazy. So much he needs me to stay here with him and not go home. So much he doesn't want other guys to talk to me or look at me. He's the only thing that feels real in my seventeen fucked-up years of life.

"Patrick, I'm sorry," I whisper. Tears spill off my cheeks onto the hardwood floor.

"I don't believe you." He grabs the bottle of Jack from the counter and takes a swig.

"I don't want to leave you."

"So don't go. Move the rest of your shit in here."

"I'm seventeen. You're twenty-two. If I leave, she'll call the cops. Plus, I've got to finish high school, and start applying for colleges. I'm an honor student. I can't just quit before my last year. As fucked up as my life is, school's the one thing I haven't totally destroyed."

He stares at me through pools of dark slate, but doesn't say anything. I can see the wheels turning in his brain. His silence, even more punishing than his fist, fills the space between us with doubt, self-loathing, and terror.

I drop to my knees, to make myself and my mistake smaller. "Please don't be mad at me. Please, Patrick. Please..." I rest my cheek against his jeans.

He takes another swig of whiskey and runs his fingers through my hair, holding my head against his groin. He puts his hand under my chin and lifts my face up, wiping tears from my eyes. He presses his thumb against my lips and I kiss it. He lowers himself down on top of me.

"My baby, my sweet little baby. You're mine," he says, and gently kisses my burning cheek.

I stare into his steely eyes, searching for my worth and his forgiveness. His muscular arms flank either side of my head. He kisses me long and hard, filling the aching empty spaces inside, suffocating everything in between until there's only him and me and this.

He unbuckles his jeans, pushes up my skirt, and buries himself hard and deep. I don't care that it hurts. I'm lost in our mutual need for pain and oblivion. He fucks me senseless and bites my neck, my lips, my breasts. I wrap my legs around him and pull him deeper into me. He pins my hands above my head and fucks me until I'm empty of everything but him.

He comes and rolls onto his back, lights two cigarettes and hands me one. We lay on the wood floor, cool in contrast to the searing July heat, and watch the spinning blades of the ceiling fan. I cry tears of gratitude and, for the first time in two weeks, imagine what my life would be like without him.

He rolls over on his side and watches me cry. I try to anticipate what he's thinking and it makes me cry harder, but I remain silent and wait for him to tell me where we go from here.

"Don't cry, babe. I'm sorry I got pissed. You just pushed me, and the thought of you away from me makes me crazy. I fucking love you."

I cup my hands over my face and sob. I don't want to say the wrong thing and break this moment. All I've ever wanted is to be loved. He folds me into his chest and strokes my hair. Once again, I'm safe. His anger a distant memory.

I wipe my face with the back of my hand, and search his eyes for signs the storm has passed. Calm, cashmere-gray skies look back at me, full of love and forgiveness. This isn't puppy love or some bullshit crush. This is messy, all-consuming, soul-changing love. "I love you so fucking much, Patrick."

He cups my face in his hands and kisses me like a man who loves a woman. "Come on, get some stuff together and I'll take you home. But leave some of your shit here so I know you're coming back."

"Of *course* I'm coming back. You're my home now."

He drops me off at Mom's. As he drives away, emptiness consumes me. I hate my mother for making me leave him. I hate everything about my miserable life, everything but him. Breathing doesn't even make sense without him.

Sick from Patrick withdrawals, I mope around the house. After Mom leaves for work, I walk to the 7-11 and ask creepy dudes to buy me beer. I pick fights with Mom over anything and everything. If I'm going to suffer, she's going to suffer too. After four days of my hellish brattiness, she finally tells me I can leave again.

For the next two weeks, Patrick and I settle back into our routine. We get high. We fuck. We occasionally hang out with some of his friends, but never mine. We sneak onto the roof of the Roosevelt

Hotel, get high, and climb the sign. I think less about college and focus more on ways to please him, to curtail his anger. It flares up at other drivers on the road, guys he works with, the government. This intensifies when he's on meth. I learn to use my body as his sedative, to anticipate when a storm is brewing.

I wake up on August fourth and realize it's our one-month anniversary. I start scheming what I can do to make it special. As I make him breakfast, I smile to myself at the thought of baking him a cake and finding him the perfect card.

"What's that grin for?" he asks, coffee cup in hand.

I transfer his scrambled eggs and bacon to a plate and hand it to him. "Can't a girl be happy?"

"That depends on what she's thinking about." A glimmer of intensity brews behind his eyes.

"You, of course. Only and forever you." I kiss his neck in reassurance.

"Keep it that way." He clenches my ass in his hands and bites my lower lip.

He eats breakfast and leaves for work. I lean against the open screen door and watch him walk down the driveway. Not walk—Patrick never just walks. He struts, daring the world to defy him, always alert and aware of everything around him. He's the Sid to my Nancy.

Before I head back into the studio, I see Fiona watching me from her kitchen window. Aside from a few words in passing, we've never actually spoken to each other. What is there to say? *Hi. It's not awkward at all we're all living on the same property. Wanna hang out and have a beer?* She holds up a hand and waves. I return the gesture, then go back inside. Patrick's warned me about talking to her. To hear him tell it, she's a fucking no-good worthless cunt who can burn in hell. I keep my nose out of where it doesn't belong.

An hour after he leaves, I get ready. He's told me a million times not to leave the house without him, but I figure just this once, what he doesn't know won't hurt him. Plus, I'm being the best girlfriend ever. He'll have to forgive me when he finds out the reason for my disobedience. And situation critical—I'm out of cigarettes.

I throw on a pair of cut-off jean shorts, a white T-shirt, slouchy black boots, black Ray Bans, and my Walkman, and head to the grocery store. I find cake supplies and cigarettes, but they don't have any good cards, so I head over to Sav-On drugs. After reading every single card, I finally find the perfect one. I also get a cassette so I can make him a mix tape. On impulse, I buy one of the single red roses wrapped in cellophane by the register.

Proud of myself, I walk back slowly, lost in love and the lyrics to Bryan Ferry's *Don't Stop the Dance* blasting through my headphones. The world looks so different than it did a month ago. Life finally doesn't suck.

Giddy like a schoolgirl, I burst back into the studio and find Patrick sitting in a chair, facing me. His face tells me I'm in trouble. The screen door slams behind me and I swallow hard.

"What did I say before I left this morning?" he asks, too calmly.

"Not to leave the house," I whisper. I set the bags down on the table by the door and wring my hands together in front of me.

"I come home to surprise you for lunch, and what do I find?"

He'll understand once you explain. I flash him my biggest smile. "Patrick, I have the best surprise for you—"

He launches up out of the chair and shoves me down on the floor. My head smacks against the hardwood. Before I can react, his right hand clenches around my throat. Panicked, I claw at his fingers, but he doesn't loosen his grip.

"You don't ever leave this house without my permission. Got it?"

My wide eyes meet his narrow ones and I nod as best I can.

"And certainly not dressed like this," he says. He puts his left hand between my legs and grabs my crotch over my jean shorts. He kisses me as I swallow tears and regret. "You. Are. Mine." He loosens his grip on my throat.

"Yours. Always yours," I grind out, trying not to let hurt and confusion show on my face or in my voice.

He stands up and extends his left hand out to me, a loving smile on his face. I place my hand in his and he pulls me up from the floor. As soon as I'm on my feet, he punches me hard in the stomach. The blow knocks the wind out of me. I gasp for air and collapse into his arms.

"Don't make me tell you again," he says, then scoops me up and carries me to the bed. He tosses me onto the mattress and pulls my shorts down over my ankles. He unbuttons his jeans, climbs on top of me and fucks me with his fury. I'm sore from the night before, dry and raw. I want him to slow down and stop being so angry with me, but in the month we've been together I've learned that words are no match for his anger.

He loves me. He loves me. I am his. I should have listened. I close my eyes and clench my teeth against his thrusts. He loves me and I love him.

He finishes and rolls over on his side, pulls me against him so we're spooning. He strokes my long hair gently, then wraps it around his hand and pulls my neck closer to his mouth where he kisses me, soft and sweet. My neck feels raw and bruised, but I don't protest.

"Why do you make me hurt you?" he whispers in my ear while pulling me closer.

The answer eludes me, and I roll over and face him, searching his eyes for redemption and understanding. "I don't mean to." Muddled thoughts swim through murky grief and confusion. "I'm sorry I made you so mad, Patrick." I swallow shattered remnants of pride. "I'll do better. I promise. Forgive me?"

"Forgiven." He kisses me and buttons his jeans, then stands up and lights a cigarette. "Where the fuck did you go, anyway?" He peeks into the bags I brought home. "What is this shit?" He pulls out the rose and card.

My previous exuberance morphs into insecurity. I answer while staring at the floor. "Today's our one month anniversary. I wanted to surprise you."

"Aww, babe." He kisses my forehead, my closed eyelids, then my lips. "Next time you want to go to the store, tell me and I'll take you. Okay?"

My bones shiver, but I nod in agreement. "Promise."

"I have to get back to work. We'll do something special later. Now let me see that smile."

I muster the biggest smile I can and hope it's good enough.

"Good girl." He walks over to his side of the bed, reaches behind the nightstand, and unplugs the phone cord from the wall. He wraps it around the phone and handset and tucks the entire bundle under his arm. "Be good, and remember what I told you." He kisses my temple.

"I will. Promise." As if I could forget.

He leaves and takes my only connection to the outside world with him.

Getting back in bed, I curl into the fetal position under the covers. He doesn't want me to leave. He doesn't want me to call anyone. School starts in less than a month. What's he going to say when I can only be here on weekends? Nausea creeps up my throat, and nagging dread tugs at my subconscious. I go to the freezer, grab a bottle of vodka and my smokes, then crawl back under the covers. *He loves me. He loves me. Be grateful. He loves me.*

It's mid-August, and over the course of six weeks I've been home for less than two. Mom has finally given up arguing with me and at least pretends to believe my bullshit excuses. Patrick and I have settled into a new routine. He uses me whenever and however he sees fit, and I try to be perfect and keep him in love with me. Every day, I maneuver around his manic violence. Littered with bruises and intoxicants, my body is a war zone. My mind, even more so. I cling to the sweet spaces between his rages and live in a constant fugue. He loves me. Why can't I just be happy? Why do I have to question everything?

Like why you're letting him beat you?

Drink. Snort. Smoke. Swallow. Fuck.

What if this were happening to Stacey? What would you tell her?

Drink. Snort. Smoke. Swallow. Try to be happy. Sleep. Wake. Repeat.

He's never going to let you go.

Ten days before school starts, I can no longer postpone the inevitable. I wait for him to unwind after work before I start the dreaded conversation. "Patrick, I've got to go home Sunday. I'll need a week to get my shit ready for school."

He clenches his jaw and the veins pop out at his temples, but he remains silent. My body tightens, waiting for the inevitable blows. Ignoring me, he lies on our bed and stares at the ceiling. His left hand rests on his stomach, his right brings a cigarette to his mouth. I lean against the kitchen counter, waiting for World War III to erupt.

"Patrick. We have to talk about this."

"Fuck you. Cunt."

I can't tell which wounds me more—his words or his fists, but I'm weary of both. "Patrick. I just want to talk. I don't want to fight."

"What *you* want. It's always about what *you* fucking want. What about what *I* want?" He stands and surges over to me. "Do you ever think about that, *whore*?" he asks, then spits in my face.

I flinch and resist the urge to curl into a ball on the floor, take a deep breath, and respond as gently as I can. "I'm not a whore, Patrick. I'm the woman who loves you." I try to make my words reach the other Patrick.

He spins me around and bends me over the counter, lifts my skirt and pins my arms painfully behind my back.

"Patrick. No. Please—"

I struggle to keep my legs together, but I'm no match for his strength. He braces my legs apart with his feet, then he's inside of me. His cock is like a dagger seeking out vengeance.

My skin tears, and the delicate thread holding my sanity together snaps. I close my eyes and focus on the cold tile of the counter under my cheek. A keyring hangs by the door. I count the keys in time with his thrusts. One. Two. Three. Four. Five. Six. In silence, I wait for my punishment to end. Mercifully, he comes and pulls out of me. I'm left hollowed and shattered.

"Useless fucking whore," he mutters, then grabs his keys. "You're nothing but a worthless hole." He slams the door behind him.

I curl into a ball on the floor, numb. Minutes turn to hours. I wait for him to come back, take me in his arms, and kiss my tears away.

There aren't enough kisses for that, Erika.

Eventually, I make my way to the shower and let the scalding water punish me. I wait for him in bed. He doesn't come home that night, or the next.

Left alone with alcohol, fear, and regret, my brain goes to the bleakest places. *What if something terrible has happened to him? What if he got arrested? What if he never comes back?*

I go to the phone to call Stacey, but stop myself. She'll ask questions I don't want to answer. I can't call Mom. Erin's gone. *She tried to warn you.*

I drink until I pass out, and wake up alone. What day is it? Friday? No, it's Saturday. You have to go home tomorrow. If he doesn't come back tonight, you can call Stacey tomorrow to come get you.

For a brief moment, I think about going to Fiona, the only other person with Patrick experience. I flash on what his reaction would be if he caught us together and I shudder. Bad idea. I fall asleep again, and wake up in darkness to the sound of a key in the door. The clock on the nightstand says it's almost midnight.

Patrick. Thank God you're home.

I sit up in bed as he walks in. In silhouette, I can see his arm draped around someone. He flips on the light and I see it's a skanky blonde girl.

"Patrick?"

"Who the fuck is this bish?" asks the blonde, slurring her words.

He kisses her the way he's kissed me countless times, and watches me while he does it. "She's nothing but a worthless cunt."

Bimbo girl laughs loudly. This is a new level of cruelty, even for him. I sit in bed with my knees curled up to my chest, helpless to stifle the sobs racking my body.

"Get the fuck out of my house, cunt."

I can't move. I stare at him and plead with him telepathically. *Please, Patrick, please don't do this. I love you.*

"Don't make me come over there," he warns.

Equally terrified and devastated, I grab my duffel bag and shove my belongings into it.

The blonde cackles and claps her hands. "Chop, chop!"

I pack, then go to the phone to call Stacey.

"What the fuck do you think you're doing? Get the fuck out, you worthless piece of shit." He looks at me as if I'm nothing.

How can I mean nothing to him? "Patrick, how am I supposed to get home?"

"Not my fucking problem."

"Yeah, not our fucking problem," echoes the blonde. "Joo got anything to drink?"

Minutes later, I'm standing in his backyard in the dark, alone, fifteen miles from home with no way to get there. From the other side of the closed door, I hear the blonde giggle. I run to the bushes and vomit. When there's nothing left in me but emptiness, I regroup. *Erika, you cannot die here in these bushes. Figure it out.*

I have only one choice—Fiona. I stand by the backdoor then look over my shoulder to make sure Patrick isn't behind me. Still alone, I knock softly. No response. *Please be home. Please fucking answer.* I knock again, on the glass this time. The porch light comes on and Fiona peeks out the back curtain.

She opens the door and looks at me, then down at my bag. She looks over my shoulder to the studio, then takes my arm and guides me into the kitchen.

"Are you okay?" she asks gently.

I shake my head. "No. I'm not okay. He...He—" I burst into tears.

"I know, Erika. Believe me, I know."

We stare at each other and speak the silent language of women who've seen too much.

"Erika. What do you need?"

A drink. A lobotomy. For Patrick to love me again. "A phone and a drink please. I'll take anything."

"In here." She takes me to the living room and sits me where Patrick was sitting when I first saw him.

Fuck, that was six weeks ago. Seems like a lifetime. She walks back to the kitchen and I call Stacey. One ring. Two rings. Three. *Please, Stacey, be home.*

"Hello?"

"Hey Stace—" I start to whimper.

"Oh my God, Erika. Are you okay?"

"Oh, Stace...everything's so fucked up."

"What do you mean? Where the hell have you been? Are you still with Patrick?"

I can't remember the last time I talked to her without Patrick looking over my shoulder. "I'll explain everything, and I know it's late, but can you please come get me? *Please."*

"Fuck. Of course."

"I'm in the front house. I'll see you when you get here." I hang up the phone and sit in silence with Fiona. My limbs are concrete and I'm certain my heart will stop beating at any moment. I'm sinking into quicksand, and I don't know if there's enough fight in me to make it out.

institutionalized

In three days, I get to die. My eyes open just a crack. I groan. I just woke up and I'm already exhausted. Dread suffocates the stale smoke and bile in my lungs and stomach. I'm a senior in high school. It shouldn't hurt to breathe.

David Bowie, Peter Murphy, and The Cure stare at me from posters on my bedroom door, silent observers of the wreckage that is me. The calendar on the wall is filled with red slashes, counting down the last days of my time on this planet. *December 23, 1987.*

I reach under my mattress to retrieve a few black beauties from their hiding spot, but my stash is gone. *Fuck it.* I pull the comforter over my head and return to the haven of sleep.

Mom half-knocks on my door and barges in as usual. "Don't forget, we have a therapy appointment at 4:00 today."

"Do we *have* to go?" I whine. "I don't think we're really getting anything out of it."

"We're going. I'm going to put in a half-day at work. I'll be back to pick you up around 3:30."

I glare at her like I can shoot laser beams out of my eyes and annihilate the possibility of therapy completely. Ever since Patrick,

I've barely been able to breathe. I can't handle one more fucking feeling.

She ignores me and leaves for work. My depression and I cuddle up together and go back to sleep.

Later that afternoon, we sit across from Nancy, our family therapist who is charged with making sense of the Worth family debacle.

I'm a fucking ray of sunshine sitting in her office, dressed in black from head to toe, legs crossed, staring at a point on her wall. *This is all almost over, Erika. Just get through this shit.*

"Erika, you have one hour to go home and pack a bag, then your mother is driving you to rehab," says Nancy.

I hear her words, but they don't register. I focus my death stare on my mother, who is suddenly very preoccupied with her cuticles. I shift my death stare directly over to Nancy. "What did you just say?"

"You have on hour to go home and pack a bag, then your mother—"

"I'm not going anywhere. You can't make me go!"

"Erika, if you don't go willingly with your mother, the Psychiatric Emergency Team will take you against your will. You will be physically restrained and put into isolation upon arriving at the facility."

I open my mouth, prepared to unleash an expletive-filled tirade on good ol' Nancy, then pause. *Did she just imply straightjacket?* That scares the bejeezus out of me, and I scrunch my eyes closed to prevent my fury from spewing out. I take a deep breath and open my eyes. Nancy sits, calm and serious, staring at me. Mom looks miserable. *Okay, Erika, get yourself out of this.*

I turn on my manipulative waterworks, complete with lip quivering and face twitching. "But...but...*(sniff)*...Mom, I...*(sob)*...didn't even get a chance to get you anything for Christmas," I whimper.

"Erika, you're going," says Nancy.

"But *Mo-om*—"

"You're going," Mom says.

Panic strangles me. *There is no fucking way I'm going anywhere. I have a fucking plan, goddam it!* I switch to rage. "What about you, *Mother?*" I snarl. "Why aren't you being locked up? I'm not the only fucked up one in this family. Whatever I am is because of *you.* This is *your* fault! *You're* the one who got knocked up by some asshole. *You're* the one who should have given me up for adoption or had an abortion, remember? *You* never wanted me, and now you're going to lock me up and abandon me right before Christmas? What kind of a mother does something like that to her *only child?*"

Like spears, my words find their target. Mom bursts into tears. Normally, the sight of her crying twists me up inside, but I sit smug with my arms crossed, pleased with myself. I'm not going to relent until she changes her mind.

"Whatever, *Mother.* You put me wherever you fucking need to. In six weeks, I turn eighteen and I can do whatever I want, and you can't stop me. And I promise you, I will *never* speak to you again. *Ever.*"

Mom looks like she might buckle and turns to Nancy, who is nonplussed by any of my rantings. "You're going," says Nancy with zero emotion.

"You're the most horrible mother in the entire universe. FUCK YOU! FUCK BOTH OF YOU!" I storm out of Nancy's office.

Mom follows me out to the car. We drive home in silence. She's going to change her mind. This is not happening.

"How could you have let her talk you into this stupid idea? What the hell are you thinking? And when did you suddenly start caring about me?"

Tears slide down to her chin, but she says nothing.

"And what about my ski trip?" *And my plan to take a sheet of acid and ski off the side of a mountain and end this ruinous existence?* "I saved for that for months, and I'll lose all my money if I don't go? WHY ARE YOU TRYING TO RUIN MY LIFE?"

Nancy must have prepared her for my resistance, because she doesn't buckle. She cries, but doesn't back down.

When we get home, I pack my things in as dramatic a fashion as possible, throwing things across the room, with loud sighs and moans for emphasis. She sits on my bed close to the door and watches me. I want to run, but I have nowhere to go.

Bag packed, we drive over the hill to Westwood and park in front of the Community Psychiatric Facility. I panic. Psych wards mean straightjackets and padded rooms.

"Um, I thought you were taking me to rehab?"

"This is rehab," she replies.

"This is a psych ward. Mom, *please*, I'll do anything you want. I'm sorry, okay? I know I've been a pain in the ass. Don't make me go in there."

"Get your bag, Erika." She gets out of the car and stands by the open trunk. She doesn't make eye contact with me, only stands calm and resolute.

A male staff member is waiting for us in the lobby, and enters the elevator with us. He puts a key in a slot and pushes the button for the second floor. As the doors close the air squeezes out of my lungs.

Mental note, Erika: You need a key for the elevator. Figure out how to get one of those.

We go up one floor. The doors open and we exit to a hallway. Directly in front of us is a common room, furnished with several blue padded chairs, blue sofas, a television, and a foosball table. To the right is a long corridor with six doors on either side. The corridor to the left is blocked by steel doors with two small windows. Several young faces peer at me through the glass.

Fuck. Get me out of here.

As we approach the double doors a *click* sound indicates the doors are unlocked, and Mom and I are escorted through the doors, through the nurse's station on the right, into a private room. An African-American woman in her mid-thirties sits at a desk, a stack of papers in front of her. One by one, she passes us papers, explains each one, then instructs me to sign on a dotted line.

"What if I don't want to sign?"

"Then your mother can sign for you. We don't need your permission to admit you if we have hers." I look down at her name tag. *Olivia.*

"And there's no way around this? There's no way for me to leave?"

"Not until you turn eighteen."

Six weeks in this hell hole? I sit, dazed, not digesting what I'm reading or what she's saying. Whatever I don't sign, Olivia hands over to Mom and she signs it. Finally, there are no more papers.

"Ms. Worth, it's time for Erika to get settled and complete her intake interview with Dr. Davis. You may say your goodbyes now."

Mom looks at me, blue eyes tinged with red. I love her and I hate her and I want her out of my sight and I never want her to leave.

"I'll come see you tomorrow before I leave for Pennsylvania," she says.

"You're still going on your trip? You're just going to leave me here? *You can't just leave me here.*" I can't breathe. "*Please...*" I beg one more time.

"It's going to be okay, Erika. I love you." She wraps her arms around me.

I stand motionless. "Fuck you."

She leaves. I am alone.

"Place your bag on the table, Erika," instructs Olivia.

I begrudgingly do as I'm told, and watch as she dons a pair of surgical gloves and empties the contents of my bag on the table.

"Something specific you're looking for, Sunshine?"

"Please remove your coat and hand it to me."

"I'm cold."

"Erika, remove your coat." She stands with a gloved hand extended to me.

I hand it to her, and she turns the pockets inside out, feels the lining. She then does the same to my empty bag.

My entire world fits on one table: a stack of black clothing, three pairs of black shoes, a pack of Marlboro reds and a lighter, a copy of Victor Hugo's *Les Misérables,* makeup, toothbrush, razor, the usual toiletries, and a journal and pen. Silently, she sorts through each item. When she's through, she removes my razor and cigarettes from the pile.

"Um, Nurse Ratched, I need those. How the hell am I supposed to smoke and shave?"

"You can shave with a staff member present, and there's no smoking in the adolescent ward."

"What do you mean, *no smoking*? That's, like, impossible. *Duh.*" Then the rest of what she said kicks in. "And a staff member present? I'm not showering with one of you creepoids watching me."

"Then you can walk around fuzzy like the rest of the girls around here."

"This place sucks to the max, in case you didn't know." I roll my eyes nearly out of their sockets to emphasize my displeasure. "Like, *totally.*"

"Thanks for your input. Now, pack your things back into your bag and follow me to your room. There's one thing I want to show you first." She walks out of the private room and leads me to a different door in the back of the nurses' station. "Look through here." She points at a twelve-by-twelve-inch square window at eye level to the door we're standing in front of.

"Ooh, so mysterious," I say, sarcasm dripping from every syllable. When I look through the window, my heart drops and plays ping pong with my ankles. Inside is a padded room. In the center is a surgical-looking table with three restraints attached to either side of the table. "What the—are you going to put me in there?" I gulp.

"Not today. This is the Level I isolation room. If you act out violently, inappropriately, or commit a major offense, you will be in this room for eight hours. If you act out while in the room, your time will start over. Today, you start at Level II, and you will be on the A wing." She points to the corridor on the right behind the locked steel doors. "The more cooperative you are, the more points you earn and you can work up to Level III and move your room over to the B wing." She points to the corridor with the foosball table and television. "Level III patients get to enjoy their meals in the cafeteria, and may earn the right to go on day passes."

"Like, does that mean they get to leave?"

"That's exactly what it means."

"How long does it take to get on Level III?"

"It all depends on the patient. Currently, there is no one on Level III. I'm going to show you to your room where you can unpack your things. Dr. Davis will be here shortly to do your intake interview."

"Who's Dr. Davis?"

"He's your psychiatrist."

"And who are you?"

"I'm Olivia, one of the nurses here. Now grab your things and follow me."

She opens the door to the A wing and I follow her out of the nurses' station. Sitting on the floor on either side of the hallway is a motley gang of seven kids. I try not to make eye contact—some of them might be crazy. I focus on the back of Olivia's braided head as I follow her down the corridor to the third door on the right.

"This is your room." She opens the door and enters.

Inside is a standard hospital room: two twin beds on the left with a nightstand between them; to the right, two matching armoires on either side of a dresser; straight ahead is a window; to the sharp left, a bathroom. The bed closest to the window has a stuffed animal on it, and various pictures taped to the wall behind it. The other bed is closest to the bathroom. It has a stack of books on it, but is otherwise uninhabited.

"This is your bed." She points to the one with the books. Dr. Davis will be ready for you shortly."

Olivia leaves me without so much as a Corona to take the edge off. I set my things on my bed and walk to the window. I open the curtains and realize in horror the window doesn't actually open. At the top of the window is a two-inch cylindrical vent that lets air in.

I sit on my bed and inspect the stack of recovery books and pamphlets people in rehab are supposed to find inspiring or useful. "Fuck this shit." I pick up the big blue book with white lettering and throw it against the wall. It makes a delicious thud before falling to the floor.

Moments later, the door opens and Olivia walks in. She inspects the book on the floor, then directs her brown-eyed gaze my way. "Problem?"

I flush purple and swallow the cotton that's formed in my mouth. "Nope. No problem. Just dropped a book."

"Good. Let's keep it that way." She exits again.

I slump on the bed, overcome by rage and self-pity. *What the fuck just happened to my life?* I'd only ever heard of one other kid at school going to rehab, but I never asked him about it. I'm a straight-A student. I had the lead in the play. I've hustled countless amounts of people for all sorts of things. I've got to be able to talk my way out of this.

A tall, lanky punk-rock girl walks in. "Hey, I'm Jeannette, your roommate." I look over her short black hair with streaks of purple and blue, piercings, black lipstick, torn black stockings, a black miniskirt, and a tattered Stooges T-shirt. I love her immediately.

"I'm Erika." I can't think of anything else to say, so I turn to my bag and start unpacking my things.

She sits on her bed, crosses her gazelle-like legs, and tucks her stuffed teddy bear on her lap. "This place doesn't suck too bad. I've been in worse places," she offers with monotone inflection.

"How many places have you been in?"

"This is my fourth. I've been here for two weeks. Trust me, this is like Club Med compared to some other ones."

Four? "What are you in here for?"

She holds out her wrists for my inspection. Scarred slashes adorn her wrists like barbed-wire bracelets. "What are you in here for?"

"I have no fucking idea, but hopefully they'll realize what a cosmic mistake they made and let me out of here soon."

Before I finish unpacking, Olivia enters. "It's time for your intake interview, Erika. Follow me."

"I'll introduce you to everyone else when you get back. See ya," says Jeannette, then leans against the wall and holds her teddy bear closer.

Underneath the morbidity, she's just a kid. Olivia leads me down the hall to an office at the end of the A wing. Dr. Davis stands when I walk in. Olivia leaves, closing the door behind her.

"Hello, Erika. I'm Dr. Davis," he says, gesturing for me to sit in a chair opposite his.

This is the guy who can get me out of here. "Hi, Dr. Davis. It's lovely to meet you," I say, flashing a smile.

He's tall with a head of thick sandy brown hair and matching full beard, wearing a charcoal-gray suit with a silver-blue tie that matches his eyes. He looks serious, but has kind eyes.

He retrieves a yellow notepad from his briefcase, a pen from an inside pocket of his suit jacket, and crosses his legs. "Erika, do you know why you're here?"

"Actually, I'm pretty sure this is all a big mistake. I know Mom and I have been fighting a lot, but there's a lot of stuff between us you should probably know about. She's a single mom and her boyfriend used to molest me. We moved into our own place a year ago, thank God, but she's got some serious issues. You should be talking to her."

"Have you ever thought about killing yourself?"

Lie. "Once, a long time ago. Who hasn't?"

"Did you tell a counselor at school that you were thinking about committing suicide?"

How does he know about that? "Oh, that." I laugh. "That was just a bad day of PMS. I'm fine. Mom just stresses me out sometimes, and all my AP classes and keeping up my GPA. You know?"

"Do you drink alcohol?"

An easy one. "Yep, but it has no effect on me. I can drink a fifth of vodka and walk a straight line. My friend, Jeff, and I split a couple cases of Lucky Lager beer and don't even feel it. Alcohol is definitely not a problem for me," I brag.

"Have you ever smoked marijuana?"

"I've smoked weed a bunch of times but I hate it. It usually makes me throw up and I just sit and stare at people and get really antisocial. I haven't smoked weed in a year."

As I answer, he jots things down on his yellow pad with his left hand while stroking his beard with his right. It's unnerving.

"Cocaine?"

"Umm, a little, but it doesn't have any effect on me. I can snort a gram and go right to sleep."

"Heroin?"

I guffaw. "No way. Only addicts do heroin." I shake my head in disgust, showing Dr. Davis how ridiculous the mere idea of heroin is. I omit the fact the only reason I haven't done it is because I never knew anyone who had any. I hate needles but, from what I hear, heroin is heaven.

"Hallucinogens?"

"Acid. Mushrooms."

"How much acid do you take?"

"The first time, two tabs. It was awesome. It was like the missing key to the universe and I understood everything. I forgot it all a second later, but it was amazing while it lasted."

"How much acid would you say you take now?"

Lie. "A few tabs here and there. It's definitely not a problem."

"Anything else?"

"Just some pills and stuff. Nothing major."

Dr. Davis is silent. More beard stroking and scribbling. I break into a sweat. After a few minutes, he tucks his yellow pad into the side pocket of his briefcase and looks at me. "Thank you for your candor, Erika."

"Sure, no problem. Can I go home now?"

"Not yet. I have some paperwork to look over. We can chat more about that tomorrow."

Just one night, Erika. And you don't want to end up in the isolation room so just chill the fuck out. "Cool. Thanks. Is that it?"

"Yes, for now." He looks at his watch. "It's almost dinnertime. They'll deliver a meal to your room. We'll talk tomorrow."

"Thanks, Dr. Davis. Have a good one." I give him a thumbs up, hoping a little perkiness goes a long way.

I leave and walk down the empty hall toward my room. As I approach my door, I'm stopped by a male staff member pushing a rolling cart stacked with thick, brown plastic food trays.

"Hi, Erika. I'm Alan." He grabs a tray from the cart and hands it to me. "And this is dinner."

"Thanks." I take it and enter my room. Jeannette is sitting on her bed, sketching. Her food tray lays untouched on the dresser.

"Hey, how'd it go?"

"Okay, I guess. I'm pretty sure he gets I don't belong here. He said we'd talk more in the morning." I sit on my bed and hold the tray on my lap, then peel off the tin foil to reveal a chicken breast covered in some kind of gravy, mashed potatoes, overcooked green beans, and a delightful-looking brownie. I can't remember the last time I've eaten, but I'm not hungry, so I grab the brownie and set the tray on the dresser next to Jeannette's. I bite into it. Dense, moist, and covered with a thick layer of chocolate icing. It's no Marlboro, but it'll do in a pinch. "Where can we get coffee?"

"Patients can't drink coffee."

"No coffee *and* no cigarettes? Are you kidding me? How do people survive around here?"

"You get used to it. They keep you so busy you don't have much time to think."

"Busy how?"

"There's breakfast and meds at seven. Then four hours of school from eight to noon. Lunch is at noon. Doctor's appointments are from one to two. Group therapy until four. Occupational therapy until five. Then they take us up to the roof for an hour until six. We have a free hour, which is usually for homework. Dinner is at seven, then free time until nine, when it's time for lights out."

"Wow, that's a lot."

"Oh, and a couple of nights a week twelve-step panels come in and talk."

"What are those?"

"They're people who used to be really fucked up on drugs and alcohol. They're clean now and come tell us their horror stories to try to scare us sober or something."

"What the fuck?"

"It's cool, though. No staff is allowed in the room for an hour. You can say whatever you want without anyone using it against you. It's only for the dual diagnosis kids."

"Dual diagnosis?"

"It's when you're mental and a druggie. Almost all of us are DD, except for Elliot. He's just mental. Wanna go meet everyone?"

I'd rather cut off my tits, eat them, throw them up, and eat them again. "Sure, I guess."

We walk out into the hallway, which is once again littered with teenage bodies. Jeannette and I slump to the floor and sit near the gang. I lean my back against the wall and cross my legs straight out in front of me, unsure who to make eye contact with first.

Jeannette breaks the silence. "Hey guys, this is Erika."

"Hey gurl, I'm Rachel. Wassup?" says a pretty brunette who talks even quicker than I do while she fiddles with her large gold-fish earrings. Brown freckles splash across translucent skin. Dark-brown feathered hair tumbles down her back. Thick black liner eclipses her eyes, almost making them raccoonish.

Next to Rachel sits one of the largest boys I've ever seen. He has gigantic hands, limbs, and feet, and a protruding forehead like Frankenstein. His chin droops nearly to his chest, and he stares in a daze at the floor. A long drip of spit escapes from his open lower lip onto his gray hoodie. For a moment, he looks over at me with an expressionless stare.

"This is Chuck," says Rachel.

Then, the tiniest and cutest pixie hippie stands up and starts hopping from one foot to the other. Under five feet tall, she's no more than twelve or thirteen years old, with a wild mane of curly blonde hair, wearing a tie-dye Grateful Dead T-shirt, blue jeans, and an impish smile. "I'm Becca, and I have to pee like a lizard on stilts," she says with the raspy voice of a heavy smoker that doesn't seem possible coming out of such a tiny human. She scurries down the hall and disappears into what I assume is her room.

"That girl is crazy," says a caramel-skinned girl with the delicate features of a porcelain doll. In another life, she could have been Cleopatra. She directs a chilly stare at me and assesses me from head to toe. "Tiffany," she says, then turns her attention back to the *Cosmopolitan* she's reading.

An African-American boy, no more than thirteen years old, stands from his place on the floor. He moves down the hall and plops down next to me. "Hi, I'm Elliot," he says, smiling. His voice cracks with puberty.

He's just a baby. They're all just babies. What the hell are they doing in this place? "Hi." I smile back.

He tilts his head and rests his ear on his shoulder in shyness, then burst into giggles. I melt from his cuteness and want to hug away whatever pain put him here.

I look over at the only girl who hasn't spoken yet, a harsh-looking chola with drawn-on, pencil-thin eyebrows, Lennox 13 gang tattoos on her arms and knuckles, and an eyebrow piercing. Her ebony hair is parted down the middle and feathered like a Latina Farah Fawcett.

"I'm Maribel," she murmurs, shifting her eyes around and then to the floor. She wraps and unwraps a tendril of her hair around one finger.

"Hi." I smile back. L.A. gangs are nothing to laugh at, but despite her tough exterior, she looks scared, unsure of herself. *Guess you're not the only one who wears masks, Erika.*

Alan opens the glass window of the nurses' station and calls down the corridor, "Chuck, come get your meds."

I look over at Chuck, who either didn't hear Alan or doesn't care. Either way, he doesn't move. Rachel nudges him with her elbow. As if waking up from a deep sleep, he raises his gigantic head, turns, and looks past her down the corridor at Alan.

"Go get your meds," Rachel instructs.

Chuck slowly stands up and lumbers toward the nurses' station. He's even bigger than I initially thought, standing at least six-foot-six.

I whisper in Jeannette's ear, "What's wrong with him? Why is he like that?"

"He's on Thorazine," she replies, as if I'm supposed to know what that is. Perhaps sensing my confusion, she continues. "He's doing the Thorazine shuffle. He can get pretty mad, so they sedate him like that to keep him under control. When he freaks out, it takes the whole male staff of the hospital to pin him down."

"Holy shit. Poor guy." I realize my only knowledge of psychiatric hospitals is from *One Flew Over the Cuckoo's Nest.* "Oh, shit! Do they do shock treatments and crap like that here?"

"Not on us kids, but upstairs is the lock-down adult ward. Those people are fucked up fo' real and shiiit," answers Rachel.

Chuck shuffles past us and into his room, just as Becca bounces her way down the hall and sits cross-legged opposite me. "What did I miss?"

It's impossible to look at her smile and not smile back.

"Nothing," says Tiffany, looking up from her magazine, bored. "I'm going to my room." She leaves.

"So..." Becca leans in closer to me. "What's your story? Are you crazy or what?"

I laugh, "Uh, kinda, but I'm sure I'm getting out of here tomorrow."

"I thought that too when they first brought me here. Been here a month." Becca laughs. "So, what kinda music do you like?"

"All kinds. New Wave, goth, classic rock—"

"Like the Dead?" she interrupts with breathy excitement.

I laugh again. *God, she's cute.* "No, but I love Pink Floyd. They're probably my favorite band of all time."

"The Wall, or Dark Side?"

"The Wall. Best album ever made.

"Righteous," she replies, bubbling with approval.

"How old are all you guys?" I ask.

"Elliott, Jeannette, and me are thirteen. Tiffany is fifteen. Chuck and Maribel are sixteen. Rachel just turned seventeen. How old are you?"

"I'll be eighteen in six weeks. Damn, I'm like a grandma."

"Elliott, Maribel, Jeannette, and Rachel, come get your meds," calls Alan.

One by one, they stand up and walk to the nurses' station.

I decide to go to my room where I can quell my sensory overload. "I'm going to write for a bit. I'll see you guys later."

"Fer sure. Toodles." Becca grins and wiggles her fingers at me like she's infusing me with fairy dust.

I enter my room, walk over to the window, and stare at the world below. Cars pass. Pedestrians walk by. People go about their lives as if the entire world hasn't just imploded. I lean my cheek against the cool glass and try to breathe. I want to run far away from imprisoned babies, medicated giants, restraints, and feelings.

I go back to my bed, crawl under my covers with all my clothes on, and let emotional exhaustion and waves of self-pity lull me to sleep. I don't hear Jeannette come back in.

In the middle of the night, an elderly man with a clipboard pops his head into our room. "Checks," he says quietly. He looks at Jeannette and me, then leaves.

For a second, I forget where I am and panic. If I was home right now, I could take something, watch TV, talk on the phone, or sneak out of the house. Here, all I can do is lie in the dark and cry myself back to sleep.

At 7:00 AM, Alan opens the door and announces breakfast. I'm still in my clothes from yesterday and decide on a quick shower and change. When I come out of the bathroom, Jeannette's already gotten my tray and set it on the dresser. Scrambled eggs, tater tots, bacon, and orange juice. Not exactly my usual handful of pills and black coffee, but a good Irish girl can never resist a potato in any form.

After I finish eating, Olivia comes for me and escorts me to the nurses' station, where a different male nurse, Robert, hands me a small paper cup with two pills in it.

I turn to Olivia. "What are these?"

"Those are your meds," she responds.

"But I'm not on any meds. These aren't mine," I protest and hand the cup back to her.

"As of today, you are. You've been put in the dual diagnosis program. You can speak to your doctor about it later."

"What do you mean I'm in the dual program? Did Dr. Davis not listen to a single thing I told him last night? Can you get him on the phone please?" The last twenty-four hours made no sense. I had a plan. I had everything under control. "And what are these? I don't want to take anything."

"Desipramine and Tegretol."

"What do they do?"

"One is an antidepressant, and the other stabilizes anger."

"I don't need them. I'm fine. It's everyone else around me you should be medicating." I cross my arms in front of me in a show of stubborn protest. "I won't take them."

"Erika, your mother signed the consent. We don't need your permission. If you don't take them, it will be considered an offense. Seeing as it's Christmas Eve and your first day here, perhaps you'd like to stay out of the isolation room today," Olivia says with a smile.

"Hmph. I *will* speak to Dr. Davis about this."

"I'm sure you will." Olivia hands me a separate paper cup filled with water.

I've swallowed pills by the handful for years with zero issue, yet these two little pills go down like golf balls. Everything in me wants to protest, but I glance over at the Level I room and surrender the small battle. Defeated, I mope back down the corridor to my room, where Jeannette is dressed and ready.

"What are we doing today?" I ask.

"School."

"We have school today? But it's Christmas Eve?"

"We have school every day but the weekends. But don't worry, it's not real school. We get to watch movies today. Come on."

She leads me to the common room.

"Normally school is at the end of the B wing, but today it's in here."

A middle-aged man with gray hair and a beard fiddles with the television and VCR, while the rest of the kids trickle in and pick their seats.

Becca bounces into the room. How can anyone be so happy in a place like this? "What are we watching, Mr. Hall?"

"*Sid and Nancy* and *Ferris Bueller's Day Off*," he responds. He finishes connecting the components then turns to me.

You've got to be fucking kidding me.

"Erika, come with me, please."

I follow him down the hall and into the classroom. Various textbooks fill the shelves along the wall. Math. English. History. Two long tables surrounded by chairs fill up what space is left by the bookshelves.

"I'm Mr. Hall and I'll be your teacher while you're here."

"Hi."

"Usually, we receive assignments from your teachers. Since you've come in during winter break, we don't have anything for you yet. And from your file, I understand you're in AP courses. Is that correct?"

"Yep."

"Well, we don't have any of that material here, so we'll have to wait until we get those assignments."

"What do I do until then?"

"Feel free to read or write during school time. It's mandatory that you're in class, but as long as you're doing something productive it'll be fine."

We walk back to the common room. Everyone settles into the sofas and chairs and we start the first movie. The irony of showing a movie like *Sid and Nancy* to a bunch of disturbed, drug addict kids is not lost on me. Graphic scenes of Gary Oldman shooting heroin remind me how great it feels to be loaded. Every cell in my body craves relief from reality. I can't remember the last time I've been completely sober. Drugs are oxygen.

Nancy Spungen screams, "Siiiiiiiid, what about the farewell drugs?" *Yeah, Sid. What about the farewell drugs?* If I'd known I was going to be taking a break, I'd have gone out with a bigger bang.

At noon, we eat lunch as a group. Rachel and Becca do most of the talking and rapid fire questions at me. Why am I here? What's my family like? How many times have I tried to kill myself? I dodge them with one-word answers in between bites of cheeseburger and fries. Cute as these kids are, I am not telling them my shit.

After lunch, I'm once again summoned and led back to the room where Olivia did my intake. When I walk in, I'm greeted by a man in his mid-forties with salt and pepper hair, caramel-colored eyes, wearing a track suit and tennis shoes. He sits at the desk and gestures for me to sit in the chair opposite him. When I do, he kicks his feet up on the desk, leans back, and clasps his hands behind his head.

"I'm Dr. Berkowitz," he says with a genuine smile. "I'm your psychologist."

"I thought that was Dr. Davis?"

"No, he's your psychiatrist. He's in charge of your meds. You'll meet with him two times a week, about fifteen minutes each time. You'll see me five days a week for an hour each day."

"What are we going to talk about?"

"Whatever you want or need to. Would you like to tell me why you think you're here?"

He's so cool and relaxed, not to mention hot, and kind of reminds me of Hawkeye from *M*A*S*H*. Maybe his hearing is a little better than Dr. Davis'.

"Look, Dr. B, I'm sure you're really awesome, but me being here is a huge mistake."

He opens a manila folder and starts leafing through documents. "It's my understanding that you're here because you have a desire to kill yourself. Is that true?"

I open my mouth to lie, but he's got my file. It's useless. Then I open my mouth to be a smartass, but he looks at me—not just at me, but through me—and his direct kindness stops me in my tracks. Unable to break eye contact with him, I respond. "Yes."

"Will you tell me what hurts so much you want to end your own life?"

The truth sits like a pill on my tongue. I can't decide whether to swallow or spit it out. "Everything."

The tears come. Not manipulative tears to distract him, nor the kind I unleash on my mother to induce punishment or guilt. These are the tears of a soul who's given up all hope of life not hurting.

Dr. B hands me a Kleenex box. I grab two tissues and cover my face in shame. "I hate it when I cry."

"Crying is a completely normal reaction to pain." He pauses, then softens his tone. "Erika, what are you afraid of?"

I pull my knees up to my chest and wrap my arms around my shins. "Fuck, Dr. B. What am I not afraid of? I'm afraid of hurting my mom. I'm afraid to live. I'm afraid to die. I'm afraid I'll fail at everything. Mostly, I'm afraid the whole world will find out what a complete piece of shit I am and throw me away."

"Why do you think you're a piece of shit?"

"*Duh.* It's pretty obvious. My own father didn't want me. My mother got stuck with me, and I ruined her entire life by being born. And then there's all the guy stuff—" I stop myself and cringe. *I can't tell him about that.*

"Start at the beginning. Tell me about your family."

"Look, Dr. B. I don't remember a lot of my childhood. My memories are like postcards underneath dingy, sticky sheets of plastic in a photo album. I get flashes of images and conversations, then huge voids of nothing. What I do remember, I'd mostly rather forget."

"There's an explanation for that if you're interested."

"Enlighten me."

"If you're walking along the forest, and everything in your life is fine, you gather imprints from your surroundings: sunlight streaming through trees, birds chirping to each other, the rustle of leaves. If all is well, you can be present in each moment. You can breathe, look around, and relax. You form memories."

"Then why have I blocked out so much?"

"Let's say one day you spot a gigantic bear across the way. Your entire focus is now on the bear. You study the bear, committing to memory each jagged tooth, the smell of its breath, the fur, protruding claws. All that matters in your entire world is that bear. Even when it's not around, you're on high alert, waiting for the bear to return. Each day you wonder if today will be the day you'll be torn apart. You stop forming memories of anything other than the bear."

"Fuck. My life is filled with bears."

"Tell me about one you can remember."

I tell him about my first memory.

I'm three or four-ish. It's winter and I want to go sledding, but Mom-Mom is taking me on a special trip and has to put her face on. I stand on the yellow fluffy toilet seat cover and watch how she puts gray powder around her blue eyes, and some peach on her cheeks and lips. When she's done with her lipstick, she lets me dab some on my mouth. I feel pretty. She stares at herself in the mirror.

"Mom-Mom, you look like Elizabeth Taylor."

Her cheeks turn into little apples. Praise always makes her smile. She moves to her closet and gets dressed: pulls up her suntan stockings, zips up her frosty blue dress, clips on her Avon earrings, and slips into beige high heels that match her purse.

I want shoes like hers. I slip my tiny feet into a red pair in her closet and try to walk. I fall every time but keep trying.

Mom-Mom finishes dressing and turns from side to side, watching herself in the mirror. Satisfied, she walks out of the room, leaving a trail of perfume behind her.

We get in her car and zoom through snowy, winding Pennsylvania country roads, past fir trees covered in cotton balls and hills covered with white blankets. Mom-Mom's driving scares most people. Not me. I like to go fast, and she lets me talk on the CB radio.

"Breaker, breaker, anyone out there?" I ask into the plastic microphone like she taught me. "This here's Cookie Monster."

"Howdy, Cookie Monster. This is Bear. What's your twenty?" a voice crackles over the radio.

I look to Mom-Mom for guidance. She takes the microphone and pushes the talk button. "Hi Bear. This is Melody," she says with a tone she only uses when talking to men.

"Well, well, Miss Melody. How are you doing today, you pretty thing?"

"Just fine and dandy, Bear. My granddaughter and I are heading into town now."

"You be careful on those back roads. They're icy in some spots."

"I will. See you soon, now," she says and winks, even though he can't see her.

"I look forward to it," says Bear in a deep voice, then he growls. I wonder if that's how he got his name.

I take back the microphone and push the button. "Cookie Monster, over and out." I beam at Mom-Mom with pride.

We arrive at Oxford Diner and sit at a booth with a man named Ray. I sit next to Mom-Mom on the inside next to the little jukebox. I get a chocolate milkshake with extra whipped cream and *two* cherries. I know not to interrupt adults when they're talking, so I swing my feet under the table and try not to slide off the seat.

Mom-Mom passes me a nickel to put in the jukebox. I flip through the pages until I see Hank Williams' face just like on Mom-Mom's eight-track. I pick him because he's one of her favorites.

"Time to go, Erika," Mom-Mom says in her sweet voice. I like her sweet voice. It doesn't make people cry.

Back in her yellow VW bug, we follow Ray down the road into a parking lot. "Stay in the car. I need to talk to Ray. I'll be back in a bit." She bundles an extra scarf around my neck, pushes the lock button down on the door, closes it, then walks with Ray along the snowy sidewalk. They disappear behind a red door.

I count all the red doors. There are ten. Pink neon letters flash on a big sign in the parking lot: *V A C A N C Y.* When I finish counting and spelling, I sing to myself and draw pictures on the frosty window. Eventually, I fall asleep.

When I wake up, Mom-Mom is gently tugging at my elbow. "Come inside, Erika. We're home."

When we walk in, Pop-Pop is sitting at the kitchen table. "Hey, Skeeter," he says to me, holding out his arms for a hug.

I run into his open arms, then jump up on his lap and snuggle into his warmth, breathing in the smell of Old Spice. I poke my finger into the dimple on his chin. "Hiya, Pop-Pop! Wanna go sleddin'?" I ask, covering his face with kisses.

"In a lil' while, honey," he says, then blows a raspberry on my neck. I giggle uncontrollably. "Did you two have a good day?"

Mom-Mom wipes the counter, then neatly folds the dishcloth into a perfect square and turns to Pop-Pop. She stares at him while he bounces me on his lap. "I had a great day, Bill. Want to know where I was?" she asks.

"Sure I do, honey. That's why I asked." He chuckles.

"I spent the afternoon in bed with a *real* man, and we did it a lot more than once."

Pop-Pop's legs stop moving. She stares at him, arms crossed in front of her like a pretzel, her chin high as she looks down her nose at him. Her left eyebrow crooks up. This Mom-Mom scares me. Tears fill Pop-Pop's eyes and his shoulders slump forward. He pulls his red bandana from his pant pocket and wipes his nose.

"All I-l-l-l try t-t-t-to do is m-m-ma-a-ake you happy. N-N-Nu-Nuf-ff-fffin' I do is ever g-g-g-good 'nuf," he sniffles. His stutter is always worse when she's mean. I slide off his lap when he stands up, and then he leaves the kitchen.

Mom-Mom grins like the fat cat from Alice in Wonderland. I want to get away from her. I leave and find Pop-Pop in the living room, sitting in his big chair next to the fireplace, sobbing. His whole body shakes and he wheezes as he cries. He wipes his eyes with his handkerchief.

I hold his hand and start to cry with him. "Pop-Pop, please don't cry." I crawl up into his lap and wrap my tiny arms around his neck. I try to hug the sadness out of him, but my arms are too little. I hate her for making him cry.

Dr. B interrupts. "This is a good place to stop. Our time is up. You did really well, Erika"

"Um, thanks, I guess."

"We'll meet again here tomorrow. Same time."

"So, we're just going to talk about stuff like this?"

"We'll talk about whatever you need to."

"And what if there's stuff I don't want to tell you?"

With unwavering intensity, he looks at me. "This is a process. It's not going to happen all at once. We've got time." He gathers the files from his desk. "I look forward to talking with you more tomorrow."

comfortably numb

I go back to the common room for drug counseling. I'm greeted by a chubby guy in his twenties. Like a bratty teenager, I give him the once-over from head to toe. He's wearing a long-sleeved shirt and vest, and black pleated pants which make his front look puffy like harem pants, a bolo tie, and high-heeled ankle boots. He's growing some kind of moustache, though it looks more like a millipede perched on his upper lip. A mop of greasy curls atop his head trails down to a mullet that ends just above his collar.

He extends a hand to me. "Hi, Erika. I'm Dave, your addiction counthelor. It's nithe to meet you."

He's got braces and a slight lisp. Several wisecrack remarks came to mind, but I stay quiet and sit in an empty chair.

The other patients and I sit in a circle and stare at the floor. My meds kick in and all I want is to nap. Instead, I listen to Dave and his lisp talk about alcoholism and addiction. I zone out, willing this nightmare to end. Occasionally, something a kid says sparks my interest, but I don't want to listen. If I listen, I'll start to care, and that's when bad shit happens.

I am in a circle of strangers talking about feelings. Like being dropped in the middle of Russia, I don't know where I am, the people, or the language. Nothing makes sense. Nothing is familiar.

"Tho, Erika, when wath your firsth drink?" Dave asks.

It takes a moment to register he's talking to me. All eyes shift my way. "Um, I don't remember. I always drank."

"What do you mean, always?"

"I'm told my stepdad used to dip his finger in scotch and rub it against my gums when I was teething. When I got a little older, he let me sip his beer. That was standard parenting in 1971."

"What about when it was your choice?" Dave asks.

"I think I was five or so. My mom worked as a legal secretary. Grown-ups always left scotch around. I didn't know what it was, but the adults were doing it, so I wanted some. I remember standing on my tiptoes and wrapping my tiny little fingers around heavy crystal glasses. That shit tasted awful, and burned my throat, but it tickled my brain like butterfly wings."

"Is alcohol your drug of choice?" asks Rachel.

Okay. Let's shut this shit down right now. "Look, you guys, I don't have a drug of choice. I know I'm in this place for a while until shit gets sorted out, but drugs and alcohol are not a problem."

Rachel chimes in again. "Then why are you in here?"

"Why are you here?" I fire back. "Are you all alcoholics and addicts?"

Everyone simultaneously looks at the floor.

"Why do you think you're not?" asks Dave.

"Dude, an alcoholic is an old guy in a trench coat in an alley with a bottle. An addict is a junkie with a needle in their arm. I'm neither of those things. I can handle drugs and alcohol, no problem."

Dave hands me a long, thin card with twenty questions typed on it. "How many of theeth can you thay yeth to?"

I go down the list and mentally say yes to every single one. A sentence at the very bottom reads: *If you have answered yes to three or more, you are definitely an alcoholic. Jesus.* "Is this some kind of trick question bullshit?"

"Nope. How many did you say yes to?"

"Fuck you, lithpy. I'm not an alcoholic."

Dave ignores my barb. "If you're not an alcoholic, why ith the thought of giving up drugth and alcohol tho difficult?"

I open my mouth to say something shitty, then realize I have no good answer to that question. It has never occurred to me to survive without drugs and alcohol. Why would I want to?

Later in my room, I think back to what a lonely kid I was. My insides always felt messy and intense, like someone turned the volume button all the way up and broke off the knob. I was an alien who wanted out. As a little girl, I looked up at the night sky as she wept tears of stars, and begged whatever put me here to come back.

Like a puzzle piece with no matching sides, I didn't fit. I had one friend, Abby, but I was even weird around her. I'd never seen a family like hers before.

Her mom, Kate, was a beautiful hippie. Chocolate ringlets flecked with gold tumbled past her tan shoulders. Make-up free, she wore crocheted halter-tops, flowing gypsy skirts, and walked around barefoot. Dylan, her dad, looked like a mountain man, with twinkling Irish eyes and a bushy beard. Her little brother, Colin, was annoying, but at least he was there. Nothing seemed to bother Abby. She was just normal and happy.

I spent as many nights over there as possible so I could study them. Kate brought food to the table, then leaned in, kissed her husband's cheek, and wrapped her arms around his neck. Dylan took her hand and kissed the top of each fingertip, then pulled her onto his lap. Colin kicked Abby under the table, and pouted when she didn't react. They talked to each other and laughed. I was enchanted.

Kate and Dylan owned a liquor store, and they always had big jugs of wine in their fridge. When everyone else went to bed, I'd lie awake, wondering what my life would be like if I'd been born into their family. I kept a running list of all the things I wasn't, didn't have, and would never be.

My brain never shut off, so I snuck down to the kitchen in my Holly Hobby nightgown, stood in front of their fridge, and guzzled cool, crisp rosé straight out of the bottle. After two trips to the kitchen, I could finally sleep.

When I was eight, Mom and I were at a dinner party with quiche and Blue Nun wine.

"Can I have some, please?" I asked and pointed to the bottle.

The adults, all in their twenties with no children, laughed at my cute request, then turned to Mom for approval. She winked and nodded, and they poured me my own glass with an inch of wine.

"Now, Erika, ladies sip their wine, and hold out their pinkie like so," someone said, followed by a proper pinkie demonstration.

I did as I was told, held the glass up to my mouth, and guzzled it all.

The adults laughed. "No, Erika, you're supposed to sip it, like we told you."

"Oh. Can I try again? I'll sip the next one. Promise." I crossed my heart and hoped to die.

I learned then that by acting cute and smiling, I could get adults to do almost anything. At parties, I was always the only kid. I went up to men and tugged on their pant legs. "Hey, can I try a sip of that?" I pointed to whatever they were drinking. The women might've blabbed to my mom, but the guys didn't care.

They looked around, made sure no one was watching, then gave me sips on the condition I didn't tell. My lips were sealed, until I moved on to the next unsuspecting partygoer and pulled on the next bit of polyester. More please.

I've never looked at my drinking and using under a microscope. It's just my life. I always needed something to take the edge off. *Probably best not to mention any of this to Dave.*

a better place to be

Mom calls me Christmas Day, but I don't take the call. Fuck her. Let her stew in her guilt.

After breakfast, we watch more movies. I'm just about to doze off when Elliot screams and bangs his head against the wall.

Becca runs over to him. "Elliot, chill out, dude. They're going to put you in Level I."

Mr. Hall also tries to calm Elliot down, but he laughs and runs away out into the hall. We clamor to the door and peek our heads out into the hallway. A male staffer grabs Elliot's arm and warns him about Level I. Elliot hits him and runs past us to the classroom.

A male voice booms over the intercom. "All male staff to the second floor. All male staff to the second floor."

Within moments, several large men emerge from the elevator doors. They retrieve Elliot from the end of the hall, kicking and wailing, and drag him into the Level I room. He screams in agony and we're powerless to help him.

The room. The restraints. They are now strapping that child down onto that table. He's just a baby.

Mr. Hall tells us to come back into the common room. Even with the door closed, his howls fill every breath of space. I don't know if they drug him or if he wears himself out, but he eventually goes silent.

At one, I see Dr. B. again. Depression weighs heavy. "Don't you have anything better to do? It's Christmas."

"I'm happy to spend it here with you. I heard you guys had a rough morning."

"That was fucked up. And there was nothing I could do to help him. I know exactly how he feels. I just keep it in, especially here. I do not want to end up in that room."

"What happens if you let your feelings out?"

My mouth goes dry. "People could get in trouble."

"People like?"

"So what happens if I tell you about something that's against the law?"

"Well, if it involves any kind of abuse, I'm required by law to report it."

I shrink into a ball on my chair, and rest my cheek against my knees.

"Erika, do you want to tell me about your mom's boyfriend. Dr. Davis said you mentioned it to him."

"Damn, do all of you guys talk to each other?"

"Yes. Since you brought it up, would you like to talk about it."

If I was going to tell someone, it would be Dr. B., but shit is crazy enough as it is. I don't need to add cops to the mix. I bite my lip and shake my head. "Nope."

"I heard your mom called you today and you didn't want to speak with her."

"Can you blame me? Would you put your kid in a place like this two days before Christmas?"

"What's your relationship like with her?"

"Oh, it's fucking peachy."

"Has it always been challenging?"

I laugh. "Challenging. It sounds so nice the way you say it." I try to remember a time when I didn't hate her, when we were something other than two people at war.

"What was it like when you were little?"

"It was always just the two of us."

"Where's your father?"

"I have no fucking idea. He met my mom when she was hitchhiking. She was nineteen. He was thirty-six and married. No one will tell me anything about him. I know he was in a work farm when I was born. He got out when I was a couple of months old. Mom said he came straight to us and held me, but of course, I don't remember. She knew he would never leave his wife, so she told him to get lost."

"Did she ever marry?"

"Once, when I eleven months old. He was thirty. She was twenty-two. They were only married a couple of years. Then he messed up their money and took off. I vaguely remember our furniture being repossessed. In Virginia, where I'm from, it takes two years to get a divorce. He kept racking up bills for two years. It was rough, so I stayed with my grandparents in Pennsylvania for a while."

"And what was your mom like?"

I flash back to when I little, as early as I can remember. Mom worked all the time, so the most I got to see her was in the mornings when she got ready for work.

She wraps her long, blonde hair around soup cans and secures them in place with bobby pins.

"Mommy, what are those for?"

"To get the fuzz out," she replies, then presses her lips around the end of a long, skinny cigarette. "We can't all have perfect straight hair like you."

"Do they make your hair smell like soup?"

She laughs. I love it when I make her laugh. "No, Erika. They just straighten my hair."

She puts on her makeup and sings along to The Beatles on the radio. She loves the Beatles more than any other band; she says George is dreamy. She licks the tip of an eyeliner brush, swirls it in a container of black powder, and paints a line from the inside of her eyelid to the outside, then swooshes it up. Then she scrapes a tiny toothbrush across black powder, raises her eyebrows, opens her mouth slightly, and toothbrushes her eyelashes until they grow long and black.

Magic. "Mommy, you're the prettiest mommy in the whole wide world," I boast. "When I grow up, I want to look just like you."

Her lips smile, but her eyes are sad. She stares back at her faace in the mirror. "I hope you don't look like me. I'm fat. My hair is fuzzy. My nose is too big. I have big teeth."

I look in the mirror, then back at her. She looks the same both places. Mommy takes another puff of her cigarette. I wait for her to be happy.

On sad days, she plays Harry Chapin over and over on the record player, and stares through me like I'm invisible. Tears melt down her cheeks like icicles.

I try to kiss them away, but I never have enough kisses. "Don't cry, Mommy. It's gonna be okay."

"I shouldn't have had you. I should have had an abortion, or given you up for adoption."

"I'm sorry, Mommy. I don't mean to make you cry."

"Go play in your room, Erika. I want to be alone."

I'm crying again, and Dr. B hands me the box of tissues. "Well, this is fun, Dr. B. Remind me to hang out with you more often."

"That must have been very painful to hear your mother say that."

"She still says it when she's pissed or depressed. I don't give a shit what she says anymore."

"If that's true, why are you crying?"

"I don't know. I guess I feel bad for that kid. No one wanted her."

"You mean you?"

"Yeah...I mean me."

"That must have felt very lonely."

"Yeah. Well, it doesn't matter anymore. And talking about this shit isn't going to change anything."

"You'd be surprised. Our time is up again, Erika. I won't see you again until Monday."

Two whole days? I've known the man a minute, and I already miss him. Then it hits me, Dr. B is the only person who's asked me what my insides feel like. Maybe ever. I've spent years hiding, and he wants to see me.

rainbow connection

1978

Maggie is the keeper of rainbows. Crystals hang in all the windows of her house. Whenever the sun is shining, prisms of color splash across every surface. When I'm eight, she becomes our new neighbor, and she lets me come over most days.

Her eyes are warm pools of hot chocolate. Even though she's only a few years older than my mom, her brown hair has streaks of silver. She has a gray cat named Ashes who purrs when I scratch her ears. Maggie smokes Camel non-filter cigarettes and drinks J&B scotch whiskey from a dark green bottle. I like the deep, raspy sound she makes when she laughs.

Everything in her home is her own kind of beautiful. Art covers her walls. I stand in front of the pictures and drink them in, each one makes me feel something.

We play double-solitaire on her living room floor, and she cusses when I win. We carve images into linoleum blocks with sharp, curved tools, then print custom cards onto thick parchment paper. We paint pictures on small canvases. We use Japanese brushes to paint watercolors. She teaches me calligraphy with a fountain pen, and how to seal letters shut with melted wax and a metal stamp.

Sometimes, I get to spend the night and sleep next to her under a vintage lace bedspread. She says my snoring sounds like a truck driver, and how could a sound so loud come out of a person so small. I tell her she snores, too. She laughs and says that's impossible.

She gives me a chunk of amethyst, because it's my birthstone. She gives me a deep-purple tie-dyed nightgown from India. She gives me a sea-urchin shell, and carved wooden block letters that spell *LOVE*. She gives me an Erté paper doll kit, and Alphonse Mucha and Queen Elizabeth coloring books. She gives Mommy a book called *The Prophet* by Kahlil Gibran. I steal it and add it to my library.

Her presents are amazing, but that's not why I love her. Maggie never talks to me like I'm a kid. She listens to the stories I make up for her. She gives great hugs. When I'm around her, my lonely goes away.

She tells me artists are special people with a different purpose in this world. She says I'm one of them and, no matter what happens in my life, don't let anyone take that from me.

Maggie gets sick and goes to Texas to see her family. Since she's far away, I talk to her on the phone.

"Maggie! I miss you so much! When are you coming home?"

"Not for a little while longer, Sarah."

"Sarah? I'm Erika, silly goose."

"Yeah. Erika. Of course. Are you taking care of your mom? Cooking her dinner?"

"Um, sometimes I guess."

"Your mother says you have a new boyfriend, and a new car. What kind did you get, Sarah?"

"Maggie...I'm ten. I don't have an icky boyfriend, or a car. It's me.

Erika." I put my hand over the mouthpiece. "Mommy, what's wrong with Maggie? Why doesn't she know who I am?"

Mommy takes the phone from me. "Maggie. We'll call you another time...okay...hope you feel better soon...love you. Bye."

"What's wrong with Maggie?"

Mommy looks at me and crinkles her forehead. "Sweetheart, Maggie has a brain tumor."

"Can the doctors make it better?"

"No. Maggie won't ever get better."

going to california

Just after my eleventh birthday, Mommy goes to Los Angeles for a two-week vacation and comes back with hearts and rainbows floating around her head. His name is George, and I already don't like him. I've seen her with guys before, but I've never seen her loopy.

They send each other cards and letters every single day. He sends her a yellow T-shirt with *California Dreamin'* on it. She sends him one back with *Virginia is for Lovers*. On weekends when long-distance rates are low, she goes into her bedroom and talks to him for hours. I stand outside her door, ear pressed against the wood, and listen to her laugh.

When she's not talking to him, she talks about him. George is so great. George is so handsome. George has a motorcycle. George, George, George. I'm glad she's happy, but why does it have to be because of him? Why can't she be happy because of me?

Three months later, she drops the bombshell we're moving to California.

"No! Why can't he come here?"

"He has a job there, and it's Los Angeles. Sunshine. No more shoveling snow. You'll love it."

"I love it *here,* in our *house.* And you have a job *here.* And friends *here.*" Pop Rocks explode in my brain. "And what about Pop-Pop and Abby and school and the theater and—"

"You can stay with Mom-Mom and Pop-Pop during the summers and on Christmas vacation, and Abby can visit once we get settled into a bigger place."

She's smiling and happy like a Stepford wife, while I'm totally freaking out. My cocker spaniel, Bentley, comes in from the backyard and nuzzles in my lap. I hug him close to me, needing something to hold on to that makes sense. We're finally happy, and now everything is going to disappear. *And how will Daddy ever find me if we move?*

"I'm not going. I'm staying here!"

"Erika, I understand you're upset, but the decision has already been made."

"Bentley and I don't want to go to stupid California."

"Well, actually, I need to talk to you about that."

She breaks eye contact with me, and I recognize her guilt just as the reality hits me. Bentley isn't coming.

"But Mommy, he's my *baby!* I can't leave him!" My bottom lip quivers.

"You're not leaving him, Erika. He's going to live in Pennsylvania with Mom-Mom and Pop-Pop. You'll see him on visits."

I wail and cry all over Bentley. Disturbed, he jumps out of my lap and runs back outside. "You are ruining my *entire life!*"

She pauses and waits for my tantrum to diminish. Then she looks right at me. "What about *my* life, Erika? Don't I deserve a chance to be happy? For *once?*"

And she's got me. More than anything else in the entire world, I want her to be happy. How can I stand in the way of that, after everything she's sacrificed for me? I'm split in two between my selfishness and my love for her.

"Plus, he might be your dad one day. Isn't that what you've always wanted?"

I'm torn between the promise of a new daddy and the hope of my real one finding me.

After spending the summer in Pennsylvania, I arrive at Los Angeles International Airport. The blond duo run up to the gate, hand in hand.

"Hi, Erika! Welcome to California."

I hug her, and look at hairy George standing next to her. He looks like Chuck Norris. Eww.

"Erika, this is George."

"Hi." I shake his hand, then look down at my feet.

"Are you hungry? Do you want us to get you anything on the way home?"

Home. "No. I don't need anything." *Except to be back in Pennsylvania with Pop-Pop and Bentley.*

We drive north on the 405, past a million billboards, cars, and palm trees. *Hotel California* is playing on the radio. I sit in the backseat, silent and helpless, dreaming of a day where I get to make my own choices and don't feel like a prisoner.

She rests her arm behind his headrest, runs her fingers through his hair, and stares at him the way Pop-Pop looks at Mom-Mom. He reaches a hand across and rests it on her knee. They're even grosser in person, but I promised I'd try to keep an open mind.

I look back out into the night as we pass Mulholland Drive, and perk up when I see a sea of twinkling lights below us. For a second, it reminds me of fireflies in the fields behind Pop-Pop's house. "Wow."

Momma looks back over the passenger seat. "This is the valley, Erika. This is where we live."

I don't want to outright punish her, but I'm not going to be doing any cartwheels from the back seat either. "Cool."

We arrive at our apartment in Van Nuys and park in the subterranean garage.

"Is this a hotel or an apartment?"

Mommy laughs. "It's an apartment, silly goose."

It doesn't look like any apartment I've ever seen. Two two-story rectangles of apartments face each other, with a big empty space in the middle where you can look down into the garage.

"There's a pool back there." She points to the rear of the building. I'm exhausted and drained, but make a mental note that California's only a ninety-nine percent failure.

We walk up the stairs and into the tiniest apartment I've ever seen. There's a sofa in front of the door and a small dining table to the right, next to an even smaller kitchen that two people couldn't stand in. Straight ahead past the sofa is a tiny bathroom, and to the right of that the one and only bedroom.

"Um, Mommy, where am I supposed to sleep?"

"I'll let you two settle in. Good night, Erika." George sets my suitcase down by the table and retreats to the bedroom.

Mommy sits on the sofa and pats it gently. "Right here, honey. This is only temporary. Now that you're here, we can get all your school supplies together and move into a bigger place."

Not only did I leave the only real house we've ever lived in, our friends, and my puppy, but now I'm sleeping on a sofa? California sucks to infinity.

Mommy makes up the sofa like a bed. "Get some sleep, Erika. Tomorrow we'll go shopping when I get home from work."

She goes into the bedroom, and I'm left alone. Well, not entirely alone. In addition to the tacky brown furniture, a large black velvet painting of a young, topless woman hangs prominently over the television.

I lie on my back, listening for the sounds of crickets, cicadas, frogs, and Mom-Mom's AM country radio playing softly through the night. Sounds of home are replaced by the whir of the air conditioner, car horns, and the rumble of an occasional low-flying helicopter outside.

The next morning, Mommy wakes me up on her way to work. "Good morning." She sits on the sofa next to me.

Half asleep, I look around and don't recognize anything. "Where are we?"

"We're in California."

My messed-up life floods back to me. It wasn't a dream.

"A couple of things. George is already at work. He should be home around 3:30 or so. I've left a key for you on the table. If you go swimming, make sure to take it with you. There are towels in the linen closet. Food in the fridge. And don't leave the complex."

"Where would I go?"

"I don't know, just stay in the building. Also, if anyone asks which apartment you live in, tell them you're just visiting. This is an adults-only building and George will get in trouble."

"M'kay," I say, desperate not to wake up too much so I can go back to sleep.

When I do finally get up, I waste no time snooping. In the kitchen, I find peanut butter and jelly supplies, Twinkies, and Pop Tarts. *Go Mommy.* In the fridge is a case of Budweiser tall cans, ketchup, mustard, and some pickles. The freezer holds several packages of frozen meat but not a popsicle in sight. *Boo Mommy.*

Next, I snoop through Georgie's eight-tracks and cassettes. Pink Floyd. The Police. Bruce Springsteen. Tom Petty. Not a single musical or Harry Chapin album. How can she be into this guy?

I decide to go for the good stuff and go into their bedroom. Around the room are framed pictures of them kissing, and pictures of Mommy. Not a single picture of me anywhere.

I hit pay dirt under the bed. George has piles of dirty magazines. Mom-Mom reads *Cosmopolitan* and *Playgirl*, and I thought those were bad, but these are *dirty* dirty magazines. *Juggs. Club. Hustler. Penthouse.* These ladies look like body parts with heads, like they aren't real people.

Disturbed, I decide to get as far away from George's stupid apartment as I can and escape to the swimming pool. Water is my new sanctuary. As my chest develops, men look at me funny, especially when I run. The jostling of flesh is disarming, so I've turned to water. In water, I'm weightless. Free.

A few weeks go by and we move into a different apartment building. It doesn't have a swimming pool, but I have my own room again with a white canopy bed. I miss everything about my old life and wonder when or if it will hurt less.

School starts, and I might as well be an alien with purple horns sticking out of my face. All the kids have known each other since kindergarten. They don't know anything about musical theater and think it's weird when I sing to myself. They wear Jordache, Vidal Sassoon, and Little Folks Shop. I wear clothes from Sears, which kids can tell by the unicorn logo where the alligator should be.

In Virginia, we switched classes and had different teachers. Here, all thirty of us sit together in the same room all day. Every hour, the teacher changes subjects, and we put down one book and pick up another.

In fifth grade in Virginia, I was doing pre-algebra. In sixth grade here, we're doing addition, subtraction, multiplication, and division flashcards. Our spelling words are *milk, pink, than, UFO*. In a week, I go through the assignment book that was supposed to last a year. My teachers in Virginia would always give us more to do if we asked, so I ask Mrs. Gage.

She narrows her eyes at me, then stands up in front of the class. "Well, students, it looks like we have a *special* student here. Erika here thinks she's better than the rest of the class." She turns back to me. "Take a seat."

I'm mortified, and Mrs. Gage has effectively started a war between me and my classmates. They corner me in the bathroom, push me on the ground at recess, and knock my books out of my arms. I never make friends easily. Here, it seems impossible.

One day, Makeba, Hilary, and Lisa ask me to be their friend and invite me to a sleepover. We eat pizza and watch *Fantasy Island,* and I feel normal for the first time since we moved here.

When I pass out, they freeze my bra and dip my hand in warm water. I wake up soaked in my own urine, with the girls huddled around me, pointing and laughing. Humiliated, I cry.

"Aww, poor widdle crybaby pee-pee pants," taunts Makeba. "Not so smart now, are ya?"

I call my mom and wait in the bathroom until she comes to get me.

On the drive home, she's angry. "Why doesn't anyone like you? Why don't you have any friends?"

"I don't know. It's not like I try to make people hate me."

"I just can't understand what's wrong with you."

I can't either, but I have never wanted to evaporate into nothingness more than in this moment. "Can I go back to Pennsylvania now?"

"No, Erika. Your home is here with us. Don't you like George? And the new roller skates we got you?"

The roller skates are stupendous, I'll give her that. White with purple wheels and unicorn and rainbow shoelaces, they are a dream come true. I feel like Olivia Newton John in *Xanadu* while I zip around the posts in the sub-garage before our neighbors get home from work.

But George, I could do without. Having a dad isn't as fun as I thought it'd be. He comes home smelling like blood and death after working at the meat plant all day. He drinks too much Budweiser. When we swim in the pool, he holds me tight against him before he throws me across the water. I've started wearing T-shirts over my bathing suit because he's always looking at my chest. Gross. Sometimes when I walk by, he pulls me onto his lap. I feel something hard beneath my butt. When I try to get off his lap, he holds me tighter. Mommy never notices, so I try to ignore him when he does creepy stuff.

School is a torture chamber. My one and only friend is Angela from the fifth grade. She lives a few blocks from me, so we walk to and from school together most days. She's got it rough. Her mom beats her and she's always covered in fresh bruises. She says she doesn't mind and that her mom doesn't mean it. Why does it hurt so much to be a kid? One day before Christmas break, we talk about

Santa. I tell her how I figured out he wasn't real because it was my mom's handwriting on the notes Santa left. Even though she's ten, she didn't know. I feel like the biggest dick for taking away the one good thing she had in her life.

My classmates start threatening to kill me. All thirty of them, led by Makeba, confront me on the playground and tell me they hate me. My neighbor, Elaine, is in the mob. I know she doesn't hate me, but I also know she can't say anything or they'll come after her as well.

My mother and I strike a deal with the principal: I get to read in the back of the room during class and am excused from all participation, and I tutor the first graders during lunch and recess so the kids can't get to me.

A week passes like a month, and I hate every moment of my life here. In June, I finally get to go back home to Pennsylvania for summer break.

* * *

Feet spread, a fist on either hip, head tilted back, and mouth slightly open, I inspect a hornet's nest up in a nearby fir tree. I'm trying to decide if it poses a threat—and, if so, what I should do about it—when I hear the low rumbling of Pop-Pop's Farmall tractor approach. When I was smaller, I'd sit on his lap, my tiny hands grasping the oversized steering wheel as he maneuvered the tractor across his land, leaving perfect stripes of mowed grass behind us.

Now I'm twelve and full of mischief. I crawl under the low-hanging branches of the tree and turn myself into an invisible ninja as he rolls by toward the barn. When the time is right, I'll jump out and scare him, which never ceases to make me giggle with glee. Minutes crawl by and anticipation tickles my skin. I check to make sure there aren't spiders crawling on me.

The sounds of clanking and shuffling emerge from the barn, but no Pop-Pop. I can't imagine what's taking him so long. Patience was never my strong suit, so I decide to move closer and investigate. Like a junior Charlie's Angel, I crawl out from my hiding spot and, hunched over, dart to the side of the barn. Pressing my back against the stone wall, I creep along until I get to the edge, then ever so carefully peek around the corner with one eye. His back is to me, and he's doing something on his work table. This could take a while, but I'm on a mission. Not to brag, but I've developed some mad scaring skills over the years. I'm darn near an expert at it. In it for the long-haul, I hunker down behind the barn door to wait.

While he putters around, I pick at the scab on my knee and swat the occasional gnat away from beads of sweat on my face. Of all the things I miss about the East Coast, humidity isn't one of them. I turn my attention to the rolling fields behind our property. I feel a hundred pounds lighter here.

The sound of boots on gravel reminds me of my mission. He's close. Closer.

I jump up from my hiding place. "BOOOOOOO!"

He holds his hand to his chest. "Dag gummit, Skeeter! You skerred the poop outta me."

I respond with intense giggling. "Just trying to keep you on your toes, Pop-Pop."

We walk side by side back to the house. He removes a red bandana kerchief from the back pocket of his Dickies, wipes the sweat off his neck, rubs it against his nose, and shoves it back. I mimic each move perfectly. He takes his baseball hat off, scratches his bald head, and puts the hat back on. I pretend to do the same.

"Yer jus' plain ornery, aren't ya?"

"Wonder where I got that from?" I wink. I'm grateful to have inherited his sense of playfulness, humor and his belly laugh. "Pop-Pop, I'm booooooooored. Let's go do something!"

"Wanna go fishing down at the crick?"

"Let's go!" He could have asked me if I wanted to stick needles in my eyes, and I would be just as enthusiastic. Anywhere with Pop-Pop is my sanctuary from the rest of the world.

We get back to the house, gather fishing gear, and stuff it and ourselves into Pop-Pop's '63 VW bug. Pop-Pop slowly makes his way down the hill, then stops at the bottom of the driveway before turning onto the main road.

"Hey, Pop-Pop, can I do the shifting?"

"You know how to shift?"

"Yep, George taught me, and he's got the same kind of car. I wait until you push the pedal in, then I move the stick around like an H."

"All right, lemme get movin'." He makes a slow right, and we make our way down the mile-long hill to the creek. Pop-Pop's left foot depresses the clutch. "Shift."

I move the stick down from first to second gear. He looks at me approvingly, and I beam with pride. "Go faster, Pop-Pop. I wanna do third!"

"Now, now, there honey. We're going fast 'nuf."

"Mom-Mom says you're the slowest driver in the whole world."

He chuckles. "Mebbe, but yer gramma is the craziest damn driver I ever seen!"

"You've got a point there, Pop-Pop."

When we get to the bottom of the hill, Pop-Pop reverses into the dirt area on the right and parks. We grab our gear, walk across the road, and dangle our legs from the bridge over the creek. I let Pop-Pop put a worm on my hook, because *yuck*, then drop my line into the water. Pop-Pop does the same and we sit side by side in silence, watching diamonds of light jump across the water.

I swing my legs back and forth, lulled into a trance by the hum of cicadas. I feel a slight tug on my line, then it goes lax. Life is simple here. Everything in California is complicated and confusing. Pennsylvania is honest. Easy. And I'm not alone all the time.

Two hours and three fish later, we're ready to head home for lunch.

"Hey, Pop-Pop, can I drive back home?"

"You know how to drive?"

"Yep. You saw me shift earlier. I know how to steer, too. I can do it, Pop-Pop. Promise." I cross my heart with my pointer finger so he can see how serious I am.

"All right, then. But don't drive like your grandmother or you'll give me a heart attack."

I slip into the driver's seat and wrap my hands around the steering wheel. The thrill of power. Pop-Pop climbs into the passenger seat, and holds the two fishing rods and bucket of fish out the window with his right hand. He instructs me to check my mirrors, put on my seatbelt, and explains what the three pedals are for.

"Yeah, yeah, Pop-Pop. I know all that. Let's go!"

"Okay, honey, with your left foot, step on the clutch. With your right, give it just a little bit of gas, then gently ease up with your left."

I nod my agreement. I press the clutch to the floor with my left foot, and do the same to the gas with my right. Then I take my foot off the clutch pedal all at once. We pop forward a foot then stall.

"Nope. You've got to ease up on the clutch. Try again."

"I got it this time, Pop-Pop." I turn the ignition key again, press the clutch, floor the gas, and let up on the clutch slower than the last time. We lurch across the road. I'm so excited with my first taste of freedom, I giggle and forget about the steering wheel. Pop-Pop grabs it with his free hand and turns the wheel left, narrowly preventing us from driving straight into the creek.

"Holy hell, I thought you said you could drive! Grab the wheel!"

I grab the wheel and, still in first gear, floor the gas pedal as I steer up the hill. "I guess I forgot to mention I've never done both at the same time," I declare over the deafening sound of the engine. Drunk on power and joy, I laugh uncontrollably. Twenty, thirty, forty miles per hour in first gear.

"Second! Shift to second! You'll blow the engine."

I press the clutch, move the stick down to second, then release the clutch, all while flooring the gas. Fifty. Sixty. "This is better than Disneyland!"

"GOD DAMNIT YOU'RE GOING TO GET US KILLED! SLOW DOWN."

It's hard to care what he's screaming about because now I'm laughing so hard I'm crying, and I pee myself. Not a little pee. I empty my entire bladder into my shorts and the driver's seat. Fish are flopping around in the bucket and he's still got a grip on the poles.

"Slow down for the turn!"

We're rapidly approaching the driveway, and I know these are my last few moments of freedom before I'm in some kind of trouble. I slow down just enough to make the turn.

"ONE WHEEL, BABY! ONE WHEEL!"

I bolt to the top of the hill, stopping right before the open garage door. I'm laughing so hard I can't speak.

Pop-Pop jumps out of the car, still carrying the bucket and poles. "Shiiiit. No granddaughter of mine is going to drive like that. I damn near 'bout pissed myself."

My grandfather never swears, so that, coupled with the fact he's bent over grabbing his privates, only adds to my giddiness. He sets everything down on the garage floor, then hightails to the bathroom.

Too soon, summer is over, and I'm back in stupid California. At least my new school is better. It's a private school—only 250 kids, where brothers Charlie and Greg are my new friends. We play chess, computer games, and Dungeons and Dragons.

Mom works overtime to pay for my tuition, so I'm stuck with more alone time with George. We play Atari, and of course, I whoop his butt most of the time. I also hang out in my room, and read or do homework. Sometimes he tries to tell me what to do, and I remind him he's not my father. She always takes his side, no matter what he says.

Our friend from Virginia, Sandy, visits us in October and takes Mom out for dinner. She's staying in my room, so I put on my fluffy red zip-up pajamas with the feet in them and go to sleep on the couch.

Shaking brings me out of a deep sleep, then stops. I keep my eyes closed and curl back into a ball.

The couch shakes like a vibrating bed, faster and faster, then stops.

I hear a *ziiiip* and cool air on my skin gives me goosebumps. Something is warm and wet on my nipples.

The couch shakes like an earthquake. It stops.

Something scratches my nipples and my skin tingles.

I lie like a possum and try to figure out what's happening. This has to be a dream. *Please, God, please let me be dreaming.*

The couch shakes again and I can't figure out what's making it move like that. Something pinches my nipples hard, then warm wetness drips down my breasts.

I'm going to open my eyes just a little and nothing will be there because this is all a weird dream. I open them just a crack and through fuzzy eyelashes I see George's head on my chest. He sucks on me like a baby. His beard scratches my skin raw.

I break apart on the inside, and I'm not me anymore.

I close my eyes and try to go back to before, when I was twelve and dreaming.

Don't cry. Don't cry. If I cry he'll know I'm awake. I grumble like I'm sleeping, roll over on my stomach, and pull up my zipper, tucking my elbows tight beneath me.

Please God. Please God. Please God. Where is Mommy? SOMEONE, PLEASE HELP ME!

No one comes—only George and his rough hands rolling me onto my back.

STOP, GEORGE! WHAT ARE YOU DOING? GO AWAY! LEAVE ME ALONE!

I scream so loud inside but no words come out. My sweet parts melt away and soon I will be disappeared.

A loud *ziiiip* pulls me back into my body, the last place on Earth I want to be.

He pulls my zipper all the way down and leans his whole body over me. He's wearing a robe and it's open and he's not wearing any underwear. He rubs his *thing* against my breast and makes it all gooey. The hair on his stomach is getting in my nose and suffocating me and I want to float like a balloon up to the sky, far away from here.

Please God, please come get me right now. I'll do whatever you want just please make this a dream. Please, please make this stop.

Like a ragdoll, he pulls me up to a sitting position. Glassy bloodshot eyes stare at me like I'm steak. He pants like a dog; his warm beer breath brushes against my cheek.

"George? What are you doing?" I whisper. Tears spill down my face. "Please...stop..."

He looks through me as he grabs my girl parts with a rough hand. His other hand grabs his penis, squeezing and shaking it really hard and fast, shaking the couch like before.

He licks his lips, grabs my tiny hand, and presses my fingers around his erection, moving my hand up and down as he keeps pinching and kissing my nipples. I've never even kissed a boy, and now I have Mom's boyfriend's penis in my hand.

He grabs my head and pulls it down toward his lap. Throbbing, pink, and wet, his penis looks angry and gross. I try to pull my head away but he hurts my neck and pushes me down closer to it. It smells like old sweat and beer, and the big round part touches my mouth. I clench my lips tight together and turn my head to the side. His penis explodes on my face. Bitter, salty beer goo gets in my mouth, my eyes, and mixes with my tears. He releases me and I sit up.

God never showed up. A million switches turn off inside and I fade away.

I wipe my face with my blanket. "Hey, George? I have school tomorrow. I have to go to sleep." I zip up my pajamas and pull my knees to my chest.

I'm really old now.

George picks up a can of Budweiser from the coffee table, tilts his head back, and empties it into his mouth. Then he gets up and stumbles down the hall back to his bedroom.

I try to stay awake, but my body won't let me. I doze off, and wake up when I feel the sofa move again.

George is naked and sitting next to me. He doesn't say anything or touch me, just stares ahead into space. Dread strangles me as I ready myself for whatever is about to happen.

Slowly, he turns his head and looks at me like an expressionless freakish mannequin from *The Twilight Zone*. My heart stops. Seconds tick by like years.

"George, I have school tomorrow. You've got to let me go to sleep."

Silence.

My heart beats in my temples. "George?"

A drunken zombie, he shuffles away to their bedroom. I sit and wonder how I'm going to tell Mom what happened. Nothing will ever be the same again.

Bone-weary and heartbroken, I decide to write a note and put it on the door so I don't have to say the words out loud. Maybe if I don't say them, they aren't real. I keep pinching myself to wake up, but none of this is a dream.

Dear Mom –

I'm sorry to tell you that something horrible happened while you were out tonight. George got really drunk and he touched me in ways he shouldn't have. I don't want to tell you, but I don't know what else to do.

Erika

I put the note on the door and sit back on the sofa, watching the minutes tick by on the Betamax. 11:13 PM. I wait for her. For the sound of his bedroom door opening.

As soon as I hear the *click* of her key in the lock, I can breathe again. Mom sits next to me on the sofa, smiling. She smells faintly of wine. The note is in her hands, still folded up the way I left it on the door. I start to sob.

"Erika, why are you crying?"

"Did you read the note?"

"No. What's wrong?"

"Oh, Mom, read it right now!"

She unfolds the note and reads it. Her forehead scrunches up, her eyes narrow. Deep crimson slashes streak across her cheeks. Her lips purse thin and tight. I've never seen her so angry.

Pale blue eyes shine bright and fierce as she stares directly at me. "Is this true?" Her eyes move back and forth, scanning mine for the truth.

Stunned, it takes me a moment to respond. "Yes Mom. It's true," I answer in a whisper.

"You swear it?" she asks, and digs her fingers into my shoulders.

"I swear it." Why is she questioning me? Where is my hug?

"Stay here," she commands, then leaves me alone on the couch and storms down the hall to their bedroom.

The digital display on the Betamax reads 1:07 AM. I pull my knees to my chest and wait. My brain replays what happened over and over again in a memory loop: sweaty, drunken smells; salty, bitter tastes; sticky, gooey touches; slurping, moaning sounds; and that hungry look in his eyes.

Muffled yelling for two hours. I can't make out what they're saying, but I'm too petrified to listen at their door. She must be giving him hell. *Mom's going to make all of this better. We'll have to move because there's no way we can afford to live here without him. Maybe now we can move back home. Just breathe.*

At 3:02 AM, their bedroom door opens and I hear Mom's voice. "Erika, come in here."

I do as I'm told and walk slowly down the hall. *Oh my God. I'm going to have to look at him.* I feel nauseous and dizzy, and the hallway seems to stretch ahead endlessly like in *The Shining.*

When I enter their bedroom I see George to the left, sitting on their bed, his back against the wall. He's naked with a sheet pulled up to his waist and his face is a mess of snot and tears. He doesn't look at me, only stares across the room at Mommy. The only other man I've ever seen cry like that is Pop-Pop, and guilt overwhelms me. *What have I done?*

I look straight ahead to Mommy standing in the corner, arms folded across her chest, her body rigid and one eyebrow raised. *Just like Mom-Mom.* All of her attention is focused at me. *Poor Mom, she's so mad she can't even look at him.*

No one is speaking, and I can't bear the silence. "Mommy, are we leaving now?"

She says nothing. George cries louder. I'm rooted to the floor praying my knees don't buckle, staring at Mommy, and waiting for her to tell me what's next.

"George admitted to everything that happened tonight," she says, shooting him a death stare. His eyes clench shut and a fresh wave of sobbing overtakes him. When she turns her stare back to me, I don't recognize the look on her face.

"And?" I ask meekly.

"This. Is. All. Your. Fault," she spews, her right index finger punctuates the air with each syllable. Her words are daggers in my chest. The air leaves my lungs. I gasp and my mouth opens to scream, to push the words back where they came from. "Mommy, what are you saying?"

Her mouth scrunches up in disgust. "You provoked this! You know you're growing and developing, that your boobs are getting bigger. You're always walking around in bathing suits and tight T-shirts, and sitting on his lap! You should know better!" she hisses, her arms folding in front of her chest.

Her words shatter my sanity. If she says one more thing I know I will explode into a million pieces and crumble to the floor. I would rather she beat me with a baseball bat from head to toe than say words that can never be unsaid. Ever.

"I...I...never...meant...to...I...er...thought..."

"You thought what?" she sneers, righteous and cold.

"I thought he was going to be my daddy," I whisper. "That's why I sat on his lap." I hang my head in shame.

"Well, he's not and never will be!"

God, let me die right now. I'm ready to go. Just get me out of here. Please. Nothing happens. God can't ever seem to find my address.

"Are we moving?"

"No. We can't afford to move right now and we're in a lease. I need time to save money."

Wait, what? We're not moving? And he's not moving? And we're all staying here together?

"Until then, you two are never to be alone together. George will stay late at work and you will stay late after school. If you're home alone and he comes home, you go somewhere else. Understood?"

This has got to be some alternate universe. Can I have my real mom back? "Yes. I understand. How long do you think it will take to save up?"

"I don't know."

I look at the clock next to the bed and see how late it is. "It's really late, Mom. Can I skip school tomorrow?"

"No. You have two tests to take tomorrow and you'd better get A's on them. And don't you dare say a word of this to anyone," she hisses.

I have no one to tell. I don't ever want anyone to know about any of this. I wish I didn't know anything about it, but I have no choice. If someone found out, would George be arrested? Maybe I would be taken away and sent to live in a foster home. I still smell his sweat and a shudder runs through me. I don't want to think for one second more. "I won't tell. I just want to sleep. Can I go now, Mom?"

"Yes. I'll wake you up in a few hours for school."

I want to collapse, but instead I turn to leave. Out of the corner of my eye I see George lower his head, a fresh set of tears flow down his cheeks.

I climb on the sofa and curl into a ball. *You are the worst person in the whole wide world, Erika Worthless. Now you've ruined*

ERIKA WORTH

everything.

hell is for children

I just closed my eyes and now Mom's hand is on my shoulder shaking me awake. For one merciful moment, I have no recollection of what happened, until I see her face. She looks at me the way Mom-Mom looks at her, with disgust.

"Get ready for school," she commands.

"But Mom, I'm so tired. Do I have to—"

"Erika, I don't want to talk about this anymore. You are going to school and that's it. Now, go get ready," she says and walks into the kitchen.

I follow her and wrap my arms around her, rest my cheek on her back. She stands motionless, her arms at her sides. After an eternity, I let my arms drop. "Yes, Mom." I grab the clothes I'd set out the night before and head to the bathroom.

In the mirror, I see red, swollen eyes and ugliness. Everyone will be able to tell. Everyone will see I'm a dirty piece of shit.

At school, I watch the unbroken kids being dropped off by loving parents who kiss them goodbye on the cheek. They smile and breathe, as if it's the easiest thing in the world to do. I'm an alien intruder in their world.

I drift through school like a girl in a bubble. Everything is surreal but vivid flashbacks of engorged penises, stubble on my breasts, and wet sounds. I lose chunks of time, and come to with a teacher asking me a question. I say I'm sick and go to the nurse's office. She asks if I want her to call my mom and ask her to release me from school. I panic and assure her I'm fine.

After school, I amble home, remembering Mom's strict instructions about not being alone with George.

Instead of going upstairs to our apartment, I retreat to the parking spaces in the back alley and settle into a corner behind an ancient Oldsmobile. From my backpack I retrieve a bottle of Liquid Paper and a plastic sandwich baggie. I pour some into the baggie, hold the plastic to my mouth, and inhale deeply. Everything disappears, and for a few glorious moments I lose the awareness I've ruined my mother's only chance at happiness.

The nothingness passes too quickly, so I huff again, deeper. Another few moments of relief wash over me, and leave just as quickly. I can't hide out in the alley all day, but my limbs are like concrete. They won't carry me upstairs.

Over the next few months, I try to adjust to my new life and try extra hard to not make Mom mad. For the most part, George and I avoid each other. Every time he looks at me, my skin crawls and I feel nauseous. Soon, Mom and I will get our own place and get far away from him. Then Mom will come back and stop being the shut-down zombie woman who only focuses dead eyes on me. She only speaks to me when she's angry or needs me to do something. Our home is a minefield and I never know where to step to avoid the explosions.

At school I bury myself in classes, the school play, and trying to fit in as a twelve-year-old, but I don't dare tell anyone about my secrets. No one seems to notice anything different about me. Almost no one.

Mr. Green is a substitute teacher who fills in when necessary. He's from Amarillo and has a Texas-sized personality to match his big barrel chest and enormous capped white teeth. He's not like any of our other teachers. He wears shorts and polo shirts, sits on the desk and swings his feet around while he tells us stories about Vietnam, movies he's done stunts in, and detective cases he's working on.

He makes everyone laugh but me.

"Hey, Erika, you gotta minute?" Mickey says in his thick drawl.

"Sure, Mr. Green."

"Look, when it's just us talking, you can call me Mickey."

"Okay...Mickey."

"Are you okay? Something seems...off."

Mom's warning flashes through my mind. I bow my head to avoid eye contact. "Everything's fine."

"Everything doesn't seem fine, Erika. I've known you for a few months now. Something seems different. You can talk to me. It'll just stay between us."

I don't know whether it's his kindness, or the fact I have no one else to talk to, but I want to tell him everything. I start and stop three times, but I don't know where to begin.

"Erika, you can talk to me. Promise," he says kindly.

"My mom's boyfriend molested me and I told her and we're still living with him and I'm so scared all the time and I don't know what to do." The second I'm done regurgitating my story on him, I'm filled with terror of what's going to happen next, especially with Mom.

Mickey puts his arm around my shoulder and I flinch. "Erika, I will never hurt you. I have a daughter a year younger than you, and I'd kill anyone who did something to her. I'm not gonna let anything bad happen to you. Promise."

I lean against his shoulder and cry. He's the closest thing to Pop-Pop I have right now. I take a deep breath for the first time in months.

"Will your Mom let you babysit?" he asks.

"I'm sure she'd love it if I was out of the house more often."

"I have an awesome friend, Amber, who has a cool three-year-old named Ben. It'll get you away from that slime ball and get you some extra cash. You interested?"

"Oh my God, Mickey, thank you! I'd love to!"

"Okay. I'll talk to Amber and see when she needs you. It's all going to be okay."

His words are the brass rings on a carousel, and I hang on to each one.

Mom agrees to let me babysit as long as it doesn't affect my grades. I swear on my roller skates *and* my Cyndi Lauper album it won't, and Mickey picks me up for my first babysitting gig. He charms Mom right away, and I'm grateful to get out of the war zone for a while. I wonder if Mickey is going to punch George, but he only shakes his hand, introduces himself, and smiles.

Not only does babysitting get me out of my house, but Amber pays me $20, gives me a bottle of vodka, and a bag of weed. She leaves me alone with Ben most of the night, then takes me to school the next day. She's the dysfunctional big sister I never had and, with a messy life of her own, isn't affected by mine.

After six months, Mom finally announces we're moving...all three of us. Together.

"But Mom, I thought just us were moving out. Why—"

"Erika, we can't afford to get our own place. Your tuition isn't cheap. This is just temporary, for a year. We can look at our options when the lease expires."

"A year isn't temporary."

"End of discussion, Erika. Go do your homework."

We settle into our new apartment, and for a time everyone finds what they need to get by. I swim in the pool right behind our unit as many hours a day as possible, although I wear extra-large T-shirts over my bathing suit to cover any body parts that might arouse men. George takes karate lessons, and Mom buries herself in overtime and pints of Haagen Dazs ice cream. Sometimes she sends me to 7-11 at 2:00 AM to get three pints. By the time I wake up for school the next morning, she's eaten them all. She gains a lot of weight and wears a big red robe around the house.

The situation with George gets more complicated. I wake up at night to find him standing over me. Sometimes he's touching himself. Always, he watches me. In the shower, I'm washing shampoo out of my hair. I open my eyes and see him standing on the toilet looking over the shower door.

"Mo-om! George is watching me take a shower again."

"George! Come take the trash out," she orders from downstairs.

We're back to being left alone together. I come home from school and he's on the sofa, watching porn and masturbating. There is no way to get to my room but to walk by him and go up the stairs. Other times, I'm in my room doing homework when I hear a loud groan. I go investigate to see if everything is okay, only to discover George had just orgasmed loudly with his bedroom door open.

Being thirteen is confusing enough without having to deal with George. In the midst of all of this, we get a new neighbor named Clyde and his seven-year old daughter, Esther. She and I become friends and frequently swim together. Esther stays in the shallow end and cheers me on as I try to perfect a back dive. Esther's adoration is sweet.

"Do it again!" She claps.

I climb out of the pool and walk over to the deep end.

"Why do you always swim with a shirt on?" asks Clyde.

Suddenly conscious of wet clothing clinging to my body, I stand dripping, hunched over so my wet shirt won't reveal any curvy bits. "Um...I don't know. Just cuz, I guess."

"You should take your shirt off. You'd be much more comfortable swimming without it."

His beady blue eyes inspect me through coke-bottle glasses as he licks his lips. His shirtless belly protrudes over his swim trunks and he casually scratches himself down below.

"No, that's okay. I'm fine, thanks." I jump back into the water.

I swim over to Esther and start playing with her. Maybe he'll go back to being silently weird and leave me alone.

"I bet you're promiscuous with a body like yours."

I am confused.

"Do you know what promiscuous means?"

I shake my head no.

"It means you fool around with a lot of different guys."

He sees it—the neon sign above my head that flashes *DIRTY GIRL.*

"I have homework. I gotta go. See you tomorrow, Esther." I scurry inside my house and close the living room curtain so he can't see inside.

I run upstairs, take a hot shower, and try to scrub away Clyde's grodiness. I come downstairs and hear a knock at my door.

"Hey, Esther. What's up?"

"Will you please come take a shower with me?" she asks with the innocence of an angel.

"I just took a shower. Why do you want me to shower with you?"

"Daddy told me to come ask you."

The hairs on the back of my neck stand at full attention. "I can't, Esther. I have to go."

I hate closing the door on her. Esther and I have more in common than I care to imagine, but there is nothing I can do for her—I can't even help myself. And I need to keep Clyde as far away from me as possible.

When George gets home, I tell him about my interaction with Clyde and Esther. From that point on, I'm not allowed to swim with Esther. When they're at the pool, George opens the living room curtains and practices karate kicks in full view of Clyde. George talks to the owner of the building, and Clyde and Esther move out. I never see Esther again.

Mom and George go out one night to the drive-in movies and leave me alone with my self-destructive nature. I open the refrigerator and decide a crisp, cool glass of boxed white wine seems like a lovely idea. I gulp the wine—first one glass, then two. Next, I pop the tab top on a tall Budweiser and guzzle it. A bottle of Jack Daniels on top of the refrigerator calls my name. I retrieve the bottle, unscrew the cap, tilt my head back, and the last thing I remember is chugging liquid fire.

I come-to and see George's fuzzy face peering down at me. My hair and cheek are caked with vomit and the room won't stop spinning. Dressed only in white panties and a bra, my robe is wide open, and I'm on my bed sprawled on my back. George can see me—touch me—do anything he wants.

"No...don' tush me," I slur.

"Shhh," he says.

From the hallway, I hear Mom's voice, "What's wrong with her?"

He calls out to her, "She's got the flu. I'll handle it." Then he turns his attention back to me.

My robe...I need to cover myself. My brain sends signals to my arms but they remain limp and lifeless. A fresh wave of nausea overtakes me and the remaining contents of my stomach mix with chunks of vomit already matted in my hair. I am thirteen and powerless.

Fade to black.

While I am passed out, an army of vicious trolls moves into my head. When I wake up, they try to bash their way out of my skull with a million little hammers. *So this is a hangover.* I reach for the glass of water next to my bed and gulp it down. Bad idea, as it comes right back up and into the bucket next to my bed. *Oh my God, kill me now.*

"Mo-om! Mommmy! June?"

George comes into my room with a fresh washcloth for my head.

"Oh...it's you. Where's Mom?"

"She went to work. I'm staying home with you today."

"Oh, well, I hope you don't get this flu—"

"How much did you drink last night?"

"I didn't—"

"Don't lie to me."

I feel too awful to be clever. "I don't remember. I was in the kitchen one minute, and the next thing I knew, I was here."

For four days, George takes care of me and my alcohol poisoning. I swear off drinking forever, until a week later when I'm at Amber's.

I need just a *little* something to take the edge off.

blasphemous rumours

At fourteen, I stop praying. God isn't listening—not to me, anyway. To make up for my awkward home life, I bury myself in perfection. I know I'll never *look* like Barbie, but I can get straight A's, and try to win every game or competition. I raise my hand at all the teachers' questions so they know I'm someone, that I matter.

As my body develops further, so does attention from grown men. I eat my feelings, hoping a layer of chubby will keep them away. It doesn't. I also realize that being over a size four is a cardinal sin, so I switch to eating and throwing up, or taking laxatives and having explosive diarrhea attacks between classes. Too messy and I'm afraid of getting caught, so I obsess on *20-Minute Workout* videos with Bess, Holly, and Arlene in matching colorful leotards, headbands, and saccharine-sweet enthusiasm. "Three more. Two more. And one more. Okay!"

Everything in my life is chaos except for my food. Food is the one area of my life I can control, so I stop eating for long stretches of time. I get down to ninety-six pounds. It still doesn't fix me.

I start high school on a mission. If I can find a boy to love me, then it'll mean I'm not the worst human ever born.

Two weeks into freshman year, my wait is over. Gary is a freshman from Notre Dame. He is tall, handsome, sweet, and perfect. We go steady for six months. I wear his letterman jacket and write him love letters during Latin class. He buys me popcorn and holds my hand when I scream myself silly during *A Nightmare on Elm Street.* We kiss, cuddle, and investigate each other's body parts, and how good they feel in our hands and mouths. He gives me my first hickey, and I give him his first blowjob. Safe in love, I know we are meant for each other and will live happily ever after, or until just after my fifteenth birthday and Valentine's Day, when our perfect love implodes.

A jealous girl tells him I cheated on him. Being unfaithful had never occurred to me, but he doesn't believe me. Heartbroken, I swim extra hours after school and pour my pain into my journal on long bus rides home. My neighbor, Jacob, sees me walking home from the bus stop one day and offers me a ride. He's almost nineteen and trouble, and the perfect distraction from my broken heart.

When he asks me out, I say yes, more to spite Gary than anything else. Mom assesses him from head to toe when he picks me up for our first date. Her one raised eyebrow tells me everything, but I ignore her and leave with him.

We eat tacos, then make out in the front seat of his car. No butterflies in my tummy or dreams of happily ever after. He doesn't kiss like Gary, and he certainly isn't as cute, but Mom hates him and he pays attention to me. That's enough for now.

I come home at curfew and find Mom waiting at the kitchen table.

"Where did you guys go?"

"To eat."

"What did you eat?"

"Mexican."

"How old is he?"

"Seventeen," I lie.

"He looks a lot older than seventeen."

"You're not getting any younger. Maybe you need to get your eyes checked."

"I don't want you to see him again. There's something about him I don't trust."

"You know all about men who can't be trusted, don't you?"

She ignores my barb. "I'm serious. I don't like him and I don't want you to see him again."

"Since when do you care what I do? I'm tired and have swim practice early tomorrow."

Mom's warnings do nothing but turn Jacob into forbidden fruit, and thereby more attractive. I am fifteen years and one month old, and can make my own damn decisions.

For the next two weeks, Jacob picks me up most days after swim practice. We eat, go to the arcade, and make out. One night, I came out of practice and find him leaning against his Datsun B210 holding three pink roses wrapped in cellophane. "There's somewhere special I want to take you today."

I get in his car, sniff the odorless roses, and watch the sunset as he navigates his way through the San Fernando Valley, Rush blasting from his AM/FM radio. We drive to the Balboa Park Air Field where guys fly miniature planes and helicopters, and park in a secluded corner. He reaches in the back seat and retrieves three more pink roses wrapped in cellophane.

"More beautiful roses for my princess." He stares intently at me.

"Aww, thanks Jacob. That's really sweet—"

He kisses me—hard—and catches me off guard. Strong hands search my body, investigating the mounds of my breasts and the heat growing between my legs. Making out with Gary had been sweet and playful. Jacob is intense and forceful. Everything about him is different—the smell of him, the taste of his kisses. I try to focus on Jacob, but all I can think about is Gary.

He unbuttons my white cords and slips his left hand into the wetness between my legs. Gary is the only other boy who has touched me down there. I squeeze my legs tight together, trying to stop his deft fingers from finding their target. I need to breathe—and for him to slow down—but every time I try to say something he kisses me harder.

His fingers find their mark, and one slips inside of me. My thighs loosen their grip and I moan.

"Oh, Erika, I want you so much."

I want to be wanted, but something doesn't feel right. "Jacob, it's too soon. I'm not ready."

With fingers still inside me, he pulls my cords and underwear down to my ankles.

I'm exposed and this feels good but it's too much and I can't think. "Jacob, I have to—"

"Shhh." He smothers my protests with his lips. He pulls my pants and underwear completely off and tosses them onto the dirty floor of his car.

I don't realize how strong Jacob is until I try to stop him and he manipulates my body like I'm a rag doll. Shifting my bare legs over to the driver's seat, he yanks on them and positions me beneath him. His kisses intensify, and I struggle beneath his weight. The stick shift digs into my back and my neck is bent against the door armrest.

"Jacob, stop. This is way too soon. I have to get home before Mom gets mad." I try to be forceful but am afraid to be rude.

He either doesn't hear me or doesn't care. He raises my shirt over my head and squeezes my nipples hard.

"Ouch! Jacob, stop! That hurts!"

He pries my legs apart with his legs and torso, and his left hand secures my hands above my head. I fight hard, but can't break free from his grip, and any way I move hurts. His right hand pulls my bra down and he bites my nipples, my neck, and then my lips, silencing my protests.

Panicked, I struggle harder to get him off me. "JACOB! STOP—"

He covers my mouth with his left hand, and with his right he pulls his penis from his pants. A fresh wave of fear washes over me.

"Look how hard you make me, princess. This is all for you," he says, then spits on his hand and begins stroking himself.

I shake my head and plead through tears, beg him with his hand over my mouth. "I don't want this. Please, just take me home—"

Blinding, excruciating pain mutilates my senses. My skin tears as he buries himself inside of me. He shreds my hymen and slams against my cervix. I scream but no sound comes out. I bite his hand to stop him and the pain.

"Oh, my sweet princess. You're so tight. You feel so good," he whispers in my ear as his thrusts come harder and faster.

The faster he fucks me, the drier I get. Like a baseball bat coated in sandpaper, he tears my flesh. Finally, he comes, then collapses on top of me.

As if waking from a daze, he looks down at me and wipes tears from my eyes with the back of his hand. "There, there, princess. It's always rough the first time. It'll get better and better each time. And you'll never forget this night. You'll always remember I was your first."

I swallow my vomit.

"You'd better get dressed. I don't want to get you home too late."

Numb, dirty, and sore, I sit up in the passenger seat, a mixture of his juices and my blood seeps out between my legs. He reaches in the back seat, retrieves a towel, wipes himself off, and hands the blood-streaked cloth to me. The parking lot is empty and dark, so I grab my filthy clothes and step out of the car. My legs wobble but I stay upright and dress next to the passenger door.

He gets out on the driver's side and stretches, then walks around to the passenger side. I shake violently, afraid of what he might do next. He leans down and kisses me, then wraps his arms around me. "You poor thing. You're so cold. Let's get you home and warm. I don't want my little princess getting sick."

I am terrified to say or do anything that might stop him from taking me home. Mom was right. Why hadn't I listened? We get back in the car and drive home in silence.

When I walk in through the back door, Mom is standing in the kitchen—waiting. She looks at me from head to toe. "Where have you been?"

"Swim practice."

Her face is a mask of disbelief. "Awfully late for practice, isn't it?"

"A bunch of us went to Bob's Big Boy after. I didn't realize how late we were." I yawn. "I'm going to go clean up."

"Next time call if you're going to be late."

"I totally will, Mom. Sorry. I wasn't thinking. We swam extra hard today. I really just want to take a shower and go to bed. I'm wiped."

She says nothing, so I walk past her and go upstairs to the bathroom. Glancing in the mirror, I see messy hair and red-rimmed eyes blotched with black mascara. Jesus. I look fucked up. No wonder she looked at me like that.

I peel my clothes off and stuff them deep at the bottom of the hamper, then step into a scalding hot shower. Bruised and bleeding, I just want to scrub every trace of him off of me.

A few minutes pass when I hear Mom's angry voice. "What's this?"

I open the shower door and see her holding my bloodstained underwear. I lie like I breathe. My survival with Mom counts on it. "I got my period. What's the big deal?"

"Have you been fucking around with that Jacob guy?"

"No, Mom." I roll my eyes at her so she'll know how ridiculous she's being. "I just got my period."

"Prove it."

"Fine, weirdo." I step out of the shower, reach under the bathroom sink and retrieve a tampon. She watches. Unflinching, I insert the cardboard applicator into the swollen raw mess of hamburger meat that used to be my virginity. "Satisfied? What the hell is wrong with you?" I stare at her. Indignant. Defiant.

She knows her instincts are right, but I know how to turn them into scrambled eggs. I lock my accusatory stare on her until self-doubt and guilt wash over her features.

I am wrapped in a towel, water drips on the floor. "Are you done with the inquisition? Can I finish my shower now?"

"I'm sorry. I thought…" and she walks out, closing the door behind her.

Mercifully alone again, I try not to pass out as I remove the tampon. I step back into the shower and let the water wash what's left of Jacob away.

The next day, I tell a kid at school what happened. Word of my de-flowering spreads like wildfire, and within a week I am known as the whore of my high school. How I lost my virginity doesn't make it to the rumor mill, only that I'm now used goods.

Girls whisper when I pass them in the hall. Prim, proper, and still pure, they look down their noses at me. I want to grab their perfect ponytails and swing them around like a lasso.

Older, athletic boys with sweet, cheerleader girlfriends suddenly want to "hang out", but never in the light of day, and never in a public place. More popular than cotton candy at a carnival, I get passed around by sticky fingers, wooed by notes and calls from boys. Sweet words pour out of their mouths like warm honey, whispered promises in my ear. I'm special. I'm wanted, if only for an afternoon.

Like a junkie, I wait by the phone for more love heroin, for calls that never come. I pass these same boys in the hallway, hand in hand with their girlfriends. They walk by me like I'm invisible. This spring, I learn about the lies boys tell.

Two months later, I babysit for Amber and nurse a bottle of vodka. Mickey comes by with Cody, a cute sixteen-year-old with a billionaire father. Mickey is paid to keep Cody company, out of trouble, and out of his father's hair. They arrive with a twelve-pack, which Cody and I drink while Mickey entertains us with stories from a movie he's working on. Ten minutes and three beers later, Cody grabs my hand and leads me to the bedroom.

Kissing leads to necking, which turns into Cody pushing me down on my knees and shoving his cock in my mouth. Through my drunken stupor and the veil of hair hanging over my face, I look up and think I see Mickey watching us through the door cracked slightly open.

"Nooooo," I slur, trying to stand up.

"I'm close, Jenny. Don't stop yet."

"Name's...nah...Jenny," I mumble.

Cody pushes my head back down onto his cock, pulls my hair at the root, and holds my head firmly in place. Without warning, he shoots a full load of warm-beer-laced-with-piss-tasting cum in my mouth. It oozes out of my nose and burns my throat.

"Swallow it all, Jenny," he instructs. "That's a good girl." Satisfied, he releases my hair and buttons up his pants.

I crawl up onto the bed, wipe my mouth with the back of my hand, and curl into a ball. Cody leaves without saying a word.

"I'll talk to you soon, Erika," Mickey's voice echoes from the living room.

I stumble to the bathroom and throw up, brush my teeth, then check on Ben. He's sleeping like an angel. I can't fathom a time when I was that innocent, or safe. How we start off so sweet and end up so fucked up is beyond me.

I make my way back to the living room and curl up with my true love, vodka, and suffocate on hopelessness. I fantasize about the easiest ways to kill myself: I could shoot myself, but I don't have a gun; I could gas myself in a car, except I don't have a vehicle, or a garage; I could take pills or slice my wrists, but with Mom constantly invading my privacy, I doubt I'd have enough alone time to complete the task; I could hang myself, but my previous attempt at hanging myself a few years ago from the bar in my closet failed miserably when the bar came crashing down.

I opt for a cigarette and more vodka. Tears for Fears tell me to shout and let it all out, but who would listen if I did? Girls don't shout. We barely whisper. We talk shit about each other, wear a lot of neon and Aqua Net, and walk around half-starved.

May 16 is a sunny, California day. I put on my red bikini, slather on a fresh stick of butter, and lay out by our pool while listening to a Depeche Mode cassette. A large shadow blocks the sun. I squint and shield my eyes with my hand, and look up to see Mickey standing over me. Fuzzy memories of vodka and Cody pop into my head, and a blush streaks across my cheeks. I've avoided Mickey for two weeks since that night, and now here he is.

"Hey, kid," he says in his Texas drawl. "Amber had to cancel tonight. Did she call you?"

"She might have but I've been out here," I say and cover myself with my towel.

"Wanna go get lunch?"

Hmm. Mickey doesn't seem weird. I must have imagined it. "Um, sure. Let me get changed."

We go to Norm's, eat BLTs and fries, and talk about the end of my freshman year and plans for the summer. He makes me laugh, and slips back into the role of being my substitute dad. For the last three years, he's been one of the only people I can be honest with, and I'm grateful for his friendship and advice.

After lunch, we drive back to my apartment. Mickey parks and pulls a small mirror out from the center console. "Hold this," he says and hands it to me. He reaches into his shirt pocket, retrieves a small brown glass bottle, and pours a mound of white powder on the mirror. He uses a credit card to divide the powder into four thin lines. He rolls a twenty-dollar bill into a tight tube and snorts two lines off the mirror.

"Ever done cocaine before?" he asks.

"Nope. I've seen *Miami Vice*. That shit makes people crazy."

"Come on, Erika. Try a little. A little won't hurt you."

As much as I love checking out, cocaine scares the fuck out of me. "No thanks, Mickey. My life's crazy enough already."

"Suit yourself," he says, then snorts the other two lines. "Yeee hawww!" He throws his head back and pinches his nostrils together. "Hey, can I come in and use your phone? I have to make a business call."

"Sure," I respond.

While he makes his call, I clean dishes in the sink. I feel lips on the back of my neck.

I spin around. "What the—"

Beady green eyes with dime-sized pupils leer at me; sweat drips from his temples into large pores on his face. He looks at me as if I were steak on a plate, and licks his capped neon-white teeth and full lips.

I try to push him away from me. "Mickey! What the fuck are you doing?"

He cups my face in his hands and kisses me. "I've watched you grow up so much these last few years," he says, placing his hands on either side of the counter behind me. He pins me between the sink and his six-foot-three, 250-pound frame.

"Mickey. You've known me since I was *twelve*. I'm a year older than your *daughter*! How could you think of me like—"

"I saw what you did to Cody, that lucky fuck." He grunts.

He saw.

He lowers his face in front of mine and growls, "I want to be in your mouth. I want you to taste me." He rubs his groin against my leg.

Tears come—tears that never help or protect me, but are unstoppable. "Mickey, not you." I whimper. "Please. You promised—"

"I want to taste you. I bet you taste sweet." He sneaks his hand under my skirt.

His huge hands are much faster and stronger than my small ones. My punches bounce off his barrel chest, as his hands pinch and probe their way around my body.

"Come on, Erika. Be a good girl."

I go numb. I have nothing in me left to protect or fight for. Mickey is just another vulture feasting on the carcass. I want to go back to when Gary loved me. Was that really only three months ago? I want to stop hurting. Most of all, I want to stop being a pincushion for men's   desires.

a girl in trouble (is a temporary thing)

Little by little, I spill my secrets to Dr. B. Talking about my past is harder than when I went through it. Outside, I had ways to numb myself. In treatment, there is nowhere to hide.

Chuck escapes one night. He pushes the release button through the nurse's window and runs down the emergency stairs. He was arrested shortly after. Tiffany leaves. She and her boyfriend both OD and die. Maribel's insurance only covered her for two weeks. I never see her again. Rachel graduates out, but doesn't come back for aftercare. Jeannette goes home, no better than when she came in.

I find it hard to care about myself, but I'm in love with these kids, and each goodbye is excruciating. Becca, Elliot and I remain as a bevy of new kids cycle through. I become the mother hen. I scream about patient's rights and help kids dodge their meds. I even teach some of them how to smoke in their bathrooms without getting caught. I am the only patient on Level III, and have my own wing. I count down the days to freedom.

Five days before my eighteenth birthday, three people come in to speak on a panel. I plan to ignore them, as usual, but one of them was in the movie version of *The Wall*, a movie I've seen no less than a hundred times. Recovery is suddenly fascinating.

I approach her after the panel and thank her for sharing her story. She asks how I'm doing. I tell her I'm great because I'm almost out of here. She asks about my plans for after. I try to sound edgy and cool, tell her I'll most likely get wasted and go from there. After almost six weeks of dissecting every horrible thing that's ever happened to me, I could use a drink more than ever.

She says there's a meeting on the beach I should check out three days from now. She tells me to try and keep an open mind, and see how I feel after. I go, but only because she suggests it.

On a crisp clear-blue Sunday morning, a psych tech accompanies me to Venice. I have history here, and none of it sober. I feel antsy, so I light a cigarette. The best part of day passes.

We take off our shoes. The cold sand squidges between my toes and shoots a chill up my spine. The sharp wind numbs my cheeks. I sit in a circle with fifty people and see nothing but differences. I'm not a man. I'm not old. I'm not rich. I'm not married. I want nothing to do with any of this.

Look for the thimilaritieth, not the differentheth. Dave's voice drones in my head. I take a deep breath and try to focus on the hypnotic sound of waves crashing into the sand. *This is ninety minutes. You're free. Relax.*

The meeting starts and a microphone and mini amplifier are passed around so people can share. None of them are like me on the outside, but when they talk, our insides are the same. Fear. Shame. Anger. Confusion.

The woman next to me is in her sixties with bronze skin, silver wavy hair, and fierce blue eyes. She wears white linen pants and a thick blue sweater the same color as the sea. She turns to me and smiles. Beautiful lines crinkle at the edges of her eyes. She radiates kindness. I have never seen someone so beautiful or at peace. I wonder what a person has to do to become like her.

Then a soft but crystal-clear voice sparks in my head. *You're one of these people, Erika, and this is your one chance. There won't be another. Pay attention.*

Goosebumps stand at full attention all over my body. Whatever that voice is, I believe it, and I am struck with a desire to live.

I go back to the hospital and shock everyone, especially Dave, when I tell them I'm staying. I sign myself in as a voluntary patient, and work my ass off for the next eight weeks.

March 31, 1988

After ninety-nine days of captivity, I'm free. Free to come and go as I please. To smoke. To shave my legs without supervision. *To get loaded and kill myself.* Now that I'm back in control of my life, I'm terrified.

I say my goodbyes and promise to come back for Saturday group. Dr. B and I will continue our sessions. Dave walks Mom and me to the elevator. "You can do thith," he assures me. "Go to meetingth every day. Call your thponthor. And I'm alwayth here if you need anything."

He's optimistic, but I know myself too well. A few months of recovery isn't going to change years of being fucked up, but it's a start.

Once back home, I sit on my bed in the room where I bottomed out. My den of depression and despair, these walls bore witness to my secrets, mistakes, teenage groping sessions, and suicide planning. The calendar still hangs on the wall with red slashes through the first twenty-two days of December. I take the calendar off the wall and throw it in the trash.

My mirrored closet doors are plastered with cutout images from magazines of girls prettier and thinner than me. I'd covered every inch of reflective surfaces so I didn't have to see what I'd become. I comb through drawers, the bottom of my closet, pockets of clothing. No stash. Nothing remains from my former life but memories of incomprehensible demoralization.

Four days of freedom and I still haven't been to a whole meeting.

I walked into the last one, saw fifty teenagers, and walked right back out. Tonight, I'm going to a meeting in Hollywood.

Taking fashion tips from Nancy Spungen, I don a black leather bomber jacket over a ripped Sex Pistols T-shirt, put on my frayed faded Levi 501s and black boots. Last night's smoky eye-make-up is perfectly smudged, needing only a fresh application of mascara on top of the several coats already on my lashes. I douse my hair in Aqua Net and tease it mercilessly with a hair pick until it's transformed into a strawberry-blonde mane.

I take a bus into Hollywood and arrive at St. Thomas Church on Hollywood and Gardner. I'm early and nervous as hell, so I lean against a brick wall and smoke a Marlboro red, hoping I look way cooler than I feel. Without the armor of drugs and alcohol, I'm naked. I pluck at the frayed gashes of my jeans while I ash into the planter nearby.

Cliques of people cluster every few feet. They all look like rock stars, aging starlets, or Hollywood wannabes. *Look for the similarities, not the differences.*

I walk up the stone steps and enter through one of the two sliding glass doors. About fifty people are inside, chatting, laughing, milling around. Coins, business cards, or other small tokens are used as seat savers. I dig into my purse and put my keys on an empty chair in the back row in case I need to make a quick exit.

I go back outside to have another cigarette. Even more people have arrived. I go back to my wall and study them. They hug, laugh, and talk to each other as if it's the most normal thing in the world to do. My skin is doing its best to crawl off my body and hide in a nearby bush.

Erika, why are you here? Nothing's going to help you. When these people realize who you are and what you've done, they'll kick your ass right out of here. They're beautiful, successful, interesting. You're nothing but a stupid, broken kid. Go home.

I make my way through the crowd, toward the meeting room so I can get my keys and leave, when someone bumps into me. I look up and see a tall, thin, black man with hair like Don King, a perfect smile except for one missing tooth, and adorable dimples.

He beams a smile at me. "Can you answer a question honestly for me?"

"Um, sure. I guess."

He puts his hands on his hips, turns his back to me, and looks over his shoulder. "Does my ass look high and tight in these shorts?"

I look down at his round, bulbous behind pushing against the seams of his cherry-red short shorts. "Uh, yep. Very perky."

He turns back to face me, sizing me up from head-to-toe as only can a fabulous gay man. "Thought so," he says, then purses his lips together. "I've been doing a lot of squats," he says, emphasizing the "s" like a hiss. His opens his eyes even wider.

I can't help but smile. "Oh...well, it shows." I give him two thumbs up.

He plucks the cigarette out of my hand, takes a drag from it, then hands it back to me. "I'd say *someone's* having a few feelings. Hmm?" He raises an eyebrow at me.

"Who? Me?" I look around to see if anyone heard him say that.

He throws his head back and laughs. "Of course, precious. Who else would I be talking about?"

"Well, maybe. One or two."

"I'm Jamal. And you are?"

"Erika."

"And how many days do you have, Erika?"

"One hundred and three. I just got out of rehab four days ago. I was in a lockdown mental ward...not that I'm mental or anything. I was in the dual diagnosis program...you know, drugs and suicide stuff. But I'm better now. I mean, I still have a lot of feelings about my mom and stuff and her creepy ex-boyfriend and I'm about to graduate high school and my mom wants me to go to some fancy college and be a somebody but all I've ever wanted to do is act and write and I'm so fucking exhausted I feel like I just need a break so I can figure out who I am, you know?"

Jamal is staring at me with wide amused eyes and I suddenly realize I've been rambling.

"And you? How much time do you have?"

He places his hands on both of my shoulders and laughs. "Oh, sweetie, I have six months, and it's all going to be okay. Do you have a seat yet?"

"Oh, yeah. My keys. Actually, I was just about to leave. I have to—"

"Sugar britches, you're not going anywhere but inside that meeting." Jamal grabs my wrist and leads me inside. Someone outside rings a bell, and everyone pours into the room, filling every seat.

At 9:30, the meeting ends and people pile out and disperse. Jamal finds me before I can cut out and once again grabs my hand before I can escape. "What are you doing now?"

"Um, I need a ride back to the valley. You don't live there by any chance, do you?"

"Sweetie, do I look like I live in the valley?"

I laugh. "No, I guess not."

"Come to coffee with us. Someone will take you home after."

"How late will we be out?"

"Ooh. Does someone have a hot date later?"

"God, no. Come to think of it, I've never actually had sex sober. I don't even know what I'd do with all of that. Jesus, what a terrifying idea. Um, no. No sex. Not now. Maybe not ever. I have a curfew."

"What time?"

"I'm supposed to be home by 11:00. I can kind of push it to 11:30, but Mom will probably be pissed. I'm still on spring break. Maybe it'll be okay. I don't know."

"Sweetie, breathe. We're going to Mel n' Rose's. You're coming."

As Jamal is now my one and only sober friend, I decide to go with. Anything is better than sitting alone, staring at the walls of my bedroom, thinking.

We arrive at the restaurant and basically take over the joint. Twenty sober people talk, laugh, and tease each other. Like

Thanksgiving at the Worth household without the barbs and bitterness.

I end up sandwiched between Dion and Joe. In his twenties, Dion is tall, thin, with slicked-back brown hair and a pencil-thin moustache and wears a white wife-beater, brown baggy slacks held up by suspenders, and a brown felt Fedora. He's a character straight out of a film-noir movie. Dion talks a lot about prison and Jesus, so I turn my attention to Joe. Joe's in his sixties with a dyed-black comb-over, has sixteen years sober, and has just inherited a villa somewhere in Spain. We make small talk, which I suck at. I realize I only know how to talk to straight men to flirt with them or get them to buy me alcohol or drugs. Joe doesn't talk about sex or blow jobs. Joe doesn't stare at my tits when he talks to me. He makes eye contact with me, and my skin doesn't crawl being next to him. Weird.

I get lost in the stories and camaraderie of these magical, weird misfits and lose track of time. The neon clock on the wall reads midnight. "Oh, fuck. I'm toast."

"What's wrong, Erika?"

"I just saw what time it is. I'm out past curfew. Do you know if buses run to the valley this late?" Anxiety plus the pot of coffee I've ingested is not a good mix.

"Where in the valley do you live?" asks Joe.

"Van Nuys."

"Hang on. My sponsee, Drew, lives there. He'll give you a ride." Joe stands, looks down to the end of our table, and yells, "Drew!"

Drew stands up and I gulp. He looks like the Terminator's younger brother, or if a Venice Beach muscle head and a mobster had a baby. Slicked black hair, black leather jacket held together with safety pins, steely eyes, square jaw, and trouble from head to toe.

"Yeah, Joe. What's up?"

Joe points to the top of my head. "You're taking this girl home."

"Okay." Drew nods, then sits back down.

"There, you got a ride." Joe smiles warmly.

I consider the fact it might be the last ride of my life, but I feel I can trust Joe, which is not something I automatically feel with most people. "And...um...Drew's a safe guy and all of that? I mean, he wouldn't—"

Joe places a hand gently on my back. "Drew's a great guy. Promise. And he comes down here for meetings all the time, so you can get rides with him."

I believe him, so when Drew comes to our part of the table, I say my goodbyes and follow him out of the diner. A huge, white anarchy symbol is painted on the back of his jacket. Black combat boots. Jeans ripped to shreds. *And hallelujah, look at his butt!* He doesn't walk—he struts like he's daring the world to fuck with him. I'm both terrified and turned on.

We walk a block and stop by a beat-up, old gray van. He unlocks the passenger door and opens it for me.

"You drive *this?*" I realize before it's too late I used my outside voice. I expected a Harley, or maybe even a Mustang, but not a van.

Drew chuckles. "I do. It's great for transporting things."

Baby Jesus, please don't let this be my last night on Earth. I climb in the van, then realize what should have been the passenger seat has been replaced with a folding lawn chair, and there's nothing holding it down to the floor. I look to the rear of the vehicle, and realize there are no other seats. This is my only option. *This is the kind of van you kidnap people with.*

"Need help?" Drew asks.

I am not a girl who needs help. "Nope. Got it. Thanks."

Drew walks to his side of the van, takes his jacket off, and drapes it on the back of his seat. *Oh. My. God. He's like a fucking Greek statue.* Tanned, bulging muscles ripple all over him, and threaten to burst through the seams of his wife-beater. I have never actually seen a body like this up close. I quell my hormones just long enough to remember he could overpower me in a second. *But Joe said I'd be okay.*

Drew pulls a pack of Camel non-filters and a zippo out of his front pocket, lights a cigarette, then throws them on the dash. He looks over at me, and seems even more intense when he makes direct eye contact with me. "Ready?"

God, that's such a loaded question. "Um, I think so? I live near Victory and Van Nuys."

"Cool. You're right down the street from me. Okay. Now hang on to the belt when we go around corners."

I look down for a belt but can't find it. He points up to a brown leather belt fastened with a bolt to the roof. "Oh, cool." *I won't need that. I can balance just fine.*

Drew steps on the gas pedal and I almost fall backward. I get a mental flash of me on my back, still sitting in the lawn chair, with my legs in the air like a dying cockroach. *Not a sexy look, Erika. Get a grip.*

We drive down Melrose, then head north on La Brea, past Pink's Hot Dogs with a line down the block, past the working boys and trans girls, drunk club goers, Angelyne billboards, homeless people covered in newspapers and plastic garbage bags. *These are my people. This should be my home, not the stupid valley.*

By the time we turn onto Hollywood Boulevard, I've got the lawn chair thing down. He's a fast driver, but in control. I have no idea how to make small talk, so I light a cigarette and stare out the window. He starts singing Aerosmith's "Dream On" at the top of his lungs even better than Steven Tyler.

I go to take a hit off my cigarette with my left hand, and inadvertently loosen my grip on the belt, just as we take a sharp turn to the right. My chair tilts so far to the left, I almost end up in Drew's lap—not like that would be a bad thing, but still. I tighten my grip on the belt and pull myself upright. I need to look cool in case Drew wants to love me in the future.

Ten minutes later, he delivers me safely to my house. We exchange numbers and I thank him, unsure if I owe him an obligatory hand job for the ride. He smiles and drives away, singing at the top of his lungs into the night.

My life suddenly has a new cast of characters in it.

Spyder is thirty-six with two years of sobriety. He's a tall, funny, dead-sexy saxophone player who wears black leather pants and has thick, long, ebony feathered hair.

Black-widow Leslie is twenty-three with a year of sobriety. She's heroin-chic thin, with straight jet-black hair, cherry-red lips, and a black widow tattoo on her shoulder.

Eddie Little is in his mid-thirties and has two years off heroin, a mullet, and is almost as wide as he is tall. His arms are covered in tattoos and bulging muscles. He frequently gets into fist fights in meetings or, at the very least, throws chairs around.

Coke-bottle Mike is a nerdy genius with thick glasses and intense halitosis who has mastered the art of close, uncomfortable face-talking. Weak on social cues, he's big on heart, but consistently relapses on heroin.

Robert is nineteen and has thirty days clean. He is a recently-retired sex worker from Santa Monica Boulevard, and was just diagnosed HIV positive.

Steve is a fifty-something musician whose brain cells have taken a beating over the years. Our sobriety birthdays are on the same day, so we take our milestone chips together.

Billy Sunshine is a homeless guy who wears a bathrobe and mumbles in the back of the room while people share. There are rumors he's the second coming of Jesus, as he randomly pops up in various parts of the country where people least expect him.

Josh is a young surfer dude who has taken too much acid. He talks about dolphins and prisms of color, and calls everyone and everything dude.

Mistress Monique is a dominatrix who used to be a psychiatrist. She has four years and comes to meetings in black leather and thigh-high latex boots, and carries a whip.

Guitar Rick lives under a bridge and is the spitting image of Riff Raff from *The Rocky Horror Picture Show*.

Then there's Chris. We meet when I am five months sober. He's nineteen years old with nine months clean, whose haunted soul mirrors my own. I lose myself in his big brown eyes and possessive kisses. In alcoholic fashion, we become inseparable the minute we meet. We hang out at Canter's Deli, Damiano's Pizza, and Oki Dog. Chris used to sell himself on Santa Monica Boulevard to support his crack habit. He tells me stories of his father, how he raped him when he was six, and his cruel step-mother. He once brought her the wrong kind of flowers on Mother's Day. As punishment, she spread uncooked rice onto the hardwood floor and made him kneel on it, then pushed down on his shoulders until the rice embedded in his bare knees. He was eight.

Now he's clean and lives in his sponsor's house in Hollywood. We make out before, during, and after meetings, and I swear, he's got the softest lips I've ever kissed. He writes me love songs and plays them for me on his guitar. Bit by bit, we reveal remnants of our shame to each other. Shame is the only feeling besides confusion we're both in touch with. Every day I wait for him to run away, but he never does. He also won't sleep with me.

I have never had willing sex sober. I'm terrified, but ready. Every time I think we're getting close, Chris pulls away.

After two weeks of soul-baring and heavy petting, he takes me to Mel n' Rose's. We share a plate of fries and ranch dressing, and I try my best to look extra seductive. He peeks at me through long dark bangs that cover his eyes, opens his mouth to say something, then stops himself. He shifts his intense gaze to a fry he now pushes around in a pool of ketchup.

Given the chance, my alcoholic mind will infuse a silent moment with every terrifying possibility. "Chris? Is everything okay?"

He fidgets, then reaches for his pack of Camels and lights a cigarette. He leans his back against the wall and extends his legs out on his side of the red-leather booth. "No, everything is definitely not okay."

My heart oozes out of my chest and plops on the diner floor. "Fuck. It's me, isn't it? That's why you don't want to sleep with me. You think I'm fat. Or you can't handle the shit about my past." My shoulders curl together and my chin drops.

He reaches across the table for one of my hands. "Are you fucking kidding me? Of course I want to sleep with you. I think about it all the time." He runs a hand through his hair, then kisses the tips of my fingers.

"Then why haven't we...you know, done it?" I ask, afraid of his answer. I went out with my first boyfriend for six months and never slept with him. We were fourteen and virgins. Aside from him, I've never waited so long to sleep with anyone.

"Because..." He drops my hand and lights another cigarette. "There's something I have to tell you first. And once I tell you, you won't want to be with me anymore."

What could he be talking about? Does he have a small, misshapen penis? Is he secretly married? I think about the horrible things I've told him. What could possibly make me run away? "Chris, I don't know what you're talking about, but nothing can change the way I feel about you. Whatever it is, it's okay. Just tell me."

My beautiful boy stares at me, searching my face for confirmation I'm telling the truth. He squashes his cigarette butt into the ashtray, then pounds both fists once on the table. He clenches his jaw and glances at the floor. When he looks back at me, tears are streaming down his face.

I move to his side of the booth and wrap my arms around him. "Chris, shhh. It's okay, whatever it is. I promise."

He starts to sob and shake. I wipe his tears with the back of my fingers, run my hand through his hair.

"You know how I used to make a living?" he asks.

"Yep, and you know I don't care about that. We both did what we had to do to survive."

"Well, I got sick from it." He pauses, his face contorts with grief.

"Like, you threw up on someone?"

His eyes implore me to understand, but I don't know what he's trying to tell me. Then it clicks, and my face mirrors his grief. I close my eyes and shake my head, as if I'll somehow be able to stop or change what he's about to tell me.

"I have AIDS."

No. No. No. No. No. Not Chris. I told him he could tell me anything. I told him it wouldn't matter. I told him no matter what, I wouldn't leave him. *But this*. He could die. I could die. I burst into tears. "Oh, Chris. I'm so sorry."

Our sassy waitress approaches our table, coffeepot in hand. "How are you kids doing over here?" she asks while chomping on a wad of gum. It takes her a moment to realize we're both crying. "Oh, crap. My perfect waitress timing. I'll get you kids some more napkins."

We pull ourselves together and go back to his house. He leaves the room dark, takes off his shirt, and lies back on his bed. A harsh glare from the streetlight streams in through the blinds, slicing shadows of light and dark across his face and torso.

We are both so fucked up and lost. Perhaps together we can find redemption. I take my shirt and bra off, and lie next to him, skin on skin. We say nothing. I rest my ear on his chest and listen to the *thump* of his heartbeat.

He gently touches my back, but nothing more. This is my choice to make. I straddle him and kiss the center of his forehead, his closed eyes, his cheeks, then the tip of his nose. His lips taste like sorrow, cigarettes, and a mix of our tears.

I move down and kiss his neck, the center of his chest, and place gentle kisses along his torso. I unbuckle his belt, then stand and finish undressing both of us. He reaches over to the nightstand and retrieves a condom.

I lie on my back, reach for his hand, and place it between my legs. He rolls over and is inside me. I wrap myself around him and pull him in deeper. Shadows splash across his face as we make love. We are lost and found, sinners and saints.

For a moment, I wonder if this is attempted suicide on my part, but I don't care. I fall asleep in his arms, grateful.

Weeks pass and I am dizzy in a love haze. We fall into a rhythm of sex, sleep, and meetings. I continue therapy with Dr. B. I expect him to restrict me from seeing Chris, but he doesn't tell me what to do. I assure him we always use condoms.

I tell Dr. B most of the truth, but paint some of it with a wide brush. I don't mention that Chris slips into deep wells of depression. I try to love him harder. Better. As if my love can somehow save him.

Chris grows manic and says things that don't make sense. He swears he sold his soul to the devil, and he'll be coming for him soon. He goes to meetings and shares he's no longer HIV positive, but everyone knows that's not true.

He pushes and pulls me away simultaneously, and I grow weary of being a human yo-yo. I ask for some time, a few days, to take a breath and handle things I've been neglecting. He becomes more possessive, and possessed. My sweet boy slips away, and I can't help him. In the passenger seat of my car on the 101, he opens the door and threatens to jump out. He needs help I can't give him. He disappears for four days and I fear the worst. Then he shows up at the midnight meeting.

I'm standing in the entry hall at the top of the stairs when Chris arrives. He stands two feet away from me and doesn't say a word as he punches his forearm through the nearby window, then lowers it onto a shard of glass. Like a crimson iceburg, it surfaces through his skin. AIDS blood is everywhere. People freak out. They all know his blood is death. He is the haunted shell of the boy I knew. An ambulance comes and takes him away, and I never see him again.

Some time after, his sponsor tells me Chris relapsed, committed some felonies, and will be in prison for at least a few years. He dies there nine months later.

under the milky way

Feelings are messy little fuckers. I try to fill the void Chris left behind with an array of men. Different names and faces—same emptiness after each one.

I parade around meetings half-naked, and get high on empty promises and attention from men. I tell myself I'm liberated. Evolved. I can sleep with whomever I please, but I never stop to ask myself why I'm acting this way. I'm too shut down to realize I'm searching for my father's love, and too filled with self-loathing to act any different.

Some women in meetings tell me to put some clothes on. They explain that people come to meetings to stay sober and not pay attention to my tits. They tell me I can dress and act like a hooker outside of meetings, but to try and have some respect while I'm in them. I dismiss them as bitchy, jealous women, but their words plant a grain of truth that will eventually sprout.

I call my sponsor, Amy, and tell her the chaos in my head and my life. She tells me to pray and run my choices by a higher power. She's a woman, so I don't trust her. I tell her God and I broke up years ago.

She tells me I can choose a different higher power, anything I want, and asks if I know a god-like person, someone pure. Good. *Pop-*

Pop. Then she asks me if I know someone who is the opposite—filled with fear and resentment. *Mom-Mom.* She tells me when I'm in a situation and I don't know what to do, to think of what each of them would say or do, and try to act accordingly.

I practice with little things. *Should I steal this lipstick?* Pop-Pop would never steal. He'd work hard, save up, and buy whatever he wanted in cash. Mom-Mom wouldn't steal, but if she didn't have the money for something, she'd seduce a man into buying it for her. I take the lipstick, but feel like shit right after. When I'm high, I don't feel guilt, just the need for more. Having a conscience is weird.

Should I lash out at someone who hurt my feelings? Pop-Pop would say no, they probably didn't mean it and might be going through something difficult no one knows about. Mom-Mom would do the exact opposite, and always go for the lowest blow. If a person had one leg, and offended Mom-Mom in some way, she'd call them a gimp or a cripple. I decide to say nothing and pretend I'm fine, but I feel like a phony. Once I know what the right thing to do is, I can't unknow it.

Instead of reacting to every feeling I have, I'm told I can pause when agitated or doubtful. I start to run my choices through this new higher power thingamabob. I can still make bad choices, but at least now I'm aware they're mine. What a concept.

I've been angry for years, and I'm really fucking good at it. But it doesn't make me happy, or make people like me. It usually makes them afraid. I pretend to be tough, but I've learned I do it for protection. Underneath the leather and confusion, I'm a marshmallow. When I get angry, I feel like Mom-Mom, and I don't want to be anything like her. Well, maybe have her shoe and purse collection, but that's it.

Amy gets loaded and calls me high one night, wants me to hold her hand while she comes down from shooting cocaine. I tell her I can't, I don't know if I could stay sober in that situation. She cusses me out, tells me what a selfish cunt I am for not being there for her after everything she's done for me.

I get a new sponsor, Mary, whose husband sponsors a guy I fuck. I share my fourth step with her, and two days later get an earful of confidential details from the guy. I switch to Gail, a sixty-something waitress. She's four-foot-nine with bright copper hair and leather skin. She chain-smokes and her voice sounds like a handful of gravel is rolling around in her throat. No matter what I ask her about, she always tells me, in a thick Long Island accent, to get down on my knees and pray.

I figure women are the problem, so I switch to Hal. He's an old guy with twelve years who clicks his dentures in and out of his mouth while I talk to him. He sponsors a bunch of guys I know and they all love him. He tells me to bring a notebook and pen to his house so we can do some step work. He sits on a blue corduroy recliner in his boxers. Instead of answering questions about step nine, he asks me how many times I masturbate. I stay silent. He tells me we need to talk about everything, because he's my sponsor. The whole time he's talking, he's rubbing his hand against his boxers. I thought sober men were supposed to be different.

I switch to Michelle, a beautiful woman with eight years. She wears see-through blouses with no bra and seems to know more about guys than recovery. I switch to Pamela, who tells me I can't wear low-cut blouses, miniskirts, swear, or have sex.

I decide to take a break from sponsors, and just talk to Dr. B instead. I want him to see I'm better, so I don't tell him everything. I spend a lot of time covering piles of crappy choices with blankets of lies, then hang air fresheners around, hoping to mask the stench of my bullshit. Maybe one day I'll wake up well.

On a Wednesday morning in November, my phone rings.

"Hi. It's George. Can we meet? I'd like to talk to you."

I know I should respond, but my mouth won't form words.

"Please," he continues. "There are some things I need to say to you. We can meet wherever you feel comfortable."

What would Pop-Pop do? My curiosity beats out my disturbance, and I decide on somewhere public and non-committal. "Saturday?

Noon? Jack in the Box on Van Nuys and Sherman Way?"

"Okay. See you there."

Sobriety is never boring. There are surprises around every corner and new feelings every three seconds.

On Saturday, I arrive thirty minutes early, get two orders of curly fries and extra ranch dressing, and sit on a stool by a window so I can watch people. A bouncy brunette with no make-up and a UCLA sweatshirt walks across the parking lot, talking incessantly. Next to her, a lanky but cute nerd hangs on her every word, and looks at her like she's made of gold dust. Distracted, he stumbles over a parking curb but rebounds nicely. He rushes ahead of her and holds the door open. She never stops talking.

I bet she doesn't live in a shitty apartment in Van Nuys with only a sleeping bag on the floor, or use milk crates stolen from the back of a 7-11 as nightstands, bookshelves, and record holders. I bet she has matching furniture and framed pictures of people who love her.

I'm the girl with two-day-old Maybelline, hair crunchy with multiple layers of ratting and super-hold hairspray, surrounded by a cloud of cigarette smoke. I absently pick at the stitching of my black leather bomber jacket. I light a cigarette, then shove a curly fry through a glob of ranch and pop it into my mouth.

I pull out my journal and go over the piece I've been writing for this moment:

George and all sick assholes who fuck with kids:

When you touch a child in a sexual manner, you mar them in ways you cannot quantify. Trauma, betrayal, abuse—those words don't begin to describe the chorus of a soul's screaming; the agony of breathing through the memory of what you've done, what you've obliterated. Beautiful fucking children were not put here for adult pleasure or amusement. Every entrance into them is a departure of their sweet spirit, an amputation of who they might have been before you infused them with your soul's sickness and robbed them of the dignity of a life void of your stench and stain. They can re-mold themselves, gather their broken pieces and re-assemble themselves into someone new, but they will never be who they might have been.

"Hey, Erika," says George next to me. He nervously clears his throat.

I slam my journal shut and turn to him, my mouth still filled with curly fry. He's aged in the last eighteen months, lost more hair. The grooves on his forehead are more pronounced, as are the lines around his eyes. He's old now. Thirty-eight.

"Hey." Somewhere between child and adult, I don't know what to do. The girl part of me who's been taught to apologize for everything wants to make him comfortable, fill the empty spaces with sugar and spice and everything nice. "What's up?"

"Thanks for meeting with me." He points to the stool next to me. "Mind if I sit?"

"Go for it." *This man stole your childhood. Kick him in the balls! Burn him with a cigarette! Throw curly fries at his head!* "Fries?" I slide the tray over to him.

"No, thanks." Before he even speaks, his eyes redden and start to water. A vein pops out from his temple, and his lips tremble. "I wanted to meet today...to say some stuff to you." His face turns bright red and he pauses.

I wonder how much Budweiser courage he needed to face me today. I take a hit off my cigarette and detect a flicker of disapproval from him. This is the first time he's seen me as an adult. He can't tell what to do anymore. I ceased being a child the night I held his cock in my hands. I take a deep drag and do my best to appear both tough and disinterested while waiting for him to get to the point.

"I want to...need to apologize to you. What I did to you was wrong and never should have happened." His face is leaking badly now, his cheek muscles twitch, and a slow drizzle of mucous escapes from his nose and seeps into his moustache. He doesn't wipe it away. The faucets open, and he starts to cry—big, ugly, messy, snot-bubble crying.

This mess of a man ended whatever semblance of childhood I might have had. He shattered my trust. His actions permanently fractured my relationship with Mom, and annihilated my self-worth.

Words clamor over each other to spill off my tongue, but I bar them behind clenched teeth and stay silent. I look at the journal, but it doesn't feel right now that he's blubbering.

In this moment, I don't hate him. I hate what he did. I hate how his actions changed me, but he can no longer hurt me. And grown men crying is my kryptonite, no matter what they've done. "George, I..." Confused. Grateful. Overwhelmed. Every second a new feeling. For one moment, there are no thoughts. No blame or judgment. An invisible fibrous chord of profound pain joins us—human being to human being. I'm not the only one with wounds.

"Erika, I don't expect your forgiveness. I don't deserve it."

The words come before I can stop them, before I can analyze, judge, and rearrange them. "No, but I forgive you anyway."

He stares at me in disbelief. I can't believe I said it, but now that I have, I know it's the truth.

"I don't want to hate you for the rest of my life. I don't want you to have that kind of power over me. And I've learned in the last year that we all make huge fucking mistakes. For every finger I point at someone else, there are three more pointing back at me."

He stares at me, listens intently. He no longer has any power over me, unless I let him.

"What happened was not okay, and I don't know what happened to you along the way to make you like that, but I hope you get the help you need. I was in rehab and they reported everything, but there was no physical evidence and too many years had passed. They took a statement from me, and if anyone ever files a charge against you, they'll call me in as a witness. I will testify on their behalf.

"I'm never going to touch anyone again."

"I hope that's true."

With each passing moment, my anger dissipates, and I'm left with pity for him. And maybe for my mom. I'm not ready to forgive her yet, but I'll get there one day...or so they tell me.

A month later, on December 23, 1988, I turn a year sober. I wear a new red dress and go to my home meeting. The whole room sings happy birthday to me and gives me a cake with one candle on it. I'm eighteen with a whole year. I fucking did it.

After the meeting, I want more—more singing, more attention, more celebration of being alive. Since it's the Christmas season, there are marathon meetings twenty-four hours a day. I go to a meeting hall on the west side I've never been to, and pick a seat in the near-empty room.

At 2:00 AM, the meeting starts. A filthy, wet drunk stumbles in and sits next to me. His clothes are disheveled. Face unshaven. His salt-and-pepper hair looks like it hasn't been washed in weeks. He rests his chin on his chest and mumbles to himself. And he stinks. Bad. *Geez, why does he have to sit next to me? He's going to ruin my whole meeting.*

Suddenly, he comes-to and looks over at me. Through drunken haze and dirt are two deep discs of blue, intensified by the bloodshot whites surrounding them. He searches my face for recognition, down at his clothes, then around the room. "Where am I?"

Weirdo. "Umm, you're at, like, the Westside Center."

He shakes his head like he's trying to wake up. "What day is it?"

Now he's just pestering me. "It's Christmas." *Duh.* It's almost time for coins and birthdays and he's interrupting my mental rehearsal of the inspiring and thoughtful things I'm going to say when I take my cake.

"What city am I in?" he asks, grabbing my forearm.

I stop thinking about myself for a nanosecond and look directly in his eyes. The hairs on the back of my neck bristle. A nagging itch in my brain tells me I may have judged him too quickly. Quietly, and with respect, I tell him we're in Los Angeles.

Grief contorts the features of his face. He clenches his eyes shut, opens his mouth as if he's in intense pain, but no sound comes out.

My stomach turns to knots. "Mister, are you okay?"

He sobs. "Two weeks ago, I had twenty-six years of sobriety. I thought I could have one drink. And I live in Chicago."

I cannot fathom being his age, or having that much sobriety, or losing everything in two weeks. What I understand with perfect clarity is that I will never graduate from this disease. There will be no certificate of completion sent to me in the mail. Being sober is not about pretty red dresses and attention, and my year clean doesn't mean shit. I will need to work at this one day at a time for the rest of my life.

love is a battlefield

July 11, 1989

Dear Diary,

I met my soul mate, and I know you've heard me say that a lot, but I totally mean it this time. Jimmy's not like the other guys. He's thirty and got a degree from Northwestern. He's cuter than James Dean (how is that even possible?) with dark hair and green eyes. He loves to smoke the ganja and can't stay sober to save his life, but I'm certain the universe put me and my eighteen months of sobriety into his life to help him find his way.

He's a brilliant actor. He even had a lead in a movie four years ago. For now, he drives a cab at night, but he's got such amazing potential.

More later.

Love, Me

Tonight, I ride shotgun with Jimmy transporting pimps, junkies, and porn stars through the seedy underbelly of Los Angeles. We wear matching black-leather bomber jackets. He rambles on like Woody Allen about his anxiety and missed opportunities, while I sit in the passenger seat, feet up on the dashboard, smoking a Red and plan our perfect life together.

"You shouldn't smoke so many cigarettes, Erika. They're not good for you."

"Neither is you smoking weed. I'm nineteen and a half and can make my own choices. Maybe if you switched from weed to cigarettes, you'd be able to stay clean."

"You might have a point. I gotta stop smoking the Mary Jane. It's killing me."

I reach my hand across to the driver's side headrest and run my fingers through his hair. "Oh, Jimmy. It's all going to be okay."

Around 11:00 PM, he starts to yawn. "I need a nap. Do you want me to drop you off?"

And miss a chance to sleep next to you? No way. "No, I'll go with you. I mean... if that's okay."

"Sure. Whatever."

We arrive at his apartment building on Vermont and Lexington, and are greeted by a cacophony of catcalls from trans hookers hanging out of their apartment windows.

"Hola, Yimmy. You lookin' good, honey."

"Jimmy, ditch that bitch. I'll do things that little girl can't even dream of."

"Come on up, guapo. I'll let you stick it in my tight little ass."

Jimmy's face is beet-red. "I gotta find a new place to live. Jesus, Erika, my family would die if they saw me living like this."

I hold his hand and give it a reassuring squeeze. "It's okay. It's just a building. It doesn't define who you are. Just think what a great story this will be when you win your Oscar."

"You're always so positive. How do you do that?"

"The power of sober living," I respond with a smile, hoping he can't hear the demons raging in my brain. *Come on, Erika. This guy is never going to love you. Why would he?* Everything is going to be different with Jimmy.

Jimmy rambles on as we ride the rickety vintage elevator up to the third floor and enter his studio apartment. The room is bare except for a single chair in the middle of the room, and a full-sized mattress in the corner. He tosses his keys and leather jacket on a pile of mail and newspapers strewn by the door, then straddles the metal chair in the middle of the floor. After running his fingers through his hair, he rests his arms on the back of the chair.

I sit on the threadbare mattress with no sheets. A small mouse skitters across the floor, so I shift my legs up onto the mattress and inspect around me to see if there are any other furry visitors nearby. I love animals, but don't think I'd enjoy one chewing on my toenails.

He lights up a joint. "Every time I quit smoking weed, I get auditions. Every single time. I know if I quit, I can work again and quit driving a stupid cab. My brother's a doctor. A *doctor.* I come from a good, Jewish family. I'm supposed to be more than this."

He's holding court, and I'm transfixed by his beauty and agony. I try to make him feel better the only way I know how. I take off my leather jacket and reveal the black bustier I'm wearing underneath.

He stops talking mid-sentence, and averts his eyes to my cleavage. "Jesus, Erika. You have the best fucking tits."

Proud he noticed, I pat the mattress next to me. "Aren't we supposed to be napping?"

"I don't know if I can sleep. I'm so fucking worked up." He paces as he smokes his joint, then blows the smoke out the open window.

"Let's try."

He joins me on the mattress, and pulls a ragged blanket up from the floor. A gaping hole covers almost half of the blanket. That mouse must have been busy while he was gone. He covers himself with the intact half, lays his head on the only pillow, and rolls over on his side facing away from me. Since there is no other pillow, I roll my jacket into a ball and use it for my head, then spoon him, for both warmth and to comfort him. As he starts to gently snore, I lie awake, plotting our future together.

He lives in a shit hole. I live in a slightly better shit hole, with actual furniture, dishes, and *four* pillows. I can never pay my rent. We hang out all the time anyway. Why not live together? With my help, he will get clean and start acting again. I will write an amazing play for the two of us to star in. It'll be perfect.

A few hours later, we're back on the road with my perfect plan in place.

I light a cigarette and open the passenger window so the smoke won't bother him. "So, Jimmy, I don't know what to do." I turn to him, my brow furrowed. "I'm having such a hard time paying my rent. And you know I have the *greatest* apartment. I'd *hate* to lose it. I wish I could find a roommate or something."

I look away from him, smirking to myself, and wait for him to take the bait. When he moves in with me, we can sleep on a real bed, with sheets and everything.

"You should get a job at Club Paradise."

Wait. Huh? "You want me to strip?"

"No, not at all. It's not stripping. I drive a lot of girls around who work there. You get paid to just talk to the guys and dance with them. Like back in the 1940's and stuff. It's totally innocent."

"Um, so, you think that's a better idea than me getting a roommate?"

"Absolutely. You don't want to live with anyone, Erika. It sucks."

My master plan is blown to bits. "Yeah. Sucks."

"Some of those Paradise girls are making a thousand a week."

"Geez, that's more than I make in a month working two jobs. I only need $700 to cover my expenses."

"It's downtown on Olympic and Figueroa. You can go down there during the day and talk to the lady in charge."

I wilt with disappointment, but can't let him see my devastation. So I smile. "Cool. Thanks for the tip. I'll call there tomorrow."

He drops me off at home, and I lie awake thinking about the lengths I'm willing to go to make a man love me.

I scroll through the mental list of willing teachers who've taught me about a man's love. At six, my cousin taught me to lick his penis like a popsicle, said it would taste like lemonade. George taught me the power of my budding breasts. The boys from high school taught me empty lies can be wrapped in sweet promises. Jacob and the memory of my first time. Mickey and his promises to protect and love me. Just because a man says something, doesn't mean it's true. Patrick taught me a man who needed to possess me *truly* loved me, until he didn't. The middle-aged men with decades of sobriety who promised to teach me about the steps, staying sober, and the magic of a higher power. Yet, somehow, I always ended up naked and sitting on their dicks.

On a rare occasion, a sweet boy would sneak past my barbed-wire barricade and get close. I love you, they said. I need you. I'll take care of you. They confused me, and it was clear to me they had issues.

A girl whose own father didn't want her, and someone who's done the things I've done, doesn't deserve love. One day, they'll see me for what I really am—broken bits of girl parts held together with glitter glue.

To show them the error of their ways, I fucked their brothers or their best friends. *Love me now?*

I turn my thoughts back to Jimmy. Things are going to be different with him. I'm so madly in fantasy, I can't imagine him leading me down a wrong road. Jimmy's smart, despite his current circumstances. He's beautiful. *Duh.* And he needs me. Maybe we can love each other into being whole.

The next morning, I call the club and make an appointment to see the general manager, Linda. I use my Thomas Guide to map my route, and navigate my way through the bowels of downtown L.A. I pull into the near-empty parking lot and nervously examine my surroundings. Debris everywhere. Homeless people sleeping under newspapers. A drunk guy stumbling along the sidewalk, yelling at cars as they drive by. Even in daylight, this is terrifying.

I hug my steering wheel, lean forward to look through my windshield, and gulp. On the side of the building is a two-story painted mural of a 1970's woman, with blonde Farah Fawcett winged hair, wearing an orange bell-bottom leisure suit. What in the hell am I doing here?

I think of Jimmy again and get out of my car. I walk up the concrete stairs, through the overwhelming stench of stale urine, and into the building. Once inside, I take a breath and look at my surrounding. Straight ahead is a decent pool table. To the left a bank of arcade games, including Galaga. No stripper poles or go-go cages, and I can get paid to play video games? This isn't so bad at all.

Behind a long counter to my right is a woman who clearly gets her make-up tips from Tammy Faye Baker or a tired, drunk drag queen. Her eyelids are covered in shimmery, electric-blue eyeshadow from the base of her lids all the way up to her badly-drawn eyebrows. Her eyelashes are like two tarantulas fighting to the death. Bright coral blush is smeared across each cheek, and matching coral lipstick is applied well past the natural line of her lips.

She eyes me up and down. "You vant job?"

I clear my throat and nod. "Yes, ma'am."

"I'm Jackie. Follow me."

I follow her past an empty dance floor to a back office. Jackie knocks twice on the door, then opens it and sticks her head in.

"New girl heah. You haf time now?"

"Show her in," says a woman's nasal voice from inside the office.

"Dis Linda. She boss." Jackie holds the door as I walk in, then closes it behind me and leaves.

In stark contrast to Jackie, Linda is a bland, non-descript mouse of a woman. Everything in Linda's office is shades of brown: faux-wood paneled walls, lackluster frizzy brown hair and eyes, brown polyester shirt, scuffed brown desk, and shit brown coffee cup. Her skin is chalky and in need of sunlight, or a smidge of Jackie's blush. I sit across from her in a worn, brown leather chair.

"Hi. I'm Linda. And you are?"

"Erika. Erika Worth."

She hands me a clipboard, with standard employee paperwork and a commission schedule, then launches into a canned-pitch explanation of the job. "You must work a minimum of two nights per week. Shifts are daily from 6:00 PM to midnight. You'll be paid for the minutes you dance per week. Clients can buy you extra minutes if they're happy with—"

"So, this is just like normal dancing, not stripping?"

She purses her lips together tightly, then continues. "Correct. No stripping. Some men want to dance. Some want to talk, play games, or watch TV. Each client is different."

"So, they pay just to hang out with us?"

Linda reaches into her desk drawer and pulls out a Tootsie Roll. She unwraps the brown candy, pops it into her mouth, and chomps on it like she's chewing cud. "Yes. You're here to entertain the clients, keep them company. Clients pay $.35 per minute for every minute you're clocked out, plus tip. The tips are yours to keep."

"And that's it? No creepy stuff?"

Linda purses her lips again and rolls her eyes. She moves what's left of the Tootsie Roll to the other side of her mouth and continues. "The rules are no drugs, no foul language, and don't do anything you wouldn't do in front of your grandmother."

Clearly, she's never met my grandmother.

"Off-duty police officers provide security and they won't tolerate any funny business."

I fill out the paperwork and return it to her. She looks it over, then reaches across the desk to shake my hand.

"That's it? I just come in whenever?"

Linda gives me a deadpan look like she's either annoyed or about to fall asleep. I can't decide which.

"That's it."

I shake her hand, thank her, and leave.

The next afternoon, I listen to Pat Benatar's *Love is a Battlefield* for inspiration while getting ready for the first night of my new job. I decide to wear a short, black-Spandex mini dress, silver stiletto heels, and tease my maroon mane to new heights. I adorn each wrist with a barrage of bangles, and drape each earlobe with an oversized chandelier earring. When some guy gets out of line, I wonder if the girls break into a shimmy dance like in this music video.

There's no full-length mirror so I teeter on the toilet seat and check myself in the mirror above the bathroom sink. I add a couple of rhinestone necklaces to my look, then head out to the club. In the car, a lump of knots tense in my belly so I sing loudly to *All Come True* by World Party. I'm Irish, stubborn, and there's no way I'm backing down now. Plus, Jimmy would think I'm a coward.

I once again ascend the stairs and walk into the club. The vibe is totally different at night. The lights are dim and the air is thick with smoke. Men lean against the walls, sit around small tables, and drink at the bar. They are everywhere, and outnumber the girls at least four to one.

Jackie sits at the counter, somehow wearing even more make-up than before. A cigarette dangles out of the side of her mouth, perilously close to her blonde bouffant. She sees me and beckons me with a neon-pink fake fingernail to join her at the counter.

She hands me my time card. "You ah number forty-two. Ven man vants talk vit you more dan vun minute you bring card heah and I clock in. No talk longer dan dat! Must bring card heah. No dance, no get paid," she says sternly.

My brain synapses fire at full blast as I try to decode her broken English and figure out what I'm supposed to do next, all while hypnotized by her tarantulashes. They really are incredible.

"Jackie, um, so where do I go? What do I do?"

"Valk around. Talk to customers. Rest feet ven tired. Go!" She dismissively waves a full hand of barracuda nails at me, then turns her attention to a couple who approached the counter. The girl hands her a time card. Jackie punches into a time clock then puts it into a rack with other time cards next to the register. The couple then walks hand-in-hand down a hallway. I'm not sure what's down there yet.

I look around, unsure where to go first. I decide to go check the high score on Galaga, but glance up and see Jackie slowly shaking her head at me. I turn left and walk down the hall, past restrooms, and enter the television room.

At first, this room seems innocent enough. Fifteen or so two-seater sofas are spaced throughout the dimly-lit room. In the center of the room is a huge projection screen with distorted red, blue, and green images of a martial arts flick. Like looking at 3D without glasses, it hurts my eyes. A groan from the corner catches me off-guard. I thought I was alone.

I look over and see the back of a man's head tilted back, mouth open. I think he's having a heart attack, but when I approach the sofa to help him, I see his suit jacket draped over his lap. His hands are wrapped around some girl's head bobbing up and down underneath his jacket.

Embarrassed, I turn and escape undetected. *Mental note, Erika, avoid the TV room.* I walk back through the game room, and enter the main lounge/dance part of the club. To the right there is a rack attached to the wall with numbered time cards. I put mine in the appropriate slot, then slowly walk around the perimeter of the dance floor. The floor lights up like in *Saturday Night Fever,* and though I'm tempted to do the Hustle, I restrain myself and instead get lost in the swirling disco ball painting twinkling stars of light around the room.

I'm afraid to make eye-contact with anyone, so I keep moving and pass a half-dozen round tables with red candles on them. Couples sit and lean in for intimate conversation. I am now seriously regretting my shoe choice, and eye one of the long red-pleather banquette sofas. There are deep indentations from years of women perched on these seats, which leads me to wonder how long this place has been here and when the last time they changed the furniture. By the looks of things, I'd say around 1972.

I sit on the sofa and smile at a couple of uninterested-looking girls next to me, but they either don't see me or ignore me. I only now realize blinding spotlights are positioned directly on our faces. We're like painted dolls on display. Trying to look calm and unaffected, I light a cigarette, hoping no one sees my hands shaking. In front of me, I discern dark silhouettes of men in the shadows, leaning into each other. Whispering. Watching. Tendrils of smoke twist and curl around their heads.

After sitting for approximately two minutes, a tiny, non-descript Asian man with thinning gray hair and thick glasses approaches me. He smells of Nag Champa incense and oranges, and looks harmless enough. He extends his right hand to me. I take it, and follow Mr. Mystery over to the wall where I retrieve my time card. In silence, we walk up to the front counter where I hand my card to Jackie. She clocks us in, then I follow my mystery date to the dance floor. *Breathe, Erika. It's only dancing.*

I expect light conversation. *Hi. How are you? What's your name?* Instead, I quickly realize this is more like vertical wrestling. My customer is five-feet-two, and with these heels on I'm five-ten, leaving my ample bosom as the perfect resting place for his head. Mister Charming locks his arms around my waist like a vice grip and pulls me close to him, while positioning both of his legs on either side of my right one. He then begins grinding on my leg like a misbehaved dog, only far less polite about it.

Nothing could have prepared me for this particular moment. Gobsmacked, I'm at a complete loss of what to do or say. My instincts are to run out of the club, down the stairs, and never return, but I stand still. Silent. I flip the switch and shut off the tender parts of me. *You need the money, Erika. It's just a dance. A thousand dollars a week. Breathe.* I tuck Erika away to the safe space where nothing can harm her. I turn on the pinup-doll fantasy girl, whose only job is to arouse men. She is powerful. Safe.

I look around and see similar struggles happening around me.

Vapid, mannequin-like faces stare into the distance while foreign hands explore various parts of their bodies. Then, because this moment could not possibly get any weirder, Tina Turner's *Private Dancer* starts playing. *I'm your private dancer, a dancer for money, I'll do what you want me to do.* Seriously? I couldn't write this shit. It's also clear in this moment that the girls and I will not be breaking into a group dance routine in solidarity, then dancing off into a pastel sunrise. This is an every-girl-for-herself kind of place.

My dance partner grips me even tighter, groans loudly, and pulls away with a satisfied grin on his face. Spent.

Aw, man. Did you really just do what I think you did?

Mr. Wonderful escorts me back to Jackie, who punches my time card again. "Four minutes. Dat's $1.40". My customer hands her a five-dollar bill, then hands me the change. My initiation is complete.

With as much dignity as I can muster, I walk back to the lounge to return my timecard to its slot. Before I complete my task, a different man grabs my hand and walks me back to Jackie.

In quick succession, one man after the other checks me out. By the end of my first night, I *danced* for 278 minutes and made $173 in cash tips.

At midnight, I hobble barefoot to my car. A beautiful French girl named Angeline appears next to me.

"Ze first night is ze worst. Zey want to see what you are made of. You did eet. You showed zem," she says with her exquisite accent, then runs her fingers through a cascade of shiny, ebony hair.

She looks like Apollonia from *Purple Rain*, and for the life of me I can't imagine what she's doing in a place like this, or what exactly I showed anyone, but I'm too tired to figure it out. My feet are so swollen I can barely drive. It hurts to touch the pedals. Twenty minutes later, I arrive home, numb and shut down, but I did it. I survived.

I put on Pink Floyd's *Comfortably Numb* and crawl into my futon bed. My exhaustion is exhausted, but my mind is on warp speed. Will there ever be more to my life than what a man wants from me? What would it feel like to be unbroken like one of the Cosby kids? And if Jimmy really cares about me, would he send me to work in a place like that?

I suffocate that thought, lest it wound me, and fall asleep to dreams of Jimmy's arms protecting me from the world.

Weeks go by. Some days I show up and tune out, other nights I stay home and hide. Most of the girls come to work with glassy-eyed courage. I envy their ability to check out. Being the only sober girl who works there, I'm present for every lascivious leer, the stench of hot breath panting on my neck, every hand reaching for more of my flesh than I'm willing to give. I fight off the crudest advances and turn down the real creepers. I hide in the bathroom as much as possible, writing forlorn poetry in my journal while sitting on the window ledge overlooking the trash-strewn alley. Jackie comes in periodically and clears out the bathrooms. No hiding allowed.

Within a few weeks, I get regulars and pride myself on not being one of the "bonus" girls who do a little extra on the side. Not sure whose grandmothers would be okay with any of this, and the off-duty officers always seem to look the other way. There are even rumors of girls disappearing and being sold into slavery.

I wear longer skirts and prom gowns, and use my dancing skills to reel in some of the nice, lonely, older guys who actually want to waltz or slow dance. Some of them talk about their wives who passed, or the girl who got away. Others, I hustle in pool or video games. They know they're being played, but like the cat-and-mouse games.

I start making great money, but it seems to slip through my fingers. I buy stacks of new clothing and fabulous shoes, yet I'm always late with my rent. I save nothing, and survive on coffee, cigarettes, and ramen noodles. I barely go to recovery meetings. When I do, I get there right as the meeting starts and leave the second it's over. I parade around like a peacock, showing everyone how *well* I'm doing. How *happy* I am. No one has a clue what the truth is except Jimmy, and I don't speak to him much. Fuck Jimmy. I add him to the list of people who have fucked with my life.

To make extra money, I start making dates with some of the guys outside of the club. Angeline warns me not to mention anything to Linda or the other girls. It's my business and I should keep it that way.

Peter is thirty-one from China. He's tall, handsome, traditional, and shy. He pays me $150 to go to dinner with him at authentic restaurants in Chinatown. He tells me about his childhood back home, and his arranged marriage to a woman he didn't know and doesn't love. He dreams of traveling and freedom, but he is duty-bound to his family and commitments. Sometimes, he stares into my eyes for long moments, searching them for something. I hope I'm able to mask the chaos and emptiness of my own life. After dinner, we walk in silence beneath colorful lanterns. When he asks me questions about my life, I redirect the conversation back to him. I don't want to spoil the illusion of who he needs me to be. He never gets handsy or tries to sleep with me, only kisses me goodnight softly on the cheek, and lingers a few extra moments, inhaling the scent of my perfume.

Jun is a fifty-year-old realtor from South Korea. He drives a gold Mercedes 500 which has a custom seat that allows him to reach the pedals and see over the steering wheel. He takes me to lunches with his clients and associates, and pays me $250 to sit with them, laugh at their jokes, and feign interest. He tells me I'm exotic and beautiful, gently plays with my red hair, and touches his fingertip to the freckles on my nose.

My favorite customer is Rudy, a forty-seven-year-old attorney from the Philippines. He's four-foot-nine without his platform shoes, has a large black Elvis pompadour, and is drizzled in gold-nugget jewelry. He wears black polyester bellbottom pants and red satin shirts open down to his bulbous belly. One lonely hair curls in the center of his otherwise-bare chest. He likes my quick wit and dirty jokes. I collect as many raunchy jokes as I can during the week, then sit with him for forty-five minutes on Fridays when he comes in. When he laughs, his belly shakes, and when he's really tickled, he slaps his knee with enthusiasm. He asks me what I'm doing working in a place like this. I smile and, with a wistful sigh, tell him how I'm going to be a rich and famous actress and writer, and this will all be an amazing story for Letterman one day. At the end of our meets, he pulls out a wad of hundreds, peels off one, and hands it to me. Then he buys me an extra 300 minutes for the night. Sometimes we go to lunch. Once when I have a bad cold, he brings me orange juice and soup.

I meet with Dr. B for a check-in appointment. I rattle on for fifty minutes about my perfect life and how happy I am. When we're done, he walks me out to the elevator. The doors open. I get in and wave a quick goodbye. He stops the door from closing with his arm.

"You know, Erika, you can always tell me the truth if you want. Entirely up to you." He moves his arm and the doors close.

I stand in silence, irritated and shaken. Right then, I decide to stop meeting with Dr. B.

On a Thursday, I pick up Rudy for a lunch date. He navigates our route from the passenger seat. We near the intersection of Santa Monica and Western.

"Turn left," he says.

I do as I'm told, and pull into the parking lot of a Best Western Hotel. I stop the car in the middle of the parking lot. "Ru-u-udy, what are we doing here?"

"It's okay, Elika. Pull up der." He motions to the office.

"Ru-u-udy, this is a hotel. I can't sleep with you yet. I'm not ready."

"Elika. Pull up." He gets out of the car and runs into the office. A few minutes later, he returns with a room key in his hand,

"Park ovah der." He points to a block of rooms.

"Ru-u-udy, I really can't do this. I respect you. I care about you. I want our first time to be special."

He gets out of the car and uses his key to open Room 108, leaving the door slightly ajar.

Seconds crawl by as I sit in my car, my hands on the steering wheel willing me to keep driving. What the hell am I doing here? How had I not seen this coming? Maybe it's not what I think. Maybe he just wants to talk, or make out. The door is open. Beckoning. And I'm being rude. I slowly get out of my car and walk into the hotel room.

The minute I walk in, I regret my choice. Mirrors cover the walls and ceiling above and around the bed. Rudy stands in the middle of the room and silently undresses. He drops his clothes on the floor and walks naked to the bathroom. I hear the shower. Rooted to the floor by self-loathing, I can't move.

I know Rudy carries a wad of cash with him at all times, at least $10,000. I could take his clothes and leave. But he knows where I live, and he's an attorney. He could have me arrested. Before I can finish my plan, he emerges from the bathroom with a towel wrapped around his waist. He leans over, reaches into his pants pocket, and retrieves the wad of cash I had just been fantasizing about. He peels off twenty $100 bills and counts them out onto the side table. My rent is due tomorrow. Of course, I have none of it.

As he looks at me, he lets his towel drop to the floor. One hand rests on his hip, and the other points to the floor in front of him.

I hesitate for only a moment, then sink to my knees, to the lowest point of my life. Within seconds, he comes in my mouth, then points to the bed. Swallowing his seed and my shame, I obey and lie like a limp ragdoll, and get lost in the picture of the girl on the ceiling. Short, chubby fingers tug her clothes off. Bulbous lips suckle her nipples. The Humpty Dumpty-shaped man climbs on top of her. Her hair is crimson lava pooled across the pillow, her skin as pale as parchment. Lifeless green eyes stare back, accusatory. His pale, flat ass pounds between her legs.

Rapid successions of memories flicker before my eyes. Spinning around in a purple ballet tutu. Running through a cornfield. Riding downhill on my bike, pretending I was flying. Pop-Pop pushing me on the tree swing. Blowing out candles on my birthday cake.

Rudy groans, and comes between my legs.

I definitely can't tell this story on Letterman.

He climbs off me, grabs his clothes from the floor, and goes back into the bathroom.

I am back in my body, suffocating on the bullshit I've been telling myself for months. This is not okay. None of this is anywhere near okay. And I'm not loaded selling myself. I'm stone-cold sober, on my back, in a Best Western Hotel, having a stare down with the corpse of the girl I used to be.

Rudy leaves. If he says anything, I don't hear him. His wetness seeps out between my legs. The salty, sweaty taste of him corrodes my mouth.

I look over at the folded bills on the table, then back at the ceiling. A sob thunders through me, so deep I fear I might shatter. I run through the list of who is to blame. My missing father. My emotionally vacant mother. Jimmy. Them. But the inescapable truth is that no one *made* me do anything. I took my inner child, shoved her in a closet, and stapled her mouth shut.

I need to get out of this hotel room. I have not stayed sober to remain a piece of shit. Forget about making men love me. How am I ever going to love me? I don't know what a life without hating myself looks like, or whether there is any part of me worth fighting for.

But I have to try.

I wish I could say I left the hotel room and wrapped myself in dignity and self-respect, but I don't learn lessons that easily. I never go back to Club Paradise, but I'm still the same girl that walked into that room—parts of me are still open, festering wounds.

I get a job at an underground bar run by some sober guys. On my way to work I get pulled over. The cop asks if I have $730 for bail money. Guess I should have paid those three speeding tickets from a year ago. I don't, and I'm arrested and taken to Van Nuys sub-station.

After forty-eight hours, Mom bails me out. I thank her and ignore the look of disappointment on her face. Even sober, I'm a fuckup.

With my new freedom, I head to Highland Grounds with my journal, hoping to find a strong cup of coffee and an open table.

From across the room, I hear a familiar voice. "Is that a jail bird I see, flying free?"

I look up and see Jamal. He stands by the door with his legs spread, knees slightly bent, and arms out wide.

"Jaaamaalllll!" I run across the room, jump into his arms, and wrap my legs around his waist. We always make a spectacle of ourselves, but I don't care.

"Well, well, well. *Someone's* been a busy little bee," he teases.

I climb off Jamal and stand on the floor. "Who, lil' ol' me?" I wave a hand in front of my face and flutter my eyelashes.

"Did we learn anything from this latest adventure?"

"That cops are stupid assholes. I was minding my own business, on my way to work, and they just had to arrest me? Like, don't they have enough real criminals to worry about? They didn't even give me a toothbrush or anything."

"Devastating. Sweetie, I want you to meet my friend. Kelly, Erika. Erika, Kelly."

I look at the pretty brunette standing near us with the sourpuss look on her face. "Hi, I'm Erika. Nice to meet you." I hold a hand out to shake.

"Hmm," she replies and shakes mine.

I ignore Ms. Judgypants and look back to Jamal. "Anyway, it wasn't so bad. I made up blues songs while I was there and started water fights. I was bored out of my mind."

"Well, isn't that an interesting way to spend a weekend?" Jamal purses his lips.

"Now I can say I've been to jail," I brag. "Of all the illegal things I've ever done, this is the one I get popped for. Can you believe it?"

"You're an asshole," Kelly says to me.

My mouth drops open. "Um, excuse me?"

"How much time do you have?" she asks.

"I've got almost *two* years," I boast.

"Not for long if you don't start doing the work. Call me when you're ready to get serious about sobriety." She scribbles her number on a piece of paper and hands it to me.

With all the smarm I can muster, I reply, "Thank you *so* much for sharing." I stuff her phone number in my back pocket. "Bye, Jamal. I'm going to go hit a meeting. Love you!" I smother his face with red-lipstick kisses, give Kelly a dismissive look, and leave.

On the drive home, I think about Kelly. Fuck her. Who the hell does she think she is, talking to me like that? *Someone who's telling you the truth.*

Every day, I sit in meetings and ask myself if today is the day I'll have the courage to kill myself. I don't share. I don't have a sponsor. I keep the world at arm's length.

At home, I put on a fresh pot of coffee, a Billie Holiday cassette, light a cigarette, and stare at my ceiling. I've fucked my life up, but do I deserve anything better? If I relapse or kill myself, all of Mom's sacrifices, the hospital, everyone who's tried to help me—will all mean nothing.

I try to avoid the scrap of paper with Kelly's number on it, but it follows me from my kitchen counter to the bathroom sink to my nightstand. I can't seem to throw it away, so I lie awake and stare at it.

After a week, I call her.

"Hello?" says a female voice.

"Um, yeah, is Kelly there?"

"This is Kelly."

"I don't know if you remember me. I met you last week with Jamal—"

"Erika, I *knew* you'd call." Her voice is smug, even over the phone. "Are you ready to do the work?"

I'm stubborn and proud. I don't like needing help. I take a deep breath and exhale. "If I don't, I'll die. What do you want me to do?"

"Can you be at my house at ten tomorrow morning? I'll make us breakfast and we can go over everything."

I have a new sponsor. Yay. Kelly kicks my ass immediately. She doesn't tell me who to date or what to wear, but she doesn't sugarcoat anything. She also makes me go to an all-women meeting. I've never gone to meetings before without trying to get laid, get a job, or at the very least attention.

Week after week, the same ten women gather at Kathleen's house and talk about anything and everything. I'm the youngest at nineteen. The oldest is in her fifties. I quickly learn that while the men in recovery grab my ass, it's the women who are saving it.

None of them are perfect, but they all have value in their own ways. They're so much more than their body parts and faces. I fall a little bit in love with all of them.

Kelly gives me an assignment to find something nice to say about every woman I meet, especially the ones I want to judge. She also makes me look directly into my eyes in the mirror and say, "Good morning, kid. You're a beautiful child of God and you're exactly where you're supposed to be. Have a great day," then end with a smile and a wink.

I think her suggestions are horrible and ridiculous, but my own ideas have brought me nothing but trouble. I do whatever she tells me, most of the time. A few times I lie to her and say I did something when I didn't. She freakishly knows every time. I don't like disappointing her, so I take her suggestions.

The more I get to know her, the more she fascinates me. She's like no other woman I've ever known before. She is confident and capable, suffers no fools, is successful and seems able to do anything. And she's only twenty-five.

I open up to her slowly. As I reveal my secrets, she tells me hers. She says she hasn't always been the woman she is now, but by doing the work and making different choices, her life changed.

I thought if I stopped getting loaded, I'd be okay. Sobriety would be enough. It turns out, alcohol and drugs weren't really my problem.

I am, and my messed-up thinking. She explains there is a huge difference between physical and emotional sobriety, and that people like us need both to be happy.

I sit at her kitchen table drinking strong coffee. I clear my throat. "If I ask you something, do you swear to tell me the truth?"

"Always."

I pause, as I can barely form the words. "Do you think I can ever be whole?" I fear her answer because she always tells me the truth. I look down at the floor.

She wraps her aroums around me as I start to cry. "Yes, Erika. If you do the work and never give up, I promise you can be whole."

cabaret

At eight years old, I decide I want to be Bette Midler as Delores De Lago when I grow up. She's got seashells on her boobs, a mound of red curly hair, and a glittery mermaid tail. Nothing could be better than that.

My aunt Sharon convinces Mom to let me audition for *South Pacific,* a musical. They dress me in a navy turtleneck and red cords. I memorize the lyrics to *You're a Grand Old Flag* and learn snazzy choreography that includes marching and salutes. The bicentennial was not long ago, so patriotism is super in.

I sing and dance my heart out. When I'm done, the adults applaud and cheer. I love the attention. I get cast in the show, and Mom and I make a whole new group of friends.

I may not have a dad, but now I have more aunties and uncles than anyone I know, and mine are way more fun. They disco dance and sing show tunes loudly in public. And they make Mommy laugh all the time.

When I'm nine, we move into a house in Arlington where none of our walls touch anyone else's. I get a cocker spaniel puppy named Bentley. Our friend, Bubba, moves in with us. He's the greatest guy I know other than Pop-Pop.

One day, he asks to speak to me alone. We go into a quiet room where he sits me down. His face looks very serious.

"Erika, I'm gay. Do you know what that is?"

"You're happy?"

"Well, that's one definition. But gay can also mean men who like to kiss other men instead of women."

"Oh, *that*. I see guys kiss other guys all the time."

"So, it doesn't bother you?"

"Well, kissing is gross no matter *who's* doing it, but why would I care?"

"Would you be upset if you saw me kiss another man?"

"As long as he's nice to you, I think it'd be swell."

He cries when I say that and gives me a big hug.

Bubba's family never comes to see him, just like my dad. I tell Bubba we'll always be his family.

My new bedroom is all purple. Purple walls. Purple bedding. I even got purple satin pants like one of the Charlie's Angels.

"Wake up!" Mommy squawks like a parrot.

I ignore her and turn my head the other way on my pillow.

She rips the covers off me and throws them on the floor. "Wake up. Time to get ready for school." She walks out of my room.

I yell after her. "Ugh! I *hate* it when you do that! You're so *rude!*" I gather up my comforter and crawl back into bed.

"Giiiit up! Giiiit up! Rise and shine, sleepy head!" Bubba screams in his Dallas drawl while bouncing on a corner of my twin bed. "It's Monday morning. Time to git up and learn."

I crack one eye open. He's in his gray velour bathrobe and white tube socks, grinning like Animal from the Muppets. He acts more like an ornery kid than an almost thirty-year-old. "Please, just five more minutes. I swear." I pull my purple comforter back over my head.

He ignores me, hops to the other corner of my bed, and continues to jump and whoop. "Git on up! The world is a waitin'!"

I can't help but giggle and crawl out from my purple cocoon. I shuffle into the kitchen for my morning Pop-Tart.

* * *

"Oh my God, Bubba. How long has it been? You look exactly the same." I hug him big and long. The smell of his Grey Flannel cologne takes me right back to the 70s.

"Well, you're all grown up. Last time I saw you was when you guys moved to California. How old were you? Eleven?"

"Yep. Ten years just flew by."

We make small talk about his life in the bay area. We fill each other in on how so and so is doing. He tells me about his work as a flight attendant. I tell him about sobriety, writing, and photography, and leave out the dicey bits. He pulls out a box of photos from the theater days. We laugh at share old stories and memories. We go quiet when we see faces of the young men who are no longer with us.

"Erika, has anyone talked to you about my status?"

My heart sinks. "Status?"

"I'm HIV positive."

I'm gutted. HIV is a death sentence.

He wags a finger at me and smiles. "Turn that frown upside down, missy. I'm okay. My T cells are a little low, but the doctors are watching it. They have me on the cocktail, and I take great care of myself. There's nothing to worry about."

"You swear?"

He crosses his heart. "Swear."

The next few hours fly by, and it's time for me to leave and drive back to Los Angeles. We hug for a long time, and I promise to come back and visit soon. One month bleeds into six, then a year passes.

"Have you talked to Bubba lately?" Momma asks.

"Well, I saw him...shit. When was that? Holy crap. A little more than a year ago, I guess."

"He's in hospice."

I cry. Hospice means dying. "That's impossible. He was just fine, flying all over the place. Happy. Handsome as ever."

"He's down to eighty-seven pounds now. He's covered in lesions. The meds he's on make his tongue swell up so it's hard for him to talk."

"I have to see him. I have to—"

"I wouldn't go up there without talking to him first. He may not want you to see him like that."

Convinced Mom is being dramatic, I call the number Mom gives me for Bubba. The once vibrant, audacious Bubba can barely say hello.

"What's...up...Sugar...Plum?" His speech is slow and labored. Unrecognizable.

I'm acutely aware that talking to me is causing him pain. I try to hold back tears, as I don't want to upset him, but it's impossible not to cry. "Oh, Bubba, I wish we could go back to when we lived on Quincy Street, when you were okay and I wasn't broken. I wish we could do theater again and I wish we'd never moved to California and I wish—"

"Erika...you can't ever go back. You can only move forward. You have to grab life by the balls and don't ever let it go. Every moment of life is precious."

The amount of pain he must have felt while saying that makes the message even more impactful. "Oh, Bubba. I love you more than I could ever say. Thank you for loving me, for being such a light in my life."

"I...love...you...too."

His voice breaks on the other end of the phone. We both cry. The thought of him alone, in a wheelchair, emaciated is too much to bear.

"Erika. You go have a big, beautiful life."

"I will. I promise."

"I love you. Bye now."

"I love you, too."

ERIKA WORTH

Bubba Garner died November 15, 1993. He was forty-one years old.

I will never understand why some people get to live and others die. I've made so many huge mistakes. I don't know why I still get to be here, but every time I think of giving up, I think of Bubba. He doesn't have any more choices. What a disservice to his life, and the promise I made him, for me to end mine.

achin', breakin heart

"Hey Mister." I tug on the stranger's pant leg and look up at him from my small part of the world. "Are you my daddy?" I've tugged on oodles of suit pants, polyester bell-bottoms, and blue jeans over the years. Men usually look scared when I ask, then glance around, probably wondering if they are on the television show *Candid Camera*. Some guys ask what kind of kid doesn't know what her own father looks like. With my inside voice, I point two imaginary thumbs toward my chest and think *this kid*.

I know I'm supposed to have a dad, but I don't feel like a freak until I start first grade and the kids question me.

"Erika, who's your daddy?"

I shrug my shoulders. "I dunno." I haven't yet learned the price of honesty.

"Did your parents get a divorce?"

"They were never married."

"What's your daddy's name?"

"I dunno."

"Where did he go?"

My cheeks burn. I should know that, but I don't.

"Erika's an or-phan," they sing.

"I'm not an orphan. I have a mommy!"

"Erika's a bas-tard."

I ask my teacher what a bastard is. When she tells me, I grow smaller. There must be something wrong with me if my own father doesn't want me.

If my life is ever going to be okay, I need to find my dad. I don't know his name, where he lives, or what he looks like. He's a big blank, so I make him up in my head. He'll be tall and strong, so he can carry me around on his shoulders like other kids' dads. He'll wrap his arms around me and hug my fears and hurts away. He'll be smart, and we'll play chess and talk about books, and he'll be rich so we can live in a big house.

I've seen more than a few episodes of *Charlie's Angels*, so I know I need more information. I pester my family about him, but no one will tell me anything. They all say the same thing: they don't remember anything, and I should just forget about him. Momma always says he's not important.

But he feels important.

I do the only thing I know how to do: I get down on my knees next to my bed, tightly interlace my fingers and squeeze my eyes shut so God can see how serious I am, and pray. "Please God, let Daddy come back and help Mommy so she won't be so sad all the time and so she won't have to work and so someone will love her and she can stay home and make me some cookies and we can be a family like normal people. Also, please bless everyone and let me have a puppy soon. Amen."

I run to the window and look out into the night. I don't know how long it will take for my prayers to be answered, and since Daddy has never been here, I worry he might get lost.

* * *

Every June after elementary school lets out, I travel from Virginia to the Pennsylvania countryside for the summer. Days are spent with cousins, chewing on humid air and swatting bloodthirsty mosquitos off our sweaty skin. We ride bikes on winding country roads. We splash in the creek—pronounced "crick" in these parts. We explore abandoned eighteenth-century stone houses. We play hide and go seek and run lightning-fast through cornfields so scary monsters don't catch us. We climb barefoot to the tops of apple trees, scraping our knees on bark as we go. We build forts with discarded branches and make pets of stray frogs and turtles.

The only rule here is we have to come back in when we can no longer see our hands in front of our faces. At dusk, we catch lightning bugs in mason jars, covered with lids speckled with air holes. We keep our prisoners on nightstands next to our beds. I watch, mesmerized, as wings expand and retract over segmented bodies. Bug butts light up every few seconds, filling the jar with a neon-green glow.

Here, no one asks me about my dad. Here, I'm never lonely. Here is home.

I follow Pop-Pop around like a puppy dog. We go down to the garden and harvest tubs of vegetables. We sit on the back porch, snapping beans and shucking corn. We make homemade ice cream with an old hand-crank machine that takes forever but tastes so much better than stuff from the store. He pushes me on the big rope swing out back he made for me.

I find him in the garage. "Watcha doin', Pop-Pop?" I study him as he maneuvers a rectangle covered in sandpaper over an old piece of furniture.

"Strippin' furniture."

"You're making it naked?"

He chuckles. "Yep. Sumpin' like 'at. C-c-come on over here,

Skeeter, and I'll show you how."

He explains about the grain, different types of wood, how some sandpaper is rough and others are soft, and how they all do something different. He's always patient, always kind.

After whatever chore Pop-Pop and I have been working on, Mom-Mom has lunch ready for us: chicken and dumpling soup and cold iced-tea in orange and brown Tupperware glasses.

Pop-Pop blows on a steaming spoon of chicken and broth and slurps it into his mouth.

"Mmm, mmm. 'At's real good, honey. Thank ya."

Mom-Mom ignores Pop-Pop most of the time. Some days, Pop-Pop and Uncle Billy go away to work, and I'm not allowed to come along. I stay home with Mom-Mom, who mostly cooks or cleans the house.

She exercises for one hour every day. Sometimes, she does calisthenics along with Jack LaLanne on television. Most days, she plays music on the eight-track and dances around the edge of the big brown, gold, and orange braided oval rug on the living room floor. She prances barefoot on her tippy-toes, wearing only one of her short nighties and no underwear. Tissues folded into long rectangles and secured with aluminum clips on either side of her head keep sweat from messing up her makeup.

"Yer cheatin' heeaarrrt...will make you weeeeep," Mom-Mom sings along with Hank.

"What are you doing that for, Mom-Mom?"

She holds out the edges of her nightie like a skirt, and smiles like one of the pretty ladies from the Miss America Pageant. "To keep my figure. My sisters were fat, disgusting pigs. Nothing worse than a fat woman, or a woman with a smelly *vagina*."

After she says the word vagina, she scrunches up her face like she just ate a lemon. I hope my vagina never gets smelly.

"I'll never be like them. I have pride in my appearance, and so should you."

"What does that mean?"

"It means you do your best to be presentable. Make sure you and your house are perfect and clean. That's why I put on fresh makeup at night before I go to sleep. If anything happens in the middle of the night, I don't want anyone seeing me without my face on."

Once a week, it's time to go into town to the market. That means two hours of prep time. First, she slathers thick Ponds cream all over her skin, and quickly pats the skin underneath her chin with the back of her hand.

"What's that for?"

"To keep my skin tight. Have you ever seen old women with necks that hang like turkeys?"

I think about it for a second. "Yes."

"Now look at my chin," she cranes her neck up, displaying her soft and supple skin.

"Yours is perfect, Mom-Mom."

She looks back in the mirror and smiles to herself with one eyebrow raised, pleased by my praise of her beauty.

Mom-Mom is in her fifties, but wherever we go, men stop what they're doing to watch her walk, her heels click across the floor. At the grocery store, most of the ladies wear sweat pants stretched thin over rolls of excess skin. Some have curlers in their hair or handkerchiefs tied around their heads. Many of them wear no makeup, and most look frazzled by motherhood. Their kids scream or pull things off shelves as they trail their mothers down the aisle.

Mom-Mom wouldn't be caught dead in public with a hair out of place. She wears a sheath dress, cape, and high heels every time we leave the house. I'm expected to look and act my best, and never embarrass her.

She takes me to nice restaurants and parades me in front of her friends. This is my little *granddaughter.* Isn't she *precious?* She's so *smart.* Such a little *lady.*

Mom-Mom never says nice things to Mommy. She tells her she's getting *fat,* or warns her that she'll never find a husband looking like a *lesbian.*

She smiles at her friends when they're together, but as soon as they leave, she talks about how much they weigh, how awful their clothes were, how messy their house was. She's got something to say about everyone.

I've never once seen Mom-Mom and Pop-Pop kiss or hold hands, although he tries all the time. He puckers up like a fish and tries to kiss her cheek, but she always pushes him away. No matter what she says to him or about him, or how many times she yells, he still loves her like crazy. They don't even sleep in the same bedroom. Married grownups are weird.

Pop-Pop is taking us to a special dinner tonight. He showers, then lets me sit on the bathroom counter and watch him get ready. I put on his large silver watch. I love how the weight of it clunks against my wrist.

He takes a long leather strap and straight razor out of the bathroom closet. He moves the razor up and down the worn leather until it's sharp. Then he wets a big blush brush and swirls it in the cup with hard white stuff, and like magic turns it into whipped cream. He whooshes the lather around his face.

"Me too, Pop-Pop! Me too!"

He dabs some of the lather on my cheeks and my chin. I grab a comb and watch him in the mirror, mimic each swipe of the blade across his whiskers. I remove my own lather with my comb.

He rinses the remnants of shaving cream off, dabs his face dry with a towel, then splashes on Old Spice after-shave. "Whooowheee!"

I know from watching him do before that the after-shave burns, so I opt out of that part of the ritual.

He takes his brown toupee off a Styrofoam head, dabs stinky glue all around the inside, and sticks it to his head. Mom-Mom says he looks gross without his hair on, but I think he looks like Paul Newman with or without it.

Pop-Pop and I finish getting ready and wait in the living room for Mom-Mom. I stand on his feet and hold his hand as we dance to Johnny Cash singing *You Are My Sunshine.* We spin and float across the floor, and don't hear Mom-Mom come down the hall.

"Oh, Bill, stop that before you break something."

She looks so glamorous in her black dress, pearls, and black cape.

He smiles at her, flashing full dimples. "Well, honey, don't you look awful purty."

"Thank you, Bill. You look nice, too...for a change."

We get in Pop-Pop's car and slowly make our way to the restaurant.

"Jesus, Bill, could you drive any slower? You could at least go the speed limit."

"I don' wanna h-h-hit no animals on these bac-k-k roads."

The one—and maybe only—thing my grandparents have in common is their love for animals. Any stray or broken bird, cat, dog, possum, or whatever comes onto their property is welcomed into the Worth house and mended with tender loving care. If only Mom-Mom loved people the way she loves animals.

"We'll be old by the time you get there," she says, and starts to chew on her thumbnail.

"Now, hon-n-ney, you just sit tight. We're gonna to have a n-n-nice night."

"We'll see about that."

He steps on the accelerator slightly as we make our way around a bend. "Two wheels, Skeeter! Two wheels!"

Pop-Pop tells that joke every time we turn a corner going more than five miles per hour, and it's always funny.

We get to the restaurant and I walk in proudly between them. The three of us out together is a rare treat.

After we look at the menu for a bit, the waitress comes up to our table. She turns to Mom-Mom, pen and pad in hand. "Do you know what you'd like?"

"Yes." Mom-Mom smiles sweetly. "A husband who lasts more than a minute in bed. Is that on the menu?"

The waitress' face turns red, and she looks at Pop-Pop with pity. "Um, I'll give y'all a few more minutes."

Pop-Pop's face starts to twitch. "N-n-n-now, why'd you hafta g-g-g-go and say sumpin' like 'at? Why can't you jus' be sweet?"

"Because it's the truth, Bill. If you'd give me a divorce and sell the house, we wouldn't have to deal with each other anymore."

"That's my house and I'm not selling it, not ever. I built that house with these two hands and I'll die there. I'll burn it down before I let you sell it."

"Well, you can eat by yourself, Bill. I'll wait in the car."

Mom-Mom storms out of the restaurant. Pop-Pop hangs his head down and cries. I hand him my napkin, helpless to take his hurt away.

"Come on, Pop-Pop. Let's go home."

"All I wanted was t-t-t-ta have a nice dinner. J-j-jus' one."

"I know, Pop-Pop. I'm sorry." I hug him tight.

We drive home in silence. Pop-Pop goes quietly to his bedroom. I walk down the long hallway and stop outside his door. His muffled sobs make my heart ache.

I go back to the living room and grab a large gold pillow from the sofa. I lie on my stomach on the dancing-rug, and kick my legs behind me with nervous energy. Mom-Mom sits on the sofa and drinks amaretto. We watch Johnny Carson, then Benny Hill.

"Everyone thinks I'm sush a bish," she slurs. "They don't know what it's like bein' married to him all these years."

The television goes off the air, and she passes out on the sofa. I'm wide awake with nowhere to go.

r o a d s

December 25, 1994

In sixteen hours, I will meet my father. I've only waited twenty-four years, ten months, and twenty-four days for this, but who's counting?

My cousin, Mary, hugs me on the train-station platform. "Good luck."

"Thank you, and thanks for the ride. Mom was so mad at me, she wouldn't say goodbye."

"She'll be fine. Give her time."

"Do I look okay?"

"You look great. He'll love you." She smiles.

Mary is living sunshine. I hug her again and climb up the stairs to the train. I make my way down the aisle and choose an empty seat by the window. I pull out my journal and pen and lay them on the seat next to me, then store my backpack under the seat in front of me.

At 4:00 PM, the train pulls out of the Wilmington, Delaware station. Mary stands on the platform, waving and smiling, all dimples and black curls. I wave back.

At 7:30 AM tomorrow, this train will arrive in Toccoa, Georgia, and

I will finally meet my father. I assess my outfit for the 532nd time: a comfy pair of holey, faded jeans, a white T-shirt, and gray men's blazer with the sleeves rolled up. My new vintage snakeskin boots are two sizes too big and have holes in both soles, but if I wear two pairs of super-thick socks, I can barely tell. They have character and I love them.

Erika, you look relaxed, yet confident. Aritstic and free-spirited, especially with your crazy red hair flying everywhere. How can he not love you?

I'm excited, but feel guilty as hell. Everything I do seems to hurt Mom, and I'm not into it anymore. There was a time when I did spiteful things to her. I'd forget Mother's Day, but bake my best friend's mom a cake, take a photo, and show it to her. When she got upset, I'd beat her over the head with my club of righteous anger. *You let him hurt me.* Righteous anger is my favorite kind. You did something horrible, and I get to remind you of it any time I want.

Two years ago, when I turned five years sober, being angry at her didn't feel cute anymore, or justified. I felt like an ass. After Kelly moved away, my new sponsor suggested I write out my mom's story without me in it. What it was like for her to be her mother's daughter. To grow up in the environment she did, and have no belief in herself. To meet my dad, and go through everything that happened between them. To fall in love with George, and finally feel like she had something good in her life, only for him to do the unthinkable. I watched Mom disappear that night, watched the precious in her break and never return.

When I finished writing her story, and stopped thinking about *me me me*, I got it. She didn't give birth to me, hold me in her arms, and wonder how she could fuck me up. She did her absolute best, and none of it was personal. I forgave her everything.

Hopefully, she can forgive me for leaving today. Two hours ago, we had the biggest fight we've had in years.

"How can you leave right now to do this?" Her eyes narrow in fury. "He's an asshole! Why do you want to meet him? And why does it have to be now? You're really going to leave your grandfather when he's got cancer? You came to Pennsylvania for Pop-Pop, not for some asshole who never gave a dime to help raise you! He never even tried to find you! Pop-Pop was your real father. You should be here, not on some train to Georgia!" On and on she goes, beating me over the head with my father's inadequacies and shortcomings.

She's right—about all of it—but I still have to go.

"I know how absent of a father he's been, Mom. I'm the one without a dad, remember? You'll never understand. You know who your parents are. You can look at them. Touch them. Yell at them. Hug them. I can't just drop it. I don't want to hurt you or Pop-Pop. But this isn't about either of you. I *have* to do this! Can you really not understand? If I don't go, I'll regret it for the rest of my life! You don't have to like my decision, but it is *my* decision. *And. I'm. Going.*"

Anger and disappointment paint her face crimson. "You don't *have* to do anything, Erika, but stay here and be with your *family*," she says through clenched teeth. "It's fucking Christmas! Why can't you plan a separate trip to meet him? You're ruining *everything*!" She angry cries.

I want her to understand, but I don't need her to. Her tears cannot sway me. "I know he was an asshole to you. I know you raised me alone with no help—and thank you for that. I'm sorry he was a dick and hurt you, but that's between you two. You tell him how you feel and keep me out of it."

"I'm not going to talk to him. I don't ever want to speak to him again!"

I stare at her, unwavering. "I love you...and I'm going."

"Don't come crying to me when he disappoints you." She gives up the argument and storms out of the room.

In my seven years of sobriety, I've rarely been as thirsty as I am in this moment. One little fifth of vodka would take the edge off this whole debacle, but I don't drink no matter what.

I go to my safety zone, the basement. Pop-Pop sits in front of fire, whittling. He's carving a simple piece of wood into a link of chains, all with a tiny pocket knife. His patience astounds me. I lift up his baseball cap, kiss his bald head, and plop on the sofa opposite him.

"Hey there, Skeeter. Watcha doin'?"

"I just told Mom about the trip."

"How'd she take it?"

"Not well at all. I don't think I've ever seen her so pissed before. Are you mad at me, too?"

"Not at all, honey. You know things weren't very nice 'tween them. She's got a right ta be upset. She raised you. He never did nuffin' to provide for either of you."

"I know, and I'm grateful to her for everything she did, but I have to meet him. This isn't about her—this is about me. Maybe by meeting him, I'll finally feel whole."

"You already are."

"I can't explain it, Pop-Pop. There's something missing inside me. I need to see him face to face and ask him all the questions I've ever wanted answers to. And I'm coming right back. I'm not spending the night or anything. It's fifteen hours each way on the train, and I'm there for twelve hours. I'm back on the twenty-seventh and staying until January 2. We'll have lots of time to hang out. Maybe you'll even finally beat me at Rummy," I tease.

"I could whoop ya if you'd quit cheatin'." He winks at me. "I love you, Skeeter. Now, pull my finger."

We both giggle.

"Oh, Pop-Pop. Gross." I bear hug him. "Geez, Pop-Pop, I'd hate to think where Mom and I would be without you."

The conductor stops at my seat and asks for my ticket. I show it to him. He writes *TCA* on a green slip and hangs it on the rack above my seat. Across the aisle from me is a zoftig African-American woman with several bags piled on the seat and the floor around her. The conductor hangs a TCA slip above her seat as well.

I'm on a train to my destiny. Talk about an Oprah moment. I want to puke one minute and cry the next. After tomorrow, I will no longer be an abandoned person. I will be my father's daughter. I drift off into my favorite fantasy of meeting him.

My train pulls into the station. The doors open and he's standing there, beaming with love and pride. I bound down the stairs into his open arms, where he swallows me in a bear hug. After more hugs and a river of tears, he holds me at arm's length.

"Let me look at you. All grown up and so beautiful." He inspects me from head to toe. "Nice boots."

"Aw, thanks Dad."

He stares at me lovingly, tears in his eyes—tears that tell me everything I've ever wanted to know. We walk arm-in-arm to the car, engrossed in conversation, exchanging stories and insights into each other's lives. He'll tell me all about my half-brothers and sisters, and we'll devise a plan for my next visit when I'll get to meet them. We'll love each other and I'll never be alone again. When I tell him about the bad stuff, he'll hug the hurt and sadness away. If I ever get married, he'll walk me down the aisle and dance the first dance with me. He'll bounce my children—his grandchildren—on his knee. I'll have a real family.

Before I get back on the train, he'll squeeze me tightly and say, "I'm so sorry I wasn't there for you, but I'm so proud of the woman you've become. You have such strength and courage. I'll never leave you again. I love you, Erika."

Doubt decides to join the party. His car could break down. Something horrible could happen to him and you'd never know about it. You could just be stuck at the station, waiting. *What if I'm not good enough for him to show up for?*

Searing pain rips through my abdomen. *He left you once. What if he leaves again?*

I turn to my neighbor across the aisle. "Excuse me, ma'am?"

The face of an angel turns toward me. Large, brown pools of

melting chocolate gaze warmly at me. Her cheeks are like two apple dumplings, and large dimples punctuate both sides of her pearly white grin. A glossy-black curly wig sits slightly askew on top of her head, and she cools herself with a cardboard church fan as she speaks. "Yes, chil'?"

"I couldn't help noticing you're going to Toccoa. And...umm...I'm going to Toccoa, too. Can you tell me about it? Are there any hotels or anything—" Adrenaline-fueled panic sears up my spine. My cheeks flush red-hot and I feel faint.

"Are you all right, honey?" she asks, concerned.

I'm not in the habit of telling deep, dark secrets to normal people. Maybe it's her eyes, or that I feel like an emotional volcano about to erupt, but I make an exception and spill.

"Well, actually, I'm going there to meet my dad for the first time ever and I'm not sure if he'll be there and I've never been there and my mom is so angry with me and my grandfather has cancer which is why I came to Pennsylvania and I didn't tell anyone I was doing this until yesterday and now Mom is furious but I had to do this and when this train gets to Georgia he'll *be there*, and, well..." Exhausted, I burst into one of the biggest cries of my life.

The angel reaches into a bag and retrieves some Kleenex. She hands me the tissue and, in a velvety Southern drawl, says, "I'm Mrs. Mae Mayes. Ah live in Jamaica Queens, New York an' I'm on mah way to see mah family in N'Awlins. We're gonna be on this train for a good, long while. Why dontcha tell me all 'bout it, honey?"

"Fifteen months ago, I hired a detective. I didn't have any information to give him other than a name. I gave him ninety dollars, and he gave me a list of three hundred possible matches and phone numbers. My dad's was the first one on the list."

"What was it like talkin' to him the first time?"

"Freaky. Awesome. We talked for about a half hour, then wrote letters back and forth." I open my journal and pass photos across the aisle to her.

"He's a hansom fella. And look at all that hair."

"Yeah. He's got a ton of hair. That's kind of a big deal in my mom's family."

"What did his letters say?"

"He told me about his wife and six of my half-brothers and sisters." I pause and scrunch my lips to one side. "My dad kinda got around."

Mrs. Mayes holds a hand up to her mouth and giggles.

"One of my sisters is six months younger than me. They don't know about me yet. That's a whole *other* thing to worry about down the road."

"What else are you worried about?"

Nerves swim in the pool of caffeine in my tummy. "My mom, for one. She's so upset I'm doing this. I get it, but I told her it was just something I have to do. And then I worry that—he" I stop myself. Saying the words aloud might make my greatest fear come true.

"What is it?"

"He could not like me. I could have waited my whole life to meet my dad, and he could think I'm awful." I dab my eyes with the balled-up tissue in my hand. "I think my heart would break beyond repair."

Mrs. Mayes smiles, reaches across the aisle, and holds my hand in hers. "Sweet baby, I've known you twenty minutes an' I already think you're precious."

Insults and anger I can deal with. I get scrappy and fight. I don't know where kindness fits. "Thank you, Mrs. Mayes. I'm so grateful I sat across the aisle from you.

"Me, too. Can you watch my bags while I use the ladies?"

"Of course."

Mrs. Mayes stands up and makes her way to the restroom. Her ample hips hit every seat as she walks down the aisle.

When she comes back, we continue talking. I feel like I can tell her anything.

I've never been on a train before so I didn't think to pack food. Somewhere around 9:00 PM, my stomach growls. With a knowing smile, Mrs. Mayes reaches down by her seat, retrieves a bucket of

Kentucky Fried Chicken, and passes it across the aisle to me.

"Take what you want, chil'. There's plenny."

Her kindness humbles me.

After we eat, Mrs. Mayes drifts off to sleep. I sneak back to the empty smoking car to have a cigarette—or ten. I read and re-read every word of my father's letter, study his photographs.

An hour later, I return to my seat. Mrs. Mayes opens a sleepy eye and gazes at me. She reaches into her endless bags of goodies, pulls out a pillow and blanket, and passes them to me. I gratefully accept and sleep for a few hours.

I wake up in the middle of the night and look over at my sleeping angel, snoring peacefully, then out at the dark, moonless sky. Hours ago, I was shattered. Now, I'm cocooned in the safety of a stranger's kindness. *Thank you, whatever you are. Thank you.*

Dawn gradually peeks over a violet horizon and paints the sky optimistic.

"Good mornin', Miss Erika. You ready?"

"I think so."

"No matter what happens, chil', you'll be jus' fine."

"Mrs. Mayes, thank you...for everything."

"It was mah pleasure to meet you. I do hope we keep in touch. I want to hear all about your meetin'."

We exchange contact information, and gather our things together.

I can barely breathe as the train slows into the station and stops. I gather several of Mrs. Mayes' bags and follow her as her hips play bumper pool down the aisle.

The door opens and she climbs down the stairs. When she clears them, I see him standing twenty feet from the door on the platform straight ahead. He's tall and striking with piercing green eyes. Even at sixty-two, he has a full head of salt-and-pepper hair. I glance at him nervously, then follow Mrs. Mayes as she walks to the left. She stops, and I set her bags down beside her.

"Is that him?" She smiles in his direction.

"Yes, ma'am, it is." I gulp and smile back.

"Go give yo daddy a big ol' hug." She winks and gives my arm a nudge.

I take a huge breath and walk toward him—a lifetime of expectation in tow. "Hi Daddy." I smile go to hug him.

He stops me, puts his hands on my shoulders, and kisses both cheeks. "That's how white people greet each other," he says coldly, then looks over at Mrs. Mayes.

Wait, what did he just say? I must have misunderstood.

"Are you done with...*all of that.*" He waves a dismissive hand toward Mrs. Mayes. This time, his intent is unmistakable.

This big, definitive moment I've waited my whole life for is not at all like I had imagined.

"I'll...um...be right back." I turn away from him and walk back to Mrs. Mayes. As soon as I turn my back to him, tears spill down my cheeks.

"Is everythin' okay, honey?" She wipes my tears away, and hugs me tight against her ample bosom.

I don't want to leave the safety of her side. I also don't want her to worry about me after everything she's done for me. I put on my bravest smile and lie, "It's perfect. I'm just so...*happy.* Thank you so much. You are my angel, and I cannot possibly tell you how grateful I am. Thank you."

"That's all right, chil'. Thanks for the good company. Now, go have a fine day with your daddy," she says with a wink, then hugs me. "Write to me an' tell me all about it when you get home."

"I will."

I wipe the remaining tears from my cheeks and turn back toward my father. Confused, nervous, and disappointed, I slowly walk back to him. My fabulous boots suddenly feel lined with concrete. "Where to?"

"To get coffee," he states, then walks to his car. I've always considered myself a fast walker, but I have to hustle to keep up with him. I follow him to a 1970s brown sedan. He is a used car salesman, and this is one of his deals. He opens the passenger door. As I go to get in, he cuts in front of me, sits on the passenger seat, and inches his way across to the driver's side. Apparently, the driver's door doesn't open from the outside. I get in and we drive in silence.

Toccoa is a little town still asleep at 7:15 AM, a fact I'm thankful for once I realize my father is the worst driver on the planet. There is no flow to his driving, and he violently jerks the steering wheel, accelerates, and slams on the brakes at random. Mr. Toad's Wild Ride has nothing on Daddy's driving, which adds to the already unsettled feeling in the pit of my stomach.

Just when I'm sure I'm going to vomit, he jerks the steering wheel to the left and screeches into the McDonald's parking lot, slamming on the brakes just before he hits a pole. He gets out of the car and strides toward the entrance, grabbing five newspapers and periodicals on his way inside.

At the counter, he orders a large black coffee, pays, then sits at a nearby table. I also order a black coffee, pay, and join him.

I sit across from him and watch as he reads the first paper, waiting for him to start some sort of conversation. He sips his coffee, finishes reading the first paper, and starts reading the second.

He doesn't seem to notice anything: my stare boring a hole into his head, my shock at his comments at the train station, the daughter he has never met before, sitting in front of him, waiting for him to love her.

Am I on *Candid Camera* or something? *Daddy, it's me! I'm here! Why won't you talk to me?*

I look around the restaurant, but there's no one else here but the staff and the gigantic pink elephant sitting on the table between us. I open my bag and pull out my trusty camera. I brought it to capture all the precious moments we are going to have today. This isn't precious, but it's a moment, so I decide to capture it anyway.

Before we met, Dad sent me old family photos and described with pride the history of our ancestors, so I know he understands the value of family portraits. "Hey, Dad, look up so I can take your picture," I say cheerfully, determined to lighten the mood.

He peers over the top rim of his glasses and stares. I ignore his glare, go into photographer mode, and begin snapping pictures. "Smile, Dad."

"You know why white people never smiled in old photographs?"

I recall countless images of stoic, rigid faces from the past. "Why?"

"So you could see their racial purity. That's why." He turns his attention to paper number three.

"That's not why, Dad. The shutter speeds were really slow back then and exposure times were long. People had to sit still so as not to blur the photos. It was easier to do when they weren't smiling. That's why *no one* smiled, not just white people."

"Hmph," he grunts and glares at me. He stands and walks away around the corner.

I can't see where he goes, but I assume it's to the bathroom. Desperate to cling to the idyllic image of my father, my hopes of the man he'd are getting their asses kicked by the reality of who he is.

A few minutes pass and he still hasn't returned. Have I said the wrong thing? Have I not said the right thing? *You shouldn't have argued with him about the photograph. Way to go, genius.* Ten minutes pass and, still alone, dread creeps up my spine. *Has he left me here?*

Unable to see the car from where I sit, I get up and peek outside. After confirming the brown heap is still there, I return to my seat. *You're so ridiculous, Erika. Of course he didn't leave you...again.* But no matter how much I try to stay positive, I can't relax.

Fifteen minutes later he returns to the table, grabs his coffee, and walks outside without a word. *Um...okay...I guess we're leaving.* I grab my things and follow him. By the time I get outside he's already in the driver's seat, the passenger door open and beckoning. Once buckled in, I decide to let him talk next, as I don't know what else to say.

He resumes his jerky driving, occasionally slamming on the brakes next to various Civil War memorial plaques along the road. Each one commemorates an event from the War, and he springs to life, going into great detail about Colonel Such-and-Such and Lieutenant What's-His-Name and the Battle of-the-Somethingorother. He's giving me a history lesson when all I want is love.

We're strangers talking about nothing when there's so much to say. As each moment passes and my adrenaline wears off, another bit of me shuts down.

"You know what just happened to your two brothers?" he asks.

"No, Dad. What?"

"The big fat Jew on the school board closed down the biggest nigger school and imported all the nigger kids into your brothers' school. Now there's fights and all sorts of nonsense," he says. His face scrunches up in disgust as if he's smelled a rotten egg.

Like Carrie at the prom who's just had a bucket of filth dumped all over her, I can't stop the barrage of crap spewing out of his mouth. I inch closer to the door. He laughs hysterically.

"You didn't know yer daddy was a racist, did ya?" He howls with laughter.

The pieces click in my brain. His first glimpse of his pure, white daughter was watching me carry Mrs. Mayes' bags. This is my own *Sophie's Choice* moment. If I can agree with him, my father will love me, but I'll have to abandon everything I've ever believed in.

In a nanosecond, my choice is made. "No, I didn't, and how in the hell could you say something like that? You're ridiculous! Are we in the 1950s? I can't believe you still have segregation down here to begin with! How stupid and inhuman is that? And of course the kids are going to fight! Their entire lives they've been taught they're different, and now you throw them together and tell them to play nice and get along? In a couple of years, no one will care. Racism isn't inherent in children. It's *taught* to them by small-minded bigots!" He isn't the only one with spunk or strong opinions in this family.

He slams on the brakes and glares at me as if I were a pile of putrid pus. I meet his gaze, unwavering. He grunts, throws the car in reverse, and backs up to a highway entrance.

"Where are we going now?" I ask, grumpy.

Silence.

I fold my arms like a pretzel. *Fine. I don't want to talk to you anymore anyway.* It's 8:00 AM. In less than one hour, my hopes of a loving relationship with my father have been eradicated. Now, I'm alone with a madman, and the only train home leaves at 7:00 PM. All I want to do is curl into a ball and wake up back in Pennsylvania, but there's no escaping the situation I got myself into. I lean my head against the passenger window and doze off.

I awake to him slamming on the brakes as he exits the highway. My watch reads 9:43 AM, and a road sign indicates we're now in Atlanta.

We park and get out of the car. Neither of us says a word, nor do we look at each other. Dad walks ten feet ahead of me. *This must be what it's like to be a woman in China.* My boots were a disastrous choice in footwear. I clunk along behind him trying to keep up with his pace. He walks like he drives—with frequent stops, starts, and random direction changes.

We arrive at a subway station. After consulting a map, he buys two tickets and we board a red line train. *Great job, Dad. I just got off a fifteen-hour train ride.* We sit on opposite sides of the aisle, and I watch him as he looks at the other riders on the subway with us.

An African-American teenage boy stands between us, holding on to the pole in the middle of the aisle. He wears baggy jeans, a white T-shirt, gold chains around his neck and an extra-large jacket. Notorious B.I.G.'s *Big Poppa* blasts from the oversized boom box he totes on his shoulder. *Good song.* I chair groove.

My dad doesn't say a word. He subtly eyes the boy from head to toe, then looks at me with an expression that seems to say, "See? Worthless."

Shame and guilt wash over me. How could I come from such a monster? This is someone's child. Someone loves him and wants him to succeed in life, to be loved and happy. My brain can't comprehend my father's bigotry.

Forty-five minutes later, we arrive at the last stop: Hartsfield-

Jackson Atlanta International Airport. He exits the train, and I thud along behind him.

"Dad, what are we doing here?" I ask the back of his head.

He barely looks over his left shoulder and replies, "This is the busiest airport in the US."

"And?" I trot a little faster, weaving around throngs of holiday tourists and business travelers. "I just spent twenty-three hours trying to get to Pennsylvania by plane. I know what busy airports are like. Can't we just go sit and talk somewhere? My feet are killing me," I groan.

He stops abruptly and I almost bump into him. He turns to inspect me, then points at my feet. "That's 'cause you wore stupid shoes."

You got me there, Dad.

We navigate our way back to the subway and take the red line to Five Corners. From there, we walk a short distance to the Atlanta Underground shopping plaza.

My father is confusing as all hell, but I understand shopping. I stop occasionally to look at different vendor booths. Dad stands fifteen feet away, hands on his hips, impatient for me to keep moving. I pretend not to notice. *I waited twenty-four years for you. You can wait five minutes for me.*

We scurry through the Underground, then scramble silently through the Coca Cola Museum. We take the subway back to our starting point.

By the time we return to the parked car, it's almost 1:00 PM. He's hungry and decides we can get lunch. He picks a greasy-spoon diner with huge Confederate flags hanging above the tables.

After twenty minutes of silent food chewing and not making eye contact, Dad points to the flag above our table.

"See this flag?"

"Um, yeah, Dad. It's kind of hard to miss."

"One out of every four Southern men died for this flag, and now the northern niggers want 'em to take it down."

There goes my appetite. "Do you have to keep using that word? And who can blame them? It's kind of like hanging a swastika around Israel, don't you think?" I retort.

He shakes his head in disgust and slams his hand on the table. "Idiot," he grunts, then gets up and walks out of the restaurant.

Asshole. I'm beyond caring what he's going to say or do next and just want to go home. I take the bill and pay at the cash register. *That's cool, Dad. I'll pay for lunch.* From the payphone, I call Amtrak and discover for $16 I can change my ticket and catch the train in Atlanta at 5:00 PM instead of the Toccoa one at 7:00. It means an extra two hours on the train, but two fewer hours with Dad. Perfect.

I call Mom next.

Please answer. Please answer. Thankfully she does.

"Hey, Mom." I say, trying to keep it together.

"What's wrong? Are you okay?"

"Yeah, I just needed to hear your voice." My voice quivers. "He's pretty awful. You were right."

"I'm sorry I was right. I know how much this meant to you. He's that bad?"

I chuckle. "Oh, Mom, he's ridiculous, but I had to find out for myself. I can't wait to get back home. We're in Atlanta now. I'm going to catch the train here instead of going back to Toccoa." Tears well up in my eyes, but I refuse to break down until I'm safely away from him.

"It's almost over, Erika. Hang in there."

"I will. Thanks, Mom." I hang up with her and glance at my watch. 2:00 PM. I want more than anything to go to a hotel, curl into a ball, and sleep this nightmare away.

Outside, Dad's car is right where we had left it. The passenger door is open. I get in and start to tell Dad about the change in plans. Before I can say anything, he reaches into the backseat, retrieves a stack of books and a card, and hands them to me. The books are from his personal library, each one chosen for significant reason to me: a book about Bette Davis because I'm an actress, a book about architecture because I shared with him I wanted to be one when I was a kid, and the last is a book about Virginians. I'm caught off-guard, until I see the accompanying card. On the front of the card is a baby deer covered in pastel glitter. It's the kind of card you give a three-year-old, not your fully-grown daughter. On the inside is a printed message:

You're such a sweet little girl. Have a very, Merry Christmas. Then he signed. *Love Pappy*

"Wow...um, thanks Dad. I didn't know we were exchanging gifts so I don't have anything for you." Awkward silence dangles between us. "I called Amtrak. There's a train leaving from Atlanta two hours earlier than the Toccoa one. That way you won't have to drive all the way back there. You can just drop me off at a hotel nearby and I can nap until it's time to take the train."

"I'm not taking you to a hotel."

"Dad, I'm exhausted and I've barely slept in two days. Please, can you just drop me off somewhere?"

"I'm not going to do it. Which train station are you leaving from?"

Stubborn old goat. I tell him where the station is and off we go on another nauseating ride. Seventeen minutes later, we arrive at the station and stand in line for tickets.

"How much is it to change the ticket?" he asks.

"Sixteen dollars."

He reaches into his wallet, retrieves a five and three ones, and hands them to me. *Wow. Thanks, Dad. That makes up for everything.*

I purchase the ticket, and we sit on a bench in silence, two virtual strangers, side by side, with a chasm of distance between us. There's so much I want to say to him—scream at him—but I'd rather stay numb.

An hour passes, and I start to think about our inevitable goodbyes. A college-aged daughter and middle-aged father walk into the station. He sets down her bags, looks up at the schedule on the wall, then down at her ticket.

"Okay kiddo. Your train leaves in twenty minutes from platform two. I miss you already."

"Miss you too, Dad."

He gives her a bear hug, lifting her feet off the ground. When he sets her down, she kisses his cheek and releases her arms from around his neck.

"Love you, Dad."

"Love you too, sunshine. Let me know when you get home."

Watching them is like being disemboweled.

Dad stands up and says, "Well—"

I extend my right hand to him. "Nice meeting you, Dad. Have a safe drive home."

He shakes my hand in return. "Yep. Don't forget to drink lots of water."

"Thanks."

He walks out of the station, out of my life. Only when I'm sure he's gone do I fall apart. I run into the bathroom so as not to make a spectacle of myself. This is the man I spent years searching and yearning for? My childhood hopes and expectations are decimated. Curled up in a bathroom stall, I have never felt so sorry for myself.

Desperate to get as far away from this day as possible, I clean myself up and board my train, and sleep the entire ride home. Mom is waiting for me at the Delaware station. I hug her tightly and don't let go.

"Thank you for raising me, Mom. Thank you for everything." I bawl like a baby. When I pull away, she's crying too. We get in the car and drive back in silence.

A few days pass, and I have ample time to stew in my thoughts and all the things I wish I'd said to Dad's face. My voice and my gumption vanished around him. He never even met the real me, just some clunky mute who looked like me.

With new clarity, I decide I want him to give me contact information for my brothers and sisters. He owes me at least that much, so I call him.

"Dad?"

"Yes?"

"Got a minute?" I ask, my voice set with determination.

"Sure. What's up?"

"I'd like to get contact info for my brothers and sisters. You and I don't ever need to see each other again, but I'd like to meet them."

"That's not gonna happen," he states firmly. "They don't know about you, and they never will know about you."

"What are you talking about? Originally, you wanted me to go back to your hours and meet everyone. You haven't even told them about me? What if I'd said yes? Were you just going to surprise them with me? 'Merry Christmas, kids! Here's your illegitimate half-sister.'"

"They would have been fine. They're great people. Not like you."

"What's that supposed to mean?" My face heats up.

"You're weak, you're pathetic and you're certainly no daughter of mine."

I gasp and my mouth drops open. Eviscerated, I remain silent.

"They wouldn't want to meet you. If they ever did, they would see how ridiculous you are. You're nothing."

His words mirror every shitty thought I've ever had about myself, but I will not give him the satisfaction of knowing that. I've been fighting my entire life: to be seen, to be heard, to be whole. He is not going to win.

My rage rises to the surface. "I'm weak? I'm pathetic? Who's the one who goes around fathering children he's never going to raise? Who's the person that never paid one penny of child support? Did you even once wonder what was happening in my life? Mom was miserable because of you. She's never been happy because of you. I was molested because you weren't there to protect me. Everything I am—and am not—is because you left! You're a complete failure as a father. Thank God you weren't in my life!"

"All you bras are the same—always complaining about what someone did to you. You didn't have a father. Boo hoo. So what? Neither did I. You don't see me crying about it. You just don't know how to cope. You're weak, like all women."

"Bras? Did you just call women bras?" I laugh. I can't stop myself.

"What's so funny?"

"You, Dad. You're fucking hilarious. I waited my whole life to meet you, and you're nothing but a ridiculous asshole. You think women are weak? They're stronger than you will ever be. My mother raised me entirely on her own, with no help from you or anyone. You couldn't even send a frigging birthday card. I will find my brothers and sisters, and you won't be able to stop me."

"You won't, and even if you do they'll see what a pathetic loser you are."

"Yeah, Dad, you already said that. You don't know the first thing about who I am, and you never will. Your loss. Have a great life."

I hang up the phone. "Fuuuuck!"

Mom-Mom saunters into the room. "Erika, we don't use that kind of language in this house."

She was eavesdropping, as usual. "Sorry, Mom-Mom. I was talking to my dad. Things got a little heated."

"Your mom told you he was no good. We all did, but you went anyway."

"I know that, Mom-Mom, but that's the last thing I need to hear right now. I had to go and see for myself."

"You should have listened," she hisses, then walks out.

I run outside to the barn where Pop-Pop is burning trash.

"What's up 'er Skeeter?" he asks good-naturedly.

I throw my arms around his neck and cover his face with kisses.

"What's all that for?" He laughs.

"Because I love you. Because you're the best dad a girl could ever ask for. Thank you for everything, Pop-Pop. I'm so lucky to have you." The tears come and I hug him hard, never wanting to let him go.

wild is the wind

"What's a guy like you doing in a place like this reading a book like *that?"*

Mr. All-American sitting at table six looks up at my question. He's not alone: Most of my customers at the pie shop are single guys. Being saucy and showing a little cleavage doubles my tips and entertains me.

He looks up and flashes me a smirk, accentuating the cutest dimples I've ever seen. "Studying," he replies, then turns his attention back to the tome sitting open before him.

"What are you studying?" I ask, pouring fresh coffee into his cup.

"Economics." He glances up from his book, but only briefly.

Handsome and smart. Nice combo. "Don't you have anything better to do?" I ask with a wink. *Hell, I'd flirt with this guy even if he didn't tip. And that hair.* It takes every bit of my willpower not to run my fingers through his thick, wavy hair whose shade matches his coffee. *Jesus, he's beautiful.*

"Nope," he says.

He puts an emphasis on the "o" that sounds distinctly Midwest. "Where are you from, handsome?"

"Okoboji, Iowa."

"Gesundheit," I tease him.

He stares at me blankly.

"Geez, I'm just teasing you. Tell me about Ohkajaweeah."

"Okoboji."

"Yeah. That's what I said." I flash him a cheesy grin.

He finally cracks a smile, teeth and all.

"Look, I'm not trying to bug you," I lie. "And I won't bite," I lie again. "You just seem like a nice guy and I'm passing time. It's been slow tonight." I set the coffee pot on the table and extend my hand to him. "I'm Erika."

"Matt." He shakes my hand.

For the next five hours, he stays seated in my section. We chat when I'm not waiting on other tables, doing side work, or ducking out back for a cigarette. With each visit to his table, he opens up a bit more. Once he gets going, he's a natural storyteller.

Jesus, how could anyone not fall in love with him? He's a fucking Golden Boy.

He tells me he just turned twenty-four, and he moved to Los Angeles six months ago to model and act. I tell him I'm twenty-six and an aspiring actress as well. I omit the part where I haven't been on an audition for two years, and that I hide out at my waitress job because I'm simultaneously terrified of failure and success.

When the restaurant closes at midnight, he walks me out to the parking lot. We stand in silence, staring at each other, then up at the few stars visible through the city lights.

"So, what are you doing now?" I ask.

"Well," he says, shifting his weight from foot to foot, "I should get home and get some sleep." He buries his hands in the front pockets of his jeans.

"I can never sleep after a shift. To me, it's like 5:00 PM. I won't sleep until the sun starts to come up."

"What do you do all night?" he asks with genuine amazement.

"Oh, just stuff I guess. I read. Listen to music. Hang out in AOL chat rooms. Go grocery shopping. It's peaceful at night when the rest of Los Angeles is asleep. No horns honking. No sun in your eyes."

"Do you ever play cribbage?"

I laugh. Of all the things men have asked me in my life, this is a first. "Backgammon. Chess. Board games. Cards. Never cribbage."

"Wanna learn?" His childlike enthusiasm is dorky but endearing.

"Now, you mean?"

"Yeppers. We can go to Jerry's Deli."

I can envision him with a stalk of wheat hanging out of the side of his mouth. There are a lot of other things I can think of doing with him, and cribbage isn't anywhere on the list, but I'll bite. "Okay. Cribbage it is. Meet you there?"

We sit at Jerry's all night, drinking even more coffee and eating matzah ball soup. He teaches me the subtle nuances of cribbage. He kicks my ass every game, which is infuriating, but his charm and humor soften the blow. We talk about the many gadgets he's inventing, his plans to invest in real estate, his family. I give him the PG version of my background. There's an innocence and a normalcy about him that's foreign to me. Most of my recovery friends have a certain amount of taint on them. Matt's wholesome, positive, and I'm smitten.

At 5:30 AM, he looks at his watch and his demeanor changes. "Oh, shit. Is it really five-thirty? I have to go. I have to be at the airport in an hour."

"Airport? Where are you going? Anywhere fun?"

"Iowa, actually." He opens his mouth to say more, then closes it.

What is he not saying? "Visiting family?"

"Uh, well, my girlfriend, actually. Chelsea." He scrunches his eyebrows together like he's coming down with a migraine.

Ever the consummate actress, I sit across from him, my face a veneer of calm indifference. *What the actual fuck? You have a girlfriend and you're just thinking of telling me this now, after we've spent the last ten hours talking about everything else? Do you think perhaps you could have mentioned that?*

As if reading my mind, he continues. "Weird I didn't say anything sooner, I know, but I didn't think we'd talk this long. She and I just started dating long-distance. We became friends in college. She's still got two years as an undergrad and we've kept in touch since I graduated."

I take a sip of my coffee and signal the waiter for the check. I look coolly back at Matt. *Whatever. It's still a douche move not to say anything and be so utterly fucking charming all night and painfully good looking but not even care how hot you are because you're also one of the raddest guys probably in the entire world except for the fact you're totally unavailable because you're dating CHELSEA.* "No biggie."

In the middle of my internal tantrum, a calm voice chimes in. *He's supposed to be in your life, Erika. Let the hurt go.* With sincerity, I respond, "You don't owe me any explanations. It is a little weird you didn't say anything, but you're cool, and I had a great time hanging out." I extend my hand across the table to him. "Friends?"

He shakes it, and our fabulous new friendship is solidified.

Matt woos and courts Chelsea for the next four months, regaling me with stories about her beauty, her purity, her ballet prowess, and her aspirations for law school. When it was time for me to fill out college applications, I was sitting in a lockdown mental institution. I'm the girl with "potential" who's slinging hash at diners. Pangs of jealousy stab me, but I remind myself of the bitter truth. *Guys like Matt do not go for girls like me. He's entirely out of my league.* And most of me wants him to be happy. Most.

I work. I go to meetings. I spend huge chunks of my free time with Matt, showing him the sights of Los Angeles. We hike up to the Hollywood sign. We rent bikes at the beach, and go on rides at the pier. On the spur of the moment, we take road trips to Las Vegas or San Francisco. I'm captivated by his ability to live each moment to the fullest with no fear.

Sometimes we hang out in my tiny, messy studio apartment in a shitty part of North Hollywood. Usually, I don't let people see where I live. There are always dishes stacked in my sink I never have the time to wash, and piles of laundry everywhere I never have the time to put away. Matt just politely pushes a mound of clothes to the side and makes a space for himself on my sofa. And for some unknown reason, I'm comfortable with Matt seeing me. All of me, warts and all.

On our way to Vegas, he stops at a payphone to call Chelsea. I stand nearby, smoke a cigarette, and mind my own business.

"Erika, here." He hands me the phone.

I look at the receiver like he's offering me molten lava, but politely take it and hold it up to my ear. "Um, hello?"

"Hey, Erika," comes an angelic voice from the other end. "It's so nice to talk to you. Matt never stops telling me how great you are."

"Really? Well, that's nice of him."

"You know Matt. He's just the sweetest ever."

"Yep. He's a peach melba, all right."

"Well, you guys have a great time in Vegas. Take good care of Matt. I can't wait to meet you when I come out to visit."

"You too. Bye."

I hand the phone back to Matt. She makes him so damned happy, and seems every bit as sweet as he says she is. She's one of those secure girls with self-esteem and an innate knowledge of who she is and what she deserves in life. *What planet does she come from?* She's not fazed by me or my friendship with Matt in the slightest. She's his emotional center, and I'm the buddy he hangs with in her absence. *Fuck it. I'm also the one who gets to be with him in Vegas.*

In the summer, Chelsea comes out to California for a visit, and Matt is pissing himself with excitement. He introduces her to me and some of his friends. She's everything he said she was—petite and perfect. She looks like she just floated off stage after a performance of *The Nutcracker.* Tiaras were invented for girls like her. Chestnut ringlets cascade all the way down her back. Her voice—gentle and soft. Her nails—perfectly manicured. Her virginity—intact. She's every single thing I'm not.

One day during her visit, a group of us are standing in Matt's kitchen, listening to him talk about creating a pancake spatula that shoots wings out of the side when you press a button. Mid-sentence, Matt burps loudly. Everyone laughs—everyone except Chelsea.

"Matt, that's disgusting," she admonishes. "Apologize to everyone right this instant."

Taken aback, I turn to Matt and wait for his reaction. Certainly, he's going to be upset with her for being so uptight.

"Sorry, guys," he says sheepishly. "That was very rude of me."

I look back and forth between Matt and Chelsea. *What the actual fuck? You have the most incredible man who's ever lived? Who cares if he burps?* I keep my thoughts to myself, at least while Chelsea's still around.

After she returns to Iowa, he asks, "So, what did you think of Chelsea? Isn't she great?" He beams like a kid on Christmas morning every time he mentions her.

"Um, yeah, she's a gem. But Matt...well...she seems a bit uptight, don't you think? I don't see you with her. I'm not saying I see you with me, but I see you with someone like me. You know, someone who's more chill and laid back."

Without missing a beat, Matt responds. "I could never be with someone like you because of your history."

And there it is, Erika. Matt can see your unworthiness. The product of a messy divorce, he wants a stable, solid marriage with an uncomplicated wife and happy, healthy kids.

Because I love him, and because I value his opinion above all others—including my own—I swallow a simple truth about myself. *I will never be marriage or mother material.* A piece of my heart retreats and hides away where it is safe and protected.

Our conversation impregnates me with a loneliness that settles deep in my marrow, nestles against my sorrow and shame, and grows with each passing day. As I watch Matt pursue Chelsea, I shove needy feelings into nooks and crannies I no longer pay attention to.

I settle into a routine. Drink coffee. Smoke. Work. Try to be happy. Smoke. Sleep. Wake up. Smoke. Pay bills. Repeat.

I construct thicker-than-normal walls of wry humor, sexuality, and a shroud of cigarette smoke to keep people from getting too close. Fuck feelings. Fuck wooing and romance. Thank God I'm a woman who doesn't need any of that crap.

I stay up late, over-caffeinate, run myself into the ground with exhaustion, sleep well into the afternoon, and occasionally sleep with guys from the restaurant.

Tim is forty-two, a rugged and handsome struggling actor. He doesn't have an apartment of his own, but he takes me to an empty mansion he's house-sitting in the hills. The only piece of furniture is a king-size sofa in front of a stone fireplace so large I can stand in it. The house overlooks the twinkling lights of the Valley. He makes love to me gently, stares at me as if I'm a memory. I feel beautiful. He asks me if I know how sensual I am. How much power I have. I don't know what to say, so I say nothing. He says he's too old for me and doesn't have his shit together. I rest my cheek on his chest while he talks, tracing a lazy pattern in his chest hair with my finger. We go out to the back yard, sit in lawn chairs, and smoke cigarettes while we look at the lights in silence. I never see him again.

Matt tells me he's designing an engagement ring for Chelsea. It's costing him thousands and he tells me it needs to be perfect, like her and the life they'll build together.

Anthony is thirty-three, an Italian beat cop from the LAPD. Tall, handsome, and virile, he stops by my house in the daytime when he's on duty and in full uniform, much to the curiosity of my neighbors. He's the simple type. He likes to talk about football, the gym, and his pecs. I turn off my brain and turn on his fantasy girl, there to fulfill his every sexual desire. He handcuffs me and fucks me over my kitchen sink, then asks me to make him a sandwich while he comments on my dirty dishes. I tell him he should make me one since I'm the one working on my feet twelve hours a day. As beautiful as he and his penis are, I decide he'd hate me if he ever met the real me, so I pick random fights with him and stop returning his calls.

Matt finishes the ring and shows it to me, beaming with pride. It's gold and gaudy, nothing I'd ever wear. But I'm sure Texas Chelsea will choke on it—er, love it. He's got the proposal all planned for her fall visit. They'll go to Hearst Castle where he'll pop the question. Of course, she'll say yes, and they'll spend the weekend not sleeping together, keeping her virginity intact for their wedding night.

Stephen is fifty-five, an attorney. After reading Anne Rice's *Sleeping Beauty* trilogy, I'm curious about BDSM and seek out answers in an AOL chat room. Titillating discussions about spankings and blindfolds via my keyboard and over the phone are fun and anonymous, but I'm not sure I can handle the real thing. Stephen explains to me a sub has all the actual power, and being dominated is not about degradation and humiliation, but freedom—from thoughts, judgment, shame. He asks if I've ever had my defenses and power removed, yet been completely safe. I laugh when he mentions safety, and tell him life always hurts, especially when other people are involved.

When he asks if he can come by the next morning with a bag of tricks, in a moment of bravado and curiosity, I say yes. The next morning, I sleep through my alarm, and awake to him knocking on my door. Still in my pajamas, I stand groggy and disheveled by my front door and tell him to go away. His muffled voice asks if we can just talk, and assures me he'll leave the goodie bag outside. I crack the door a bit and see a short Jewish guy with a white comb-over, coke-bottle glasses, a huge schnoz, who weighs about 110 pounds soaking wet. I decide he poses no threat and let him in.

We sit on the sofa and chat about nothing for ten minutes. When he asks if he can kiss me, I say yes, because what else can I say when

I'm sitting on my sofa in my pajamas in front of a total stranger who's got a bag of dildos, floggers, and nipple clamps perched outside my front door? He kisses me passionately, pulls my hair with expertise. Moments later, he pulls me across his lap, yanks down my pajama bottoms, and spanks me. He asks me if this is what I want. In a breathy voice, I respond yes. The pain is exquisite and delicious and I come almost immediately, then flush with shame at my body's betrayal of my sense of decency. *You're not supposed to enjoy shit like this, Erika. It's humiliating. You're an evolved, empowered woman now.*

As I battle with guilt and shame, he does a spot-on impersonation of a vibrator with only his mouth, and his fingers probe, pinch, and penetrate in ways that make me forget my own name. *Way to go, old guy.* I orgasm so many times I lose count, and my brain does the unthinkable and shuts the fuck up. In this moment, I'm completely vulnerable, all defenses have been stripped away, and instead of feeling frightened and defensive, I'm liberated. *Jesus, I'm one of those people.*

He keeps his clothes on and asks for nothing in return. When I'm on the verge of collapse, he says I need rest. Shaking from muscle exhaustion, endorphins, and euphoria, I don't argue. I put my pajamas back on, then the two of us stand in the middle of my tiny, messy life. He tells me the feelings I'm having are normal and not to ignore them. I smile politely and show him the door.

He calls and wants to meet again. He leaves me long messages on my voice mail, which I never return. He tells me my body was made for this and that I will always need an element of this in my life to be happy. I never speak to him again.

However, three years later when speaking at a meeting in front of two hundred people, who should be sitting in the front row?

Chelsea comes out for the big visit and, of course, she says yes. Mr. and Mrs. Soon-to-be-Fabulously-Happy announce they'll be married the following December. They need a year to plan the perfect wedding.

I try to find my own kind of fulfilment, the kind that doesn't involve marriage and children, but lies somewhere between intense passion and responsibility. I have a God-given right to enjoy my body while in a loving relationship. Can I be empowered sexually and available emotionally? I'm not the shattered girl of my teens, but, as Matt established, I'm not the marrying kind, either. My friends are getting engaged, starting to have children. I know I'm supposed to want that, all of that, but I want something else. Something different, something extraordinary. I look for mirrors in my peers, someone to echo my independent sentiments, but all the females I know are obsessed with men and the size of their asses. Is there more to being a woman?

Friends who see Matt and me together ask me why I don't date him. We should be together. We get along so well. *Bleck!* I respond. He's like my brother. Most of the time, I believe it. After swallowing shovelfuls of my own bullshit over the years, I'm used to the taste.

Late at night while Los Angeles sleeps, I drive my red Fiat convertible down the 101 to Topanga Canyon, and wind my way to Malibu. I find an empty beach, lie in the cool sand, and stare at an ink-stained sky searching for a God who'll give me answers. I find only uncertainty and stars.

When I least expect it, I meet Jason. He comes in to the restaurant one night with a large group of recovery people after a meeting. Deep pools of blue stare at me intently over a menu, and follow me as I refill coffees and take orders. He looks like Ralph Fiennes from *Schindler's List*: tall, blonde, the kind of guy my Dad would cream himself over. Blondes are not my thing, as I usually go for dark hair and eyes—*like Matt*—but his attention demands reciprocation. Even better, he's got almost three years of recovery, and isn't intimidated by the fact I've got over eight years. He asks for my number before he leaves. I jot down my home and pager numbers on a scrap of paper.

I come home after work and find Jason's left me a voicemail. He wants to see me the next day, and tells me to call him back no matter what time I get in. It's almost one in the morning, but I call the number I've written on the back of the *Rolling Stone* magazine lying next to the phone.

"Well hello, gorgeous," Jason says as he answers the phone.

"Um, do you always answer the phone like that?" I chuckle.

"When I'm expecting a call from a gorgeous redhead, I do. What are you doing tomorrow night?"

We make small talk and plans for the next night. I meet him at an intimate Italian bistro. Every word out of his mouth feels like foreplay. He feeds me across a flickering flame, grabs my foot from under the table and nestles it between his legs. He removes my shoe and massages the ball of my foot, then each individual toe. This is better than any diamond ring. After dinner, we walk around Studio City. Uncharacteristic for Los Angeles, it begins to rain, and neither of us have umbrellas. I take my shoes off. We hold hands and splash in puddles. He pulls me close to him and we slow dance in a parking lot. His gigantic hands cradle my face, and he bends down and kisses me sweet and soft. Jason's the perfect distraction from my humdrum life, and I immediately fall into deep obsession with him.

We spend the next two days in bed together. I forget everyone who came before him, and he cures me of my Matt obsession. *Mostly.* In true alcoholic fashion, Jason and I are inseparable. Months go by, and my world gets smaller. He likes keeping tabs on me, and doesn't like it when I talk to other guys. I rarely go to meetings, opting instead to spend most of my free time with him. Or waiting for him to call. Or thinking about seeing him again. When I do see Matt, I brag to him about awesome Jason. *See? I'm lovable.*

Matt is happy I'm happy. I think this is what normal is supposed to feel like. I decide to call Dad. It's been over a year since we've spoken. I'm happy and want to gloat, and remind him what a shithead he is.

"Hello," says Dad, slightly slurring his words. It's 1:00 AM there, and he sounds like he's been drinking.

"Hey, Dad. It's your daughter, Erika."

"Well, howdy."

"Howdy yourself. How are you?"

"We're all fine here. Healthy. No complaints. Making enough to get by. Anything more, the government would take."

"How are my brothers and sisters?"

The moment I ask this, a knot forms in my intestines. Somewhere out there are others like me. Dad's fathered a lot of other children, nineteen to hear him tell it.

"Everyone is good. You married yet?"

The question irritates me. I still care what he thinks of me, although I will never admit that to another living soul. "No, Dad, but I am dating a great guy. You'd love him. Tall. Blonde. Blue-eyed. German." *Why are you trying to impress him?*

"That's wonderful! Now, are you pregnant?"

"Jesus, Dad, what a segue. No. We've only known each other a few months. And I've told you before, I have zero desire to have kids."

"Now, now. If you put it off too long, your eggs'll dry up. Then you'll have wasted your life."

"Damn, Dad, you're a piece of work. A woman's life is wasted if she doesn't have kids? Do you really believe the shit you say, or do you just say stuff like that to start fights with people?"

"Now, don't go getting hysterical. A woman's purpose is to have children. It's just that simple. No woman has ever done anything substantial in this world other than that."

"You're a barbarian. What about agriculture? The domestication of animals? Marie Curie and all that? All worthless?" My voice is shrill, and I hate myself for letting him get to me.

"You bras always get so hysterical." He laughs. "Women's insanity."

"I love how you just rip through women's lives, populate the world with children you never raised or even bothered to find, then talk about women's insanity. Do you ever take responsibility for anything? Do you ever admit you're wrong, about anything?"

"I never did anything with a woman she didn't want to do,

including your mother. You didn't need me. None of you did. All you needed was my genes, which I gave to you freely. What you do with that is up to you. Have children. They live on through you. That's all that's important."

"Unless they don't even know your name or who you are. Then they just have a void the size of Death Valley in them for the rest of their lives." I sigh. "I don't know why I even waste my time. Bye." *Asshole.*

I click the off button on my cordless phone, suddenly missing the days when I could slam the receiver down in a fit of frustration. I bask in my anger. If I dig under it, I'll have to feel his abandonment again. It was bad enough the first two times. I'll stick to anger and hiding my skeletons from my new relationship.

I lose track of everything when I'm with Jason. He feasts on my senses between sex and sleep, seasoned with Italian-roast espresso and Marlboro reds. Wait, who does he remind me of? A familiar queasiness makes its way through my intestines.

Patrick.

But this is different, Erika. Jason's sober. You're sober. *But you almost didn't survive Patrick.* Hush, old conscience of mine. That was almost ten years ago, and I'm busy falling deeply in love and will not be sidetracked.

I get out my extra-large bucket of green paint and slop it over red flags as quickly as they pop up. Jason talks mostly about himself. *A little green paint here.* Jason doesn't go to a lot of meetings. *A little extra dollop there.* Jason doesn't like the word no. *I might need two coats here.* Jason doesn't have any friends. Jason wants to dominate all of my time. Jason doesn't like my friendship with Matt. *An extra can of green over there.*

After three months of semi-smooth sailing with Jason, one night in mid-December, I get a 9-1-1 page on my beeper from him.

"Hey, sweet lips. Zat you?" Jason slurs on the other end of the line.

"Jason? What's wrong with you?"

"Come overrrrrr and play with meeeeeee."

"Jason, I thought you were out of town. And what's wrong with you? You sound weird."

"I'm jus' fine and dandy. Come over an lemme see your tits. I love yer fuckin' tits."

A shiver runs up my spine. "Jason, are you drunk?"

He laughs. "Yessirree Boobie."

"Jason, I'm on my way over. Don't go anywhere."

I hear a shuffling noise from the other end of the line, then a *click*. I've never relapsed, but have seen too much of it, and it's never pretty. I imagine the amount of self-loathing, regret, and shame he must be feeling right now. I need to bring him right back into sobriety.

I rush over to his house and find the front door unlocked. I enter his pitch-black apartment and flip on the light switch by the front door. Nothing. "Jason?" I flick my Bic and slowly make my way forward to the lamp by the sofa and turn the knob. Nothing. I reach under the lampshade to check the bulb and discover it's been removed. I head left toward the kitchen and hear something clink at my feet. When I hold my lighter over the source of the noise, I see a half-dozen empty whiskey and wine bottles. *Shit. He hasn't wasted any time.* I call into the dark again. "Jason? Where are you?" Silence.

I reach the kitchen and flip the switch for the overhead light. The fluorescent bulb flickers to life, illuminating the disaster zone that is now Jason's kitchen. His normally-immaculate kitchen is now littered with empty beer cans smashed on the kitchen counter, cigarette butts floating in coffee remnants, and greasy In-N-Out wrappers strewn on the floor.

I hear a groan from the adjacent dining room, and look over to see Jason on the floor in the corner, his long legs stretched out in front of him, his face and torso hidden behind a curtain.

I move the curtain aside to look at him. "Jesus, Jason. What are you doing?" His head is resting against the wall, his mouth slack and open, vomit caked on his chin. A steady stream of drool is making its way from the side of his mouth down the front of his shirt, which is also caked in vomit.

He squints as if to focus. "Zat you, tits?" He laughs.

I squat down next to him and gently brush his bangs off his face. "Jason. What the fuck happened? I just saw you a few days ago. I thought you were going out of town to see your dad?"

"Didden make it."

"Have you been here drinking the whole time?"

He looks at me, then starts sobbing. "Oh, Erika. I fucked up. Jus' go 'way. I don' want you to see me like this." He grabs the back of a dining room chair and tries to stand, but his legs don't stay solid underneath him. He drops to his knees and begins crawling across the floor toward his bedroom.

I walk behind him, powerless to do anything but watch. His bedroom is dark, so I move ahead to the bathroom and turn the light on, illuminating enough of his path for him to find his way.

He puts his elbows on the king mattress, and I help lift all six-foot-three of him onto the bed. He lands face first, groans, then rolls over onto his back. He sobs louder. A dark stain seeps through the front of his jeans. I weep in silence for the pathetic spectacle in front of me.

"Erika, don't leave me," he whimpers.

"I'm not going anywhere Jason." I go to the bathroom and get a warm washcloth, then retrieve a large cooking pot, glass of water, and a bottle of Advil from the kitchen. I place the pot on the floor next to the bed, and the water and Advil on his nightstand. I undo his belt and pull his soiled jeans and boxers off him. I remove his T-shirt, then wipe him down like an infirmed child.

I remove my clothes and crawl into bed next to him, spooning him tightly in a cocoon of arms, legs, breasts, and a mane of red hair, willing him back to sobriety. Baffled and heartbroken, I have no idea what to do next. If he keeps drinking, he's going to change dramatically. If he gets sober again, he'll be a newcomer, and not equipped for a relationship. Either way, this isn't going to end well. I push my fears aside and hold him tighter.

In the middle of the night, I'm stirred awake by him reaching between my legs. In my sleep fugue, his relapse and my hopelessness are forgotten. My lover rolls his weight on top of me, pushes himself inside me. His kisses taste of stale whiskey, vomit, and grief, and my memory returns in full.

I tear at his flesh, trying to pull him deeper inside me. His ragged breath whispers at my neck. As he purges his sins in the folds of my forgiveness, I flash through the myriad of men who've found refuge in a body that's never felt like my home. I've welcomed the broken ones, the cruel ones, the distant and dishonest ones.

His urgent thrusts bring me back to the present. Jason comes, rolls back over to his side of the bed, and passes out. I lie beside him, awake and empty. *Is this what you want, Erika? Is this what love is?*

For two weeks, I avoid Matt, making various excuses to not see him. He shows up at my house and knocks on my door. I try to ignore him, but there's nowhere to hide in my tiny studio apartment. He knocks without stopping until I finally open the door.

"Wanna go skydiving?" he asks with the same enthusiasm a kid would use to ask if he could go to Disneyland.

His innocence is infectious, and interferes with my wallowing, self-pity, and depression. "Well, that's random. I'd love to, but it's too expensive. Can't."

"Okay. Vegas?"

I turn away from him and go sit on the sofa. "Suuuper busy right now. Can't. Sorry."

He sits on the other end of the sofa, stretches out, and pokes me in the leg with his sneakers. "Well, how are you? How've you been? What have you been doing? How's Jason? Have you been writing at all?"

I haven't told him about Jason's relapse, or his steady decline over the last two weeks. "Oh, you know. Work and stuff. Jason's great. Just been really busy working and stuff." I lie, averting my eyes to the ground. Matt is in the perfect relationship, and my life has suddenly become *Leaving Las Vegas.* Going to war with someone's alcoholism is exhausting.

"Hey. You okay? You seem...sad or something."

I walk over to the kitchen and pour myself a fresh cup of stale, black coffee. I chew the inside of my cheek as I contemplate the next lie I can tell him. He follows me into the kitchen and stands in front of me. I just can't do it. I rest my forehead against his chest. He pulls me to him and bear hugs me. I drink in his warmth, the smell of his cologne. *Why can't I have something simple and uncomplicated like this?* That voice is silenced by another one. *Quit wishing for shit you can never have.*

I pull away abruptly. I can't close like this with Matt. "Jason's drinking again."

"Oh, shit. That's bad, right? I mean, he's an alcoholic and stuff?"

"Yep. And when someone with a few years relapses, it gets ugly fast."

He thinks about what I've just told him as he rubs his chin between his thumb and pointer finger, like he's pondering a complex math problem. "Geez. That's rough. Are you going to break up with him? You don't need that stuff in your life."

Even though Matt is two years younger than me, I often feel like he's the only adult in the room. My life is emotion-based, a reaction to a feeling, a hormone, or a situation. Matt's internal compass is always set due north. Mine spins in random, wild directions.

I cringe at the thought of leaving Jason, and even more at the idea of failing at yet another relationship, in plain view of Matt. "It's not that simple, Matt. My Dad left. Not once, but twice."

"But Erika, this situation is entirely different—"

My voice gets louder as I try to convince him, and myself, why I'm staying with Jason. "I can't just abandon someone, especially when they're down. It sucks to be left behind. I can't do it."

"But you shouldn't have to take care of another person. Don't you deserve to be happy? Have someone look after you for a change?"

Matt's one of the few people I can't manipulate into believing whatever bullshit I'm slinging around at any particular time. "Isn't that what you're for?" I deflect.

He crinkles the space between his brows. His concern feels like pity, which feels like a punch to the gut. The last thing I want is for Matt to feel sorry for me. I want so much more.

I want to wrap my fingers through his thick hair and kiss him. I want to tell him how I think we're made for each other. What a mistake I think he's making. How hurt I am by what he said to me. How much I love him, how I don't think I'll ever love another man the way I love him. How in another life I wouldn't be so fucked up and he'd love me and we'd be together.

But I can never speak those words to him, or even admit those feelings to myself. "I'll be fine. Aren't I always?"

He looks at me skeptically.

"Come on, who's your scrappiest friend?"

Two more weeks pass. My life is a blur of work, denial, and a slow descent into the hell with Jason's ongoing relapse. On December 23rd, I go to a meeting, then over to Jason's.

His apartment is lit only by a few candles. I find him sitting on his sofa, drinking a beer.

I drop my overnight bag and keys by the door, then lean over the sofa and kiss him. "Hey, babe."

He tilts his head back and kisses me, reaches for my breast and squeezes it. "Hey, tits. What took you s' long?" he slurs, as is usual for him now.

In the last month, I haven't asked for a single thing for myself. Not a hug. A meal. An orgasm. Lost in his chaos, ego, and neediness, I exist to hold him together. But today is my special day, and I want to share it with him.

"I was at a meeting. I'm nine years sober today, babe." I smile at him, hoping there's a part of old Jason in there, who remembers how good it felt to be sober.

He turns to me, bleary-eyed, and holds his beer up in a toast. "Happy birthday, tits. Wanna beer?" He laughs, cold and mean like a school-yard bully.

His words are a sucker-punch to the gut. "Jason, how can you say something like that? You know how fucked up that is—"

"Yeah, yeah. Go cry about it atta fuckin' meeting, ya cunt."

His cruelty ignites the fierce part of me, resurrects her from the emotional graveyard I'd buried her in. She sizzles to the surface. *This man may drag you to hell with him to try to save himself, and you might never get back out again. You must love yourself more than you love him.*

The shroud of grief I've been hiding under ignites and disappears. I'm awake. Finally. I look at Jason, mumbling to himself incoherently. In an instant, I lose my taste for cruel, broken, emotionally-unavailable men.

I go into his bedroom and retrieve the personal items I've previously left there, then into the bathroom to grab my toiletries.

"Hey, tits, where'd ya go?"

I walk back into the living room and shove everything into my bag.

"Aw, come on, babe. Where're you going? Don't be mad at me. Iz just jokin'."

I remove his key from my keychain and leave it on the table by the door. I walk out and never see him again.

Leaving was easy. Once I get home, I'm smacked with the reality that I'm single again, and start to second guess my decision. Even though I know I've made the right one, I'm wracked with guilt over my abandonment of him—and myself—for so long. And if leaving was the right thing to do, why does it feel so shitty?

I stay up all night flipping through channels on my remote, smoking countless cigarettes. At dawn, I drift off to sleep.

At 7:00 AM, there's a persistent knocking at my door that can only be Matt. I ignore it and smash my extra pillow over my head, but his knocking only intensifies.

"Go away," I groan.

From the other side of the door, I hear Matt's unmistakable voice. "Buffet." Matt is addicted to buffets in general, but particularly Denny's breakfast buffet. And he never just says the word "buffet." He sings it in a high voice with a lilt. B*uuuufayyyy*.

I continue to ignore him.

"Buuuuufaaayyyy."

"Matt, it's seven in the morning. I am not going to a fucking buffet with you. I need sleep."

He continues to knock on the door. "Breakfast buuuuufaayyyy."

"Oh my God, Matt! I am not going to Denny's with you. *Go! A! Way!*"

The knocking on my door stops.

"Thank God," I mumble into my pillow as I try to drift back to sleep.

A few moments later, I hear tapping on the window on the side of my house, which he had to climb through bushes to get to. "Buuufayyy buuufayyy buuuuuuuffayyyyyyyy."

I roll over on my back and give up the idea of sleep. "Geez. You're like the Land Shark from SNL!" I shout as I roll my sorry ass out of bed. Even when I'm exhausted and heartbroken, Matt makes me laugh. I shuffle over to the front door wearing men's boxers and a white T-shirt. I light a cigarette and glare at Matt as he walks in.

He's happy, beautiful, and ready to seize another day of life. "Good morning, sunshine." Dressed in a blue baseball cap, gray T-shirt, and blue jeans, he is the walking epitome of America.

I, on the other hand, am a wrecked dark cloud. "What's so good about it?" I grab the large Starbucks cup he's holding and take a swig.

Completely nonplused by my mood, he responds yet again with one word—"Buffet"—then flashes full dimples at me.

Not fair. "I'm not hungry. I broke up with Jason. I feel like shit and I'm a complete fucking mess."

"Okay, Miss Grumpypants. Get dressed."

"Matt, did you hear what I just said?"

"Yeppers." He rummages through the pile of clothes on the sofa, and retrieves a pair of jeans and a black T-shirt. "Put these on while I use your restroom."

While he's occupied, I throw on my jeans, black Chucks, and my New York Yankees baseball cap. I blast Nick Cave and the Bad Seeds' *Do You Love Me* from the stereo, then look in the mirror. Between the crying and my leftover eye makeup, my eyes are like pink marshmallows with charred edges. Nick sings about his lady of the various sorrows like he's singing the story of my life.

The chorus starts, and Nick and the Bad Seeds start asking *do you love me?* From behind the closed bathroom door, Matt sings back-up off-key, "Do you love me?"

I can't tell what's funnier, Matt singing Nick Cave, or him doing it while he's doing God knows what in my bathroom. Despite my misery, I belly laugh.

After an eternity, Matt emerges from the bathroom, followed by the stench of the dead.

"Matt, why do you always wait until you get to my house to take a dump?"

He smiles, and with no shame responds, "I love your bathroom. It's so comfortable."

"Grrr. It's a good thing I love you."

Matt repeatedly drops by unannounced. He doesn't say it, but I know he's checking on me. He sees my dark spaces and tries to flood them with his light. He would almost be unbearable if I weren't so grateful for his friendship.

One night after a particularly rough shift at work, I come home and find Matt standing on the back of my sofa hanging Christmas lights along the ceiling. I had mentioned once in passing how happy they made me, and how I used to hang them in all my other apartments, but just hadn't gotten around to doing it in this one. I've lived here six months and still haven't unpacked half my boxes. There's no point in settling down when I'm just going to move again.

Not only has he strung lights around my entire apartment, but he's folded all the clean clothes, done the dishes, and made my bed. He doesn't even do that in his own apartment, yet he's here, doing it in mine.

I have no clever quip. No sarcastic response. Matt's love strikes me harder than any fist, and I have no defense against it.

"Happy birthday," he says, grinning like the Cheshire Cat.

"But...I can't believe you...it's not even my birthday yet."

"I know. I wanted it to be a surprise."

the other side

"Three. Two. One. Fly!" Igor's voice commands in my ear.

I let go of the side of the plane and fly like a bird 14,000 feet above the ground, with a one-hundred-forty-pound Yugoslavian man strapped to my back. Wind kneads my cheeks like silly putty, and I'm smiling so hard it hurts. I breathe in every moment of pure, ecstatic, life-changing joy.

As a child, I flew in my dreams. I walked on blades of moonlit grass, then pushed off with my toes and soared above the earth towards the moon and stars. I was free of everything but my curiosity. At some point, I stopped flying.

At thirty-three, life is so fucking hard I can't breathe. So hard, I'm afraid I'll never be whole again. So hard, I might shatter into a thousand pieces and vanish into nothingness.

So today, despite my toxic head and broken heart, I choose to do something life-affirming. On a clear-blue, seventy-five degree, September day, I am jumping out of a perfectly good airplane.

The videographer floats in front of us, a camera attached to her helmet. She waves, and I give the camera a thumb's up and a perpetual grin, legitimately from ear-to-ear as I can almost feel my cheeks smacking against my earlobes. I've been warned not to break my freefall form, lest we might spin out of control. The videographer floats around us, capturing various angles of my daredevil antics.

The sound of falling at 120 miles per hour is deafening. Below us is the barren patchwork of the Mojave Desert. Blue sky blankets the beige horizon as far as my eyes can see. The altimeter ticks down. 6,000. 5,000. I put my hand on the ripcord, ready to pull when we get to 4,000 feet.

Igor signals me and I yank the ripcord. After some resistance, it gives way and the parachute opens. We're catapulted violently upward, like a boulder shot out of a giant's slingshot. As the chute opens, the harness straps bruise my inner thighs and tighten around my chest, but I'm too high on adrenaline to care.

Then silence. I'm floating on a swing. Matt would love this as much as I do.

Igor grunts and groans behind me. We spin out of control and drop altitude rapidly. "Chit," he says with a distinct Yugoslavian accent.

This is not what I want to hear from the skydiving expert strapped to my back. We spin like a giant yoyo unraveling at the end of a long string. I'm nauseous, and closing my eyes makes it worse. I look up and see our blue and violet parachute, not fully opened, flapping in the wind like a massive, crumpled bedsheet.

"Veer goink to haf to cut avay," says Igor. "Veer goink to fall again, fast, den I deploy emergency chute. Hank on."

No panic. No dread. My life doesn't flash before my eyes. If this is it, I'm ready to go.

Igor releases the malfunctioning chute, and we freefall again. The spinning stops, but the ground swells and expands beneath us. Tiny dots below enlarge and morph into buildings and cars. 3,500 feet. 3,000 feet. Even with my virgin skydiving experience, I know we need to deploy the chute by 2,500 feet.

He pulls the chord for the emergency chute, and we're once again catapulted. The skin on the inside of my thighs feels is raw, and my stomach is now in my throat. I look up and see the white nylon parachute fully open.

Igor issues a warning in my ear. "Vee are too low to slow down all da vay. Vee vill haf wery hard landing. Keep feet up."

"Whatever you say, Igor."

Igor pulls the tethers, and we drift left and right as he maneuvers us towards a somewhat clear patch of desert. "Keep legs up until I say, den valk!"

The ground looks like sandy concrete interspersed with spiky tumbleweeds and cacti. We're going to crash. This is just like what happened to the Bionic Woman. I brace myself for impact.

"Now!"

I move my Corgi-legs as instructed, but instead of landing on our feet, we somehow land on my stomach, and bounce our way across the desert, eventually stopping in a cloud of dust. I have dirt in my mouth. My eyes. But I'm alive.

"You put feet down too soon," says Igor in my ear, still strapped to my back.

It's hard to breathe with the weight of him on my back. "Can't...breathe." I also can't feel the lower part of my body. I feel the weight of him on my torso. I feel the rawness in my inner thighs and tightness in my chest. I wiggle my feet. I feel one of them move against the solid ground, but not the other.

Igor unhooks himself from my back and stands up. I roll over but am afraid to look down for fear a foot is missing, or twisted into a ghastly, misshapen appendage. A few moments pass. I brace myself for the worst, look down, and see two intact legs and feet.

"Are you hurt? Can you move eweryting?"

I wiggle both feet and see I am indeed intact. "Yep. I'm okay."

He extends a hand to me, and his slight but sinewy arm lifts me to a standing position. Once I'm on my feet, he squints his eyes and searches the landscape. "Road is dat vay. Help me get chutes."

Igor unhooks the good one from the harness and hands it to me. "You grab dis von, and make sure you don't tear it. Be wery careful," he warns. With that, he darts across the desert like the Road Runner to retrieve the first chute fifty feet away.

You just had a parachute malfunction and a very rough landing, and you are still alive. Guess it's not your time, kid. In a daze, I bundle up the disarray of white nylon and strings, trying not to tear it on any rocks or rough foliage. I can't see over the massive billows of fabric, so I lean my head to the side and see Igor has bundled his chute and is making his way towards the road. I shuffle along behind him.

We are on a desolate road, and luck out when a lone, maroon van stops next to us.

A grizzled man in his fifties rolls down the passenger-side window. "You two make an unscheduled landing?" He flicks a toothpick from one side of his mouth to the other.

Igor raises his bushy, charcoal eyebrows halfway up his forehead in an amusing look of relief. "You could say dat."

"Where ya headed?"

"California City drop zone."

"I know it well. Damn, you two. You landed about four miles from your target."

"Vee are lucky to haf landed at all."

"Name's Doug. Hop on in."

Igor and I climb into the rear passenger area, trying to keep our chutes in check. All in, Doug closes the side door, and he drives toward the drop zone. In a fitting ending to today's adventure, Tom Petty's *Free Fallin'* blares out of the AM/FM radio.

"So, Igor, how often does stuff like this happen?"

"Vat you mean? Malfunction?"

"Yes. Has that ever happened to you before?"

"Of course! I train Yugoslavian army tirty years. I have turteen thousand jumps. Today was twelve time malfunctioned."

"In thirty years, you've only malfunctioned a dozen times?"

"Skydiving wery safe sport. Today vas exception, not rule. You wery lucky."

"To be alive?"

"No. To haf malfunction first time. Means prolly no more malfunction for you. You can jump vit no worries, although you must learn landing." He then bursts into a smile, and gorgeous lines crinkle next to each eye. His gaunt, harsh features soothe and soften, and he laughs.

His laughter is infectious, and I start to giggle. "Well, thanks Igor, for not letting me die. I really appreciate it."

"Don't tank me. You die, I die. It vas self-preservation." He winks at me.

A mile down the road, we see the black drop-zone van ahead of us.

Igor calls out to Doug, "Dats our people. Can you pull next to dem?"

Doug pulls beside the black van and motions with his thumb for the other driver to look in the back. William, the owner of the skydive company, looks over and sees our faces smiling at him from the side window. His blue eyes widen with what looks like relief, and both vehicles pull over to the side of the road.

Igor and I change vehicles and head back to the hangar.

The van pulls into the parking lot, and I see my fear friend, Mallory. I've nicknamed her Em, short for Emallem, for her love of Eminem. She sits on a metal picnic bench, smoking. As I walk up to her, blue-lagoon eyes swim with grief and she looks away. She's made of iron, but the last month has been trying on her.

"I thought...I thought you were..." she sits motionless, arms at her side, unable to finish the thought.

"Oh, my sweet Emallem, I'm not leaving you." I wrap my arms around her and give her a suffocating squeeze.

She remains non-responsive. I let go, and she takes another drag from her cigarette and turns her head away to exhale. Tough. Tender. Wounded. Wonderful. This girl is my heart.

"So, are we done with this skydiving shit now? Can we go home?"

She stands up and puts her cigarette out in the nearby ashtray, then brushes the bottom of her pants off.

I look at her, trying to gauge how she'll take this next bit of news. "Actually, I want to go again tomorrow."

Her expression looks as if I've told her I'm going to tattoo a large penis across my forehead and she's trying to figure out how to respond.

"I talked to Will. We can stay here at the Drop Zone tonight, camp in the back with everyone else, or even in the extra rooms in the hangar if they're unoccupied."

"Are you out of your fucking mind? You're going to do another tandem?"

Oof. She's really going to hate this next part. "Well, no actually. I'm going solo. I have to do some extra training with Will, but I'll be ready for my first AFF jump by noon tomorrow hopefully."

Mallory sits back down on the top of the picnic table and lights another cigarette. "What the fuck is AFF?"

"Accelerated Freefall. I'll go out of the plane with two jump masters. They'll make sure I'm stable in the air. When it's time for me to pull the ripcord, they'll break off and I'll be on my own."

"What do you mean on your own? How will you get down?"

"I'll have earphones, and be guided to the landing zone. You can be there and watch me land!" I offer her my childish enthusiasm.

"Yeah," she huffs, "like where I was today? All the skydivers came down one after another, and you never did. We saw you spinning like crazy. We saw you fall really fucking fast. And then you disappeared... We thought you guys were dead!"

The words unleash a torrent of tears. She knows what it's like to be left behind. It's one of the things that bonded us when we met seven years ago. Her face twists with grief. She folds her arms across her knees, and rests her head down on them.

I sit next to her but know not to touch her when she's in porcupine mode. She's like a younger version of me. In some ways, I know her better than she knows herself. I light a cigarette and inhale deeply, thinking of the irony of smoking after a near-death experience. *I'll quit at some point, but it sure as hell won't be today.* "Em..."

Silence.

"Em. I didn't die. I'm okay. It's not my time to go yet."

She laughs up to the sky. "How the fuck can you know something like that?"

"I just do. And the guys said on the way back malfunctions are rare. Something like twenty-five people a year die worldwide from skydiving. It's a safe sport. The malfunction was a complete fluke. The chances of it happening again are astronomically slim."

"Why is everyone so hell-bent on leaving me?" Her voice is like glass. She smashes out her cigarette and storms into the hangar.

A fresh wave of grief rips through my chest like a samurai sword. "I don't want to leave you. I just want to be closer to him," I whisper.

One year earlier

After a particularly stressful day at work, my phone rings at ten at night.

"Buuufayyyy."

The sound of his voice is like an adrenaline shot to my heart. "MAAATTTTT! How the hell are ya? How's Texas? How's life? What's going on? I miss you!" I rattle off in breathy excitement.

He chuckles softly, then responds, "I miss you, too. Umm, there's a lot going on, actually. That's part of why I'm calling you."

"Wait, it's midnight there. You're like an old geezer. You never stay up late. Are you okay? What's happening?" My brain starts jumping to conclusions, which is bizarre since Matt is the most-okay person I've ever met in my life.

"I'm fine, I just need to make some changes. I've talked to my job, and they've agreed to let me work remotely. I was thinking of moving back out to L.A. for a while and giving acting another shot."

Matt? Here? Close? I almost burst. "Oh my God, Matt, that's

213

awesome! When are you coming?" In my excitement, I forgot that Matt has a life and a wife very much in Texas. "Wait. What about Chelsea? Is she coming with you?"

"Um, not exactly. She's got the house here, and she works long hours at the law firm. It'll just be me."

"Are you guys okay?"

"I can't really talk now, but I'll tell you all about it when I see you. Which brings up the next part. Can I stay with you?"

My roommate, Steve, and I share a miniature two-bedroom condo in Van Nuys, and I go through the logistics of where everyone will sleep. *Fuck it. It's Matt.* "Of *course,* you can stay with me! Steve's in the extra bedroom, but we can work it out. My condominium is your condominium. I even have extra office space across the street if you need it."

"Okay. Thanks. And if it gets too cramped, I can stay with Julio as well."

"No way. It'll be perfect. When are you coming?"

"I'm not sure yet. I'll let you know when I work everything out."

"I cannot wait to see you! Love you to the moon and back."

"Love you, too."

A month later, I'm sitting at a Starbucks when two hands cover my eyes. I turn my head and see Matt. "Oh my god! You're here!" I throw my arms around him, get drunk on the smell of his Tommy Hilfiger cologne, and the feel of his arms around me. "Welcome back! How did you know I was here?"

"I stopped by the house and Steve told me where you were. Okay if I sit?"

"Of course, silly. Wow. Look at you. You're all growsed up!" At thirty, fine lines have settled in around his eyes, and gray hair lightly salts his thick, ebony hair. His boyish good looks have hardened slightly, making him look wiser, more mature. *He's still the most beautiful man in the world.* "So handsome, as always. Geez, you're the spitting image of Billy Crudup. Anyone ever tell you that?"

"I still get Jim Carrey sometimes."

"That's bullshit. You look exactly like Billy Crudup with Orlando Bloom's eyes. Tell your future agent that's your type." I wink at him.

"I will. So, what's going on with you?"

"Fuck that. I have nothing to talk about. Since starting my own detective agency, all I do is work. No complaints, though. I'm glad to not be doing surveillance sixteen hours a day and peeing in bottles in the back of my SUV anymore. It's much more fun to be the boss." I grin.

"You made it through your first year. Impressive."

The slightest praise from him still makes me giddy, as if it only counts if Matt knows about it. Even though I've long since moved on from the idea of ever being with him, he still takes my breath away when I least expect it. "I don't feel very impressive. I feel stressed and exhausted most of the time. But truth be told, I love every moment of it. I hope I don't ever have to work for someone else again. I don't know why I waited so long."

"I always said you could do anything." He flashes his dimples.

"And I'm eternally grateful for your belief in me. You always pushed me to do better. If it weren't for you, I'd probably still be working at the restaurant. I'm just sorry it took me so long to believe you. You were right."

"I was what?" Matt smiles and puts his fingers behind one ear, leaning in closer as if to hear what I'd said better.

"You losing your hearing, old man?" I tease. "You were right. In my defense, I had some killer demons to work through. It took a little longer for me to catch up." Suddenly self-conscious, I change the subject. "Enough about me. How long has it been since we've seen each other?"

"Two years, I think. When you and Mallory drove through on that road trip to Georgia."

"Oh wow, that was two years ago? Time flies. Are you happy to be back in L.A.?"

"Very." Matt looks around, then down at the table, lost in thought.

"Hey, buddy, what's going on? Why the move to Los Angeles? And Chelsea's okay with this?"

Matt takes a sip of his coffee and doesn't make eye contact with me.

"Matt?"

"Things aren't going so great."

"With Chelsea?"

"Yeah. I think I want out."

"Out? Like, *out* out?" I'm stunned. It's like hearing there's no Santa Claus. "I don't understand. You guys are Mr. and Mrs. Perfect. What's going on?"

"Things aren't always what they seem, Erika. I haven't been happy for a long time."

"I know you said there were issues in the bedroom, but that was a couple of months after you got married. How long have you felt like this?"

"Honestly? When I saw her walking down the aisle toward me."

"On your *wedding* day? Holy shit! Why did you get married then?"

"It was too late at that point, but I knew in my gut I was making a mistake."

"But why? I thought she was perfect? What the fuck happened?"

"Well first, she's frigid."

"What do you mean, frigid? I mean, I know what the word means, but how is she frigid?"

Matt squirms in his seat and takes another sip of coffee. "We've never successfully had sex."

Mind. Blown. She's married to Matt and doesn't make his toes curl on a nightly basis? That's a sin. "Now, wait just a minute. You're going to need to give me specifics, Matt. I can't even comprehend what you're talking about."

"On our honeymoon, obviously, we tried, but she said she couldn't feel anything...you know, down there. No matter what I tried, nothing worked. I haven't slept with a ton of women, but enough. I've pleased women before. I know what I'm doing."

"Oh, I have no doubt. And she can't feel anything," I motion around my pelvis, "at all? Down there?"

"Well, um, she says it's kinda numb. I've tried...you know, all the usual stuff, and nothing works. She hates sex, so we stopped trying after a while."

"What's awhile? You guys have only been married five years."

"We've had sex," Matt looks up in the air and starts counting on his fingers, "maybe a dozen times total."

"A dozen times a month, maybe, but in five years? I've heard from married friends that sex dwindles after marriage, but when you never even had sex to begin with, shouldn't you at least do it like bunnies for the first year or so?"

Matt chuckles. "Straight to the point, as always."

"Well, Jesus, Matt. I just had no idea. I don't think I could stay in a relationship like that. You must be climbing the walls. And wait, is that why you guys don't have kids?"

"Physically, yes, but I also don't want to have kids with her."

"Matt, what the fuck? Clearly, it's been too long since we've talked. You were made to be a dad. You've always said you wanted two kids. Why don't you want to have kids with her?"

"All she cares about is money. She's cold. Ruthless. Everything is about appearances with her, and I'm sick of it." His tone is bitter.

"Wait a minute. Sweet little Chelsea? Perfect little ballerina Chelsea?" This is the woman I envied. The one I compared my shortcomings to. And somehow, she's inspired the ire of Matt. In all our years of friendship, I've never seen him angry with anyone.

"She's not so sweet. It started with little things. My sisters came to visit, and she wouldn't let them stay at the house, so they'd go stay at a hotel. She failed the bar exam twice, and made me lie to everyone about it. She hangs photos of herself everywhere. There's a full-length photo of her when you walk in our front door. She's just not the person I thought she was."

"Damn, Matt, I'm really sorry." I stand up and go over to him, wrap my arms around his neck. I always secretly wished he'd break up with her, but now the moment is here, I'm not as gleeful as I thought I'd be. "I know how much marriage means to you."

"It does, but not like this."

I sit back down next to him. "Have you filed papers yet?"

"Nope. I need to come up with some money first for the attorney and settlement costs. I've given her everything she wants: the house, a semester at Oxford, ridiculously expensive furniture. It's time for me to figure out what I want for a change."

"Well, that part of it is awesome." I hold my latte up in a toast. "To new beginnings."

He taps his paper cup to mine.

Months pass, and Matt and I settle into being roommates. He helps me paint the bedroom, and hangs white Christmas lights around like old times. He hates smoking, so I promise to make the bedroom a smoke-free zone, but the rest of the house and my office across the street are fair game. Our roommate, Steve, spends most of his time alone in his room playing Xbox, so we hardly ever see him.

Matt has way more free time than I do, and wants to go see movies, skydive, and take road trips like old times. My excuse is always the same. "Can't. Gotta work."

My company is in its second year, and I work seven days a week, no less than twelve hours a day. I'm exhausted most of the time, fueled by insane amounts of coffee, nicotine, and endless ambition, but I love the challenge of creating something from nothing.

Matt goes to bed by ten, and I usually crawl into bed a few hours later. It's hard to lie next to him and not think of making sexy time, but I remind myself Matt's like a brother. Nothing more.

One night, I come home and find Matt stretched out on the long green sectional sofa, watching television. "Well, look at you, lazy bones. You hardly ever watch TV," I tease him.

"Come over here," Matt moans, and holds his arms up in the air like a lazy couch zombie.

"Aww. Did someone have a hard day playing in the sunshine?" I sit on the edge of the sofa next to him, then look at the TV to see what he's watching.

He wraps his arms around me and pulls me close to him, throws his heavy left thigh over my legs. "Cuddle with me."

Matt and I never cuddle, yet my face is now buried in his chest. For a fraction of a moment, I forget he's not mine. That we're just friends. That romance has nothing to do with who we are or who we've ever been to each other. I breathe in the exquisite perfection of this one moment. Then it's gone.

"Matt, what are—"

"Shhh."

As I nuzzle closer to him, my head screams. *This is Matt and he's married and your best friend and life is complicated enough right now without you pouring kerosene over every inch of it and burning it to the ground.*

But the smell of him...

I'm afraid to speak. Afraid to break whatever perfect spell has come over him. I place my lips gently ever so gently against his chest.

Matt pulls away enough to look at me. Lust swims through pools of molten espresso. I want to ask what he's thinking and feeling, but I remain mute.

His fingers softly caress my cheek. His thumb traces my eyebrow, down my face, across my lips. He leans closer and gently places his lips on mine. There has never been a more perfect kiss.

I'm defenseless. The feelings about him I've always suppressed now burst in my chest. I have always been and always will be in love with him.

His kisses intensify, and he rolls over on top of me. He kisses my ear, then my neck. His hand is on my breast over my shirt. He stands, grabs my hand, and leads me to the bedroom. By the light of white Christmas lights, we disrobe in silence on either side of the bed, then slip under the covers. He is a chiseled Adonis. Perfection. I am chubby and seriously regret the amount of fast food I've shoved into my mouth this last year. *And when's the last time I shaved my legs?*

ERIKA WORTH

Matt and Erika naked, lying under a sheet, K-I-S-S-I-N-G. I'm never nervous about sex. It's my thing. But suddenly I feel like a virgin on my wedding night.

In a show of gratitude and love, I pull back the sheet and let my kisses speak the words I cannot say. I work my way down from his mouth, to his neck, across his chest, and slowly down his torso. I trail kisses down his stomach, then between his thighs, finally taking him in my mouth.

Like a crimson curtain, my hair shields my face and my racing thoughts. His body tenses. His torso rises. He runs his fingers through my hair, then pulls my head away before I make him climax.

"Not yet." Matt rolls me over on my back and reaches between my legs. It's my turn to be breathless. He positions himself on top of me and gently slides into me. In the dim light and silence, this feels like a delicious dream. Only when I open my eyes, Matt is staring down at me, grinding slowly between my legs. This is too honest. Too intimate. I slam my eyes shut and quicken the pace.

"Slow down. I'm not in a hurry." He braces his elbows next to either side of my head and kisses me sweetly.

I suddenly feel like the dirty ex-whore fucking America's golden boy. His love making is equally exquisite and repulsive. This tender shit is too dangerous. I gave up on love and chose ambition. *But this is Matt.* I want this to stop. I don't ever want this to stop. I don't ever want to be anywhere but right here, with him buried inside of me.

He rolls over on his back and positions me on top of him. Oh my God, now he's going to see my tummy rolls, and he'll totally be able to see how lopsided my boobs are. *Why did I leave the lights on?*

I know how to fuck. I know how to shut down. I know how to run. I have no idea how to handle that Matt is naked and inside me right now, trying to make sweet, tender love to me. I look down at my beautiful friend, then away. This is all too much—fear, vulnerability, love.

Auto-pilot kicks in. My mission is to make Matt come. I close my eyes, feel his hands on my breasts, and ride him faster. Matt grips my hips tighter and his face contorts. *Oh, look. There's Matt's "O" face.* He comes. I pretend to, and try not to stress about the fact that neither of us even mentioned birth control.

I roll over to my side of the bed and stare at the ceiling. *What did we just do?* "I need a cigarette."

"You promised not in the bedroom."

"Matt, this situation above all other situations in this world calls for a cigarette. I'll open the window. Be right back." I get up, painfully aware that Matt is probably looking at my naked behind as I walk to the living room. I grab two glasses of water from the kitchen while I'm at it, then return to the bedroom and resume staring at the ceiling from my side of the bed.

I smoke that cigarette like a motherfucker. I try to exhale away from Matt, but he still waves his hand in front of his face and coughs. He'd love nothing more than for me to quit smoking. I'd love nothing more than to be lovable. But we can't always get what we want.

Matt rolls over onto his right elbow and looks at me. "Watcha thinking about?"

Jesus, that's a loaded question. "Chelsea. You. I hadn't gotten much past that."

"What about her?"

"Um, I don't know. The fact that she's your wife, and even though I'm your friend and not hers, sleeping with someone's husband is still a shitty thing to do."

"Don't feel too guilty. This wasn't my first time sleeping with someone else."

I look over at him, shocked. How did I not know any of this? I'm supposed to be the fucked up one. I'm the one with the damaged past who wasn't good enough to marry and have kids with. Is everyone destined to be fucked up?

"You had an affair?" I take another drag off the best cigarette I've ever smoked in my life.

"About five, yeah."

"Wait, five? When did all of that start?"

"About a year ago, I guess. I knew I'd never be happy with her, so when the opportunity came up, I took it. It wasn't something I ever thought I'd do. It just—"

"Sort of happened, I know. Story of my life. I just never thought you'd do something like this."

"Me neither. This isn't what I had planned."

"Yeah, well, life has a way of happening when you're making plans. I didn't think I'd live to be eighteen, let alone thirty-three. They teach us in recovery to make plans, then show up for whatever arrives at your doorstep. If it's a pile of shit, get out the shovel and start digging, and don't dump it into your neighbor's yard. If it's a Mercedes with a big red bow on it, get in and enjoy the ride. "

"Sounds like good advice."

"Uh huh," I reply absently. My cigarette has burned down to the filter and I'm contemplating my life without it. Sadly, I extinguish it in the ashtray I carried in from the living room, then take a sip of water. I hand the other glass to Matt. "I need another cigarette." I head back to the living room, but Matt stands and blocks my exit from the bedroom.

"Not yet. Not now." He's naked in front of me, tracing his fingertips down my arms, which I'm now holding in front of me to cover my less-than-L.A.-perfect breasts.

He takes each of my wrists in his hand and unfolds my arms, drinking in my nakedness. He leans over and takes my breast in his mouth, then kneels before me and kisses my stomach. Tears of gratitude well up in my eyes, but I wipe them away before he can see. He buries his face between my legs, and I steady myself by running my fingers through his thick hair. The feeling is delicious, but I'm too in my head to come, so I fake it again.

Seemingly pleased with himself, he stands up, an irresistible smirk on his face. He's ready to go again.

"Way to go with the short recovery time, Matt."

He gets in bed and sits with his back against the wall. I sit on his lap facing him, and wrap my whole self around him. I'm whole. I'm home. I don't want to feel this with him. I don't ever want to feel this with someone else.

Through tangled passion and pain, and despite my better judgment, I make love to Matt. This time when he comes, I come with him. Afterwards, he spoons me from behind.

What should be a tender, sweet experience leaves me choking on fear. I wait until I hear his familiar light snoring in my ear, then slowly untangle myself from his heavy limbs. I grab blue jeans, a hoodie, and my black Converse and get dressed in the living room. Grabbing my keys, wallet, and cigarettes, I head down to the garage, get in my car, and drive into the night.

I want to run wild like when I was a kid. Run so far, so fast, until there are no thoughts left, just a symphony of breath and bone in perfect harmony. I've been an emotional runner most of my adult life, but my escape routes are dwindling. I can't drink or do drugs. No gratuitous sex with strangers. No stealing. No bulimia or anorexia. What do I have left? Cigarettes and driving alone at night. Doesn't seem like much.

Under a blanket of smog and stars, I drive west and listen to Coldplay's *The Scientist* on repeat. Chris Martin sings about going back to the start. How far back would I have to go to be undamaged? What parts of my history could I have erased for Matt to have chosen me instead of her all those years ago?

I arrive at Zuma beach and park in the lot near a lifeguard station. I walk up the ramp and sit with my legs dangling down, lean my arms against the wooden rails. My teeth chatter, but I don't care. Consumed with fear, I don't know where else to go.

Behind the mask of workaholism, I feel accomplished, like maybe my life amounts to something. When I stop pushing myself 5,000 miles per hour, my inner critic rails on me, tells me I'm still the broken girl doll playing at being a grown-up. So I don't stop. I push harder and I don't let anything get in my way.

Mouth on skin. His hand on my cheek. Matt coming inside of me. I shake my head and try to dispel the memories of us together. I can't ever be with Matt. Not him. When he sees my broken bits up-close, he'll leave me behind. It's too dangerous to let him love me.

I should reach out to my higher power and try to connect with something other than my fear, but I don't deserve to feel comfort now. It's easier to retreat into the safety of emotional distance.

I smoke. I think. With each wave that breaks against the sand, I grow colder and more distant. When I'm numb, I drive back to the house and fall asleep on the sofa.

The next morning, I awake to the smell of fresh coffee, and the sight of Steve and Matt standing in the kitchen. Steve is in boxers and white tube socks, holding a cup of coffee in his left hand, and stirring his creamer thirty-six times with his right. Matt is in black sweats and a grey New York City marathon T-shirt, making his usual morning protein shake. I get up from the sofa still wearing the clothes I fell asleep in, make a pit stop to the bathroom, and then cram into the tiny kitchen with the boys. I reach for my jumbo mug and fill it with black coffee.

"Good morning, Erika. We didn't mean to wake you," says Steve. He sips his coffee, then stirs it a few more times.

"You didn't. It's probably time for me to get up anyway. What time is it?" I yawn and wipe my eyes.

"Seven," replies Matt, sheepishly looking at me as he drinks his shake.

I avoid eye contact with Matt and instead focus on the steam rising from my cup. "Mmm. Good coffee."

Steve scratches his hairy chest and asks, "Did I hear one of you go out super late last night?"

Matt looks over at me, eyebrows raised. I turn slightly away from him, and take another chug of coffee. "Umm, yeah. That was me. Couldn't sleep."

"Where'd you go?" asks Matt.

"Well, aren't you the nosy one?" I say in a tone snarkier than I intended. "I just drove around for a bit. Went to the beach." I look at

Matt. If last night had been with anyone else, he'd be the one I talked to about all the shit running through my head today. He'd tell me when I was being stubborn and full of crap. Now, he's the last person I can say anything to. "Sorry if I woke you, Steve."

Steve smiles and is oblivious to the awkwardness between Matt and I. "You didn't. I was up late anyway playing Doom."

"You went to the beach by yourself? At night? Alone? That's dangerous," Matt says with a parental undertone. Or a boyfriend one.

"Well, lucky for you I'm an independent woman you don't have to worry about. I've somehow managed to survive thirty-three years of life without anyone looking after me. I can handle myself." I stare at him, defiant.

He looks hurt and holds his hands up defensively. "Whoa! I never said you couldn't."

Matt and I stare at each other, a palpable, pregnant distance between us.

Steve looks back and forth between us. "Okey dokey. I'm going to get ready for work. See you guys later."

Steve retreats to his bedroom, leaving Matt and I alone in the kitchen. He sets his shake on the counter, then moves closer and wraps his arms around me, kisses the top of my head. Frozen in indecision, my brain short-circuits and I stand, unresponsive.

"What are you doing later? You wanna go to Mogo's for dinner tonight? Mongolian buuufayyy," Matt says, flashing his megawatt dimples.

I'm too absorbed in self-protection to let my guard down. "Hmm. Maybe. It depends on how much work there is. Can I let you know later?"

"Sure. I'm gonna hit the gym. I'll see you later at the office. I have a few hours of work to do."

"Okay. Later."

There is no later. I find excuse after excuse to not spend time with him. When he's happy, I'm bitchy and rude. When I'm happy, he's preoccupied, moody, and distant. In almost eight years of friendship, we never fought. Now, we bicker daily, and it's exhausting. The only time we come together is occasionally in bed, but sex only widens the distance between us.

Sometimes, he doesn't come home for two or three days. I don't know whether to feel relieved, jealous, or worried. I opt for apathetic. When he does come home, he doesn't offer an explanation, and I don't ask for one. We do an emotional tango for a couple of months until late June. He comes to my office on a Monday and says he's moving back to Texas.

"But, you've only been here ten months. I thought you hated it there? Why are you going back?"

"There's going to be a big strike at my company. As a supervisor, they'll need me to work twelve-hour days seven days a week for about three months."

"That's harsh."

"Yeah, but I'll make more money in three months than I normally do in a year. I'll be able to get away from Chelsea, settle our accounts and property, and come back permanently."

"When are you leaving?"

"Thursday."

"As in, three days from now?"

"Yep. My mom is getting off work Friday. I'm going to stop in Phoenix, pick her up, then we're gonna go hike the Grand Canyon."

He's leaving in three days. There's so much to say. "Cool."

"Sorry about the short notice with the office and stuff."

"Doesn't matter." Blunt. Cold. Uncaring. I can be such an asshole.

"Okay then."

We stare at each other. He turns and starts to leave, then I blurt out, "Hey, Mogo's on Wednesday night for old times' sake? Buuufayyy?" I offer him an awkward smile.

He half turns to me and smiles back. "Sure. Sounds great."

"Cool. Okay. Wednesday night then. Seven?"

"Okay. Also, I want to see some friends before I go back to Dallas. I may not be around much the next few days."

"I totally get it. I'll see you when I see you."

Wednesday morning, Matt and I spend most of our time side-stepping around each other. I hide out in my office and try not to stress about our impending dinner conversation.

Em comes in and closes the door behind her. "Have you figured out what you're going to say tonight?"

"I think so. Can I practice on you?"

"Shoot."

"Okay. I'm thinking something like, 'Matt, I love you. I'm sorry for being such an unbearable bitch these last few months. I've had big, messy feelings I don't know what to do with. I should have talked to you about them instead of pushing you away. You're my best friend in the whole world, and I don't want anything to come between us. You mean everything to me. I love you more than words could ever say.' Something like that. Think it'll work?"

"Yes. Now can you two just make up already? Being around you guys is like watching mom and dad fight. It sucks."

"Tell me about it. Okay. Wish me luck."

She leaves, and I try to focus on work, but it's hard to concentrate. I have no idea what he's going to say in return. I hope the damage between us isn't irreparable. The thought of him hating me sends a boulder careening through my stomach. *Happy thoughts, Erika. Just tell him the truth, and you guys can figure out the rest when he comes back.*

At noon, Matt comes into my office. "Got a sec?"

I swivel around in my chair. "Of course, what's up?" I smile, feeling more like my old self now that I've decided to take the bull by the horns and finally tell him the truth.

"Well, my mom just called. She got tomorrow off work, so I'm going to head out today instead of tomorrow."

"But, dinner—"

"I'm not going to be able to go to dinner. It takes six hours to get there, and we're going to head to the Canyon first thing in the morning. I'm leaving now."

His expression looks weary, but for the life of me, I can't figure out what he's thinking. Is he sad to be going? Is he going to miss me? Did we fuck everything up? Does he just want to get as far away from me as possible?

"I know it's unexpected, but now I get to spend an extra day with my mom."

"Your mom. Of course, moms are important. Wanna grab lunch then?" *I was hoping we could talk.*

"I can't. I really need to hit the road."

Don't be pathetic, Erika. Don't beg. "Okay. Cool. Do you have everything packed? Do you need help?" I walk into his office and see he's already cleared it out. The space looks like he was never here.

"Everything's already packed and loaded into the Cherokee."

He wants to leave so bad, let him. Fuck it. "Oh. Perfect." I call to the next room. "Hey, Jodi, we can use this extra office for the microfiche machines. Can you move them in here?" My voice is icier than I intended, but I'm hurt. "Well, I've got to get back to work. Have a safe drive and let me know when you make it to Texas."

"I will." He walks out to his Jeep parked by the back door.

I walk next to him, silent. *Tell him. Tell him. Tell him.*

"Thanks again for everything." He gives me a polite hug.

I pat him twice on the back. "Yep. No problem."

He gets in the Jeep and rolls the window down. "See ya."

I hold up my hand in a dismissive wave and walk back inside before he drives away.

Em is in my office when I walk back in. "So? Did you guys talk?"

"No. He couldn't get out of here fast enough."

"You didn't say anything to him? That's bullshit."

"No. What's bullshit is he couldn't take an hour to get lunch or coffee. He wanted to leave? Now he's gone."

"Jesus. I don't know which of you is more stubborn."

"It doesn't matter, Em. I have no time to waste on foolish romantic dreams or people who don't want to be in my life. I have real shit to deal with. Employees to pay. Clients to make happy. Vendors to manage. I'll deal with Matt another time." I swivel my chair around and turn my back to her, signaling the end of this conversation.

Two weeks later, I still haven't gotten my period, nor have I talked to Matt. My new daily mantra is *nothing but work matters*, but there's an unshakable, underlying sadness to each day. *What are you going to do if you're pregnant? He's always wanted to be a dad...but not with someone like you. Especially now. He probably hates you.*

I shove my emotional messiness deep into the vault and get back to business. The vulnerability of hope can kill a person if they're not careful. I'm an ambitious woman with a company to run, with no time for weepy nonsense.

But sometimes at night, the mask of self-control falls off. I wear Matt's marathon shirt he left behind, lie on his side of the bed, and curl around the pillow that still smells like him. Tender Erika comes out of hiding and plays with the possible future with Matt. Fingers interlocked and eyes clenched shut, I pray like a child. *Please, whatever is out there, if I'm at all worthy and if you're at all listening, please let me have this one thing.*

Two weeks later, the blood comes, and washes away my hopes of redemption and happiness. I plant my feet firmly back in reality, and step into the stark truths of my life: *No matter how successful I become, I'll always be the woman with the sordid history, the one who's just a little too messy, a little too loud, and with a few too many rough edges.* Matt will never be mine. I take the shirt off, light a cigarette, and embrace reality.

Steve moves out. I leave the bedroom Matt and I shared untouched, and transfer my stuff to Steve's room.

A few days later, my phone rings late one night.

"Hey," Matt says quietly.

"Oh. Hey." *It's so nice to hear your voice.*

"I made it to Texas."

"Mallory told me. How's the strike going?" *I miss you so much.*

"It hasn't happened yet. They're saying now it might not happen at all."

"Oh?" *Come back. I'm so sorry.*

Long pause.

"Yeah. It's pretty disappointing."

"Sorry." *For everything. I've been such an ass.*

Longer pause.

"How's everything there?" he asks.

"Oh, the usual. Work. Sleep." *Say something. Say you hate this as much as I do.*

"Well, I guess that's it."

"Guess so." *It's not the same without you here.*

"Well...I guess we'll talk soon."

"Sure. Sleep well." *Do you miss me at all?*

"Bye."

"Bye." *I love you.*

Click

Mid-August, Mallory comes into my office and hovers near my desk until I acknowledge her.

I pry my eyes away from my computer and look at her. "What's up?"

"Have you eaten today?"

"Not hungry." I turn back to my monitor.

"When's the last time you ate?"

"I don't know. What time is it?" I glance at my clock. Ten in the morning. I search my memory for the answer. "McDonald's Big Mac Value Pack last night around eight."

"Figures." She walks over to my desk and places a vitamin and a handful of almonds on the paperwork in front of me.

The art of self-care eludes me. What would I do without my precious Emallem? I spin around to face her. "Thank you. Seriously, you're the best."

"I worry about you."

"You're paid to, and you're amazing at your job, but I'm okay. Really. Just busy."

Instead of leaving, she sits across from me, sets her arms on my desk, and clasps her hands in front of her. "I talked to Matt."

I stiffen at the mention of his name. I've become comfortable with the forgetting of things, and have buried my inconvenient feelings for him deep down where I don't have to deal with them. *Most days.* "And?" I ask, casually lighting a cigarette.

"He said you guys still aren't talking."

"I just talked to him, like...well...I guess about a month ago. He didn't have much to say."

"He said things felt weird when he left."

"Things were weird long before he left, Em. There was plenty of time to talk when he was here, but he wasn't interested then. Look, I really don't have time for this. We're buried in searches, and he's the one that left a day early. We could have gone to lunch or coffee or something. He's the one that ran off," I inhale deeply, hoping the smoke will fill the hollow space that's formed in my chest at the mere mention of his name.

"He thinks you couldn't wait for him to leave, that you were already moving stuff into his office before he was even gone."

"Whose side are you on, Em? We needed the space for the microfiche machines. And he had everything packed and ready to go by the time he told me he was leaving. He couldn't wait to get out of here, away from me."

"He thinks you hate him."

I gasp. "What? That's fucking ridiculous." I turn my back to her, anxious for the conversation to end. *I can't deal with any of this.* "I have shit to do. If he's got something to say, he can say it to me himself."

"Erika…"

I keep my back turned to her, "Not now, Em. I'm *busy*," with a tone that lets her know I'm not interested in pursuing this conversation any further.

I hear the office door close, and turn around to confirm she's gone. Finally alone, I try to focus on work, but my righteous anger distracts me. *I'm right, aren't I? Why should I be the one to call him? He's the one who left.*

And he thinks you hate him.

I'm gutted. How could he ever think that? He changed my whole life, pushed me to be more than I thought I ever could be. He was the only person who believed in me when I started my company. When I struggled financially the first year, he offered me his savings account, told me he knew I'd pay it back in no time. I didn't take the money, but the offer was incredible.

It's impossible to measure the impact he's had on my life. How much have I achieved merely for the sake of impressing him? No one's opinion has ever mattered more. Matt matters to me more than life. *You sure don't act like it.*

I stare at the phone. My fifteen years of recovery tell me to put my pride away for five minutes, pick up the phone, and call him. I need to clean my side of the street and stop focusing on how dirty his side is. I lift the receiver, but it weighs a ton, so I set it back down on the base.

I can speak in meetings in front of hundreds of people, openly share the most painful mistakes in my life, walk through my hellish childhood and come out the other side, survive alcoholism, abusive relationships, but I can't make a simple phone call? I know I'm being a chicken, but I don't want to say anything I'll regret. I decide to call him when I'm home and relaxed.

I go home and pass out from exhaustion. The next day, I don't feel like calling him. The day after that, I work through most of the night and sleep through much of the next day. When I think of calling him again, it's too late in Texas. Each day, a different excuse.

The week before Labor Day, the man who was most like Em's father-figure dies at age forty from a brain tumor. Her entire family is devastated. On Saturday, I attend the funeral with her and her family. She's never lost anyone close to her before, and the loss of Dan is devastating for her. I spend the rest of the weekend and Labor Day taking care of her for a change, holding a space for her grief. She doesn't want to talk, and I don't want to leave her alone.

Tuesday morning at 9:02, I walk into my office. My phone rings.

"Good morning. Investigations."

"Can I speak to Erika Worth, please?" a woman's voice asks on the other end of the line.

"This is she."

"Hi Erika. It's Judy. I work with Matt."

"Oh, hey Judy! I've heard so many great things about you. What's up?"

She pauses. "Erika...Matt's missing."

No air. There is no air and the blood in my brain rushes forward and assaults my temples with a thousand tiny fists. "What? What do you mean, missing?" Panic creeps in.

"He's been missing since Saturday. He was on his way to Iowa. There was a flood...and he..."

Saturday. Saturday was Dan's funeral. Today is Tuesday. *Breathe, Erika.* This is Matt. He's fine. He's just out somewhere. Judy is obviously confused.

"I'll let you know when I know something more. I have to make some more phone calls."

"Um...of course. Have Matt call me when you find him. This is crazy." I hang up the phone, stunned. *Why can't I breathe? Where are my cigarettes? Where is Matt?*

I dial his number, and my call goes immediately to voicemail. "Hi. You've reached Matt and I can't come to the phone right now. Leave me a message and I'll call you back." I hang up and try again. "Hi. You've reached Matt." Again. "Hi. You've reached—" His battery is dead. That's it. Just. Fucking. Breathe.

I light a cigarette and stare at the phone, willing Matt to call. One minute passes. Five minutes. Twenty-six minutes. I try to work, but heavy clumps of wool invade my brain and I can't concentrate.

The phone ringing startles the hell out of me. I grab the receiver. "This is Erika!"

"Hi, Erika. It's Judy again."

"Oh, thank God they found him. Where was he?"

"Erika...Matt's dead. They just found his body..."

She keeps saying words and won't stop talking.

"There was a flood...his car was stuck on a turnpike...he kept going back in and rescuing people...family in a minivan...mother and four children died...news story on the internet...pictures..."

Why is she still talking? My vision narrows down to a pinhole like the opening of a James Bond film. Grief strangles breath from my lungs. Clenches my heart with a merciless fist until it shatters into a million pieces. Death roots in my belly. Sorrow enters every pore, attaches itself to every nerve ending and sets them ablaze. Violent sobs rattle through bone and skin.

I try to swallow the vomit making its way up my throat, but I can't stop my body's violent rejection of her awful words. I throw the receiver down, drop to the floor, and throw up in the trashcan under my desk. Her voice buzzes like a chattering insect. I've stopped listening.

Matt is dead.

"NOOOOOOOOO!" My scream shatters what is left of my sanity. "Please, God, I'll do anything you want. Take anything. Please, not Matt."

I will myself into oblivion, pray for the earth to swallow me whole. But I don't die. I'm forced to breathe and feel and bear witness. Unable to dissociate, the pain is merciless, unyielding. I hyperventilate.

Jodi runs into the office and finds me under my desk, the phone receiver dangling over the edge. "Oh my God, Erika. What happened?"

I can't say the words out loud.

Jodi kneels by me and gently touches my arm. "Erika, what happened?"

"Matt—" my voice cracks. I can't.

"Matt? What about him? Is he okay?"

I drown in a fresh wave of hysteria.

Jodi hangs up the phone, then dials a number. "Mallory. Come to the office right away...I don't know. Erika is hysterical...just get here."

I waiver between catatonia and hysteria. At some point, it occurs to me they may be wrong. Maybe it's not him.

I pull myself up from the floor and sit in front of my computer. I Google the details Judy told me. The first image is Matt's red Jeep Cherokee smashed like a pancake. He was just here. He drove away in that car and he was fine. *And you didn't even say goodbye.*

Page after page, image after image, I read about the accident. Seven cars stuck on a turnpike over a creek. Twenty inches of rain in twenty-four hours. Water rose and entered his vehicle. Matt got out of his car and went to the vehicle of a seventy-nine-year-old woman. Her doors and windows wouldn't open, so Matt pulled her out through the sunroof and carried her to safety. She asked what his named was. He told her it didn't matter, only that she was safe. He went back into rapidly rising water. He and another good Samaritan pulled two teenage girls out of their car and led them to safety. Repeatedly, he went back into rising flood waters, rescuing six people altogether.

A family that consisted of a father, mother, and their four children stayed in their van in the rising water. Three times, Matt tried to get the family out of the van, but the father refused. After the third attempt, Matt walked away as a seven-foot wall of water washed the turnpike away. The man escaped through the driver's window. His wife, four children, and Matt all perished. The bodies of three of the children were located immediately. Matt, the mother, and fourth child were discovered a few feet from each other today.

Matt's kindness and strength is in every story. He's a hero. *Was. He was everything.*

Mallory walks in and stands behind me as I watch a video of the accident scene. "Jodi said I had to get here right away. What's going on?"

Still unable to say the words out loud, I turn around, hug her, and point to the screen.

"What is that? That looks like Matt's—" Mallory sits at my desk and watches the news footage, reads the eyewitness accounts on CNN. "Matt's *dead*?"

She turns to me, our faces mirror images of shock and despair. We hug each other tightly, our sobs a cacophony of grief.

* * *

William comes out of the hangar and walks over to the bench where I'm sitting, trapped in a memory I can't get out of. Was that really less than month ago? "Hey, what's going on with Mallory? She seems pretty upset."

"We both lost some significant people in our lives in the last month. And today's malfunction really freaked her out."

"Oh shit. That's totally understandable."

"She left after I told her I was going to jump solo tomorrow."

"You still up for it?"

"Nothing in the world could stop me. What time are we starting in the morning?"

"Eight will work. Look over the study materials tonight. If you grasp everything tomorrow and I feel confident in you, I'll put you on a jump before noon."

"Sweet. Thanks, Will. I'm going to go find Em."

"She was in the first bedroom in the hangar a few minutes ago."

"Okay. See you later."

I go into the hangar and knock on the closed bedroom door. There's no response. I open the door and find Em sitting on the bed alone, back against the wall.

236

I sit at the foot of the bed. "Em, the last thing on earth I want to do is leave you."

"Then don't jump tomorrow."

"Em, when I was up there..." I get lost in the memory of freefalling, then briefly floating for a few blissful moments, before the chaos hit. "I can't explain the feeling of what happened today. How close I felt to him up there. I need to go back, alone. It felt like he was with me."

"Matt?"

"Yeah."

"So risking your life is going to make you feel closer to him?"

"I did a little experiment last night and wrote out my obituary. I thought about what people would say if I died today."

"Well, that's just fucking wonderful, Erika. And today, you almost do."

I search for the words that will make her understand. "Matt fucking lived, Mallory. He didn't make excuses. He didn't let fear stop him. Ever. He didn't waste a second of his life. And what did I do with the time we had? I fucking blew it off at every turn. He wanted to go skydiving. I told him it was too expensive. He wanted to go on road trips. I said I had to work. He wanted to eat out. I told him I wasn't hungry, and instead stayed in, smoked cigarettes, and worked all night."

"But... but you guys did stuff! You went places. Vegas. San Francisco. You hung out all the time."

"Em, he was going to Nepal in November to climb to Base Camp One. Four hundred people showed up at his funeral to pay respects to the man who touched their lives. People don't really know me."

"But you sponsor people. People know you. I know you."

"I know you do, but you're one of three people who are even remotely close to *knowing* me. Not the tough façade. Not the businesswomen. Not even the woman with fifteen years. Those are all shells. Shields I hide behind. People see me as they need to see me. Tough. Ambitious. Bitchy. Whatever. But deep down, Em, my insides are twisted up. I keep people at arm's length. I always have. I pushed Matt away because I knew wasn't good enough for him. I figured it would hurt less to push away rather than be rejected. I fucking blew it, Em, and I know you know what I'm talking about, because you do the exact same thing. Abandonment issues were parting gifts from our fathers."

"So, this is what you got from writing your obituary?"

"It's what wasn't there, Em. No one comes to my home. I ask people how they're doing, but never talk about anything intimate or personal, only work and the number of clients we're getting. People come to me with their problems and I come up with solutions. I get shit done.

"I even do it when I date guys. I find projects, never peers. When they bring stuff up about me being distant or not letting them in, I deflect and point at their issues and insecurities. I manipulate them with words, anger, and blowjobs, then leave before they get too close. My reasons seem logical at the time, but are truthfully more about getting out before I get hurt. I've wasted years of my life on fear. I wasted so many precious moments I could have had with Matt. And now I'll never—" I choke on the words.

Mallory moves closer to me and hugs me. Both of us are shit at falling apart, but someone else's grief gives us a purpose. I'm hers until I can pull my shit together for more than ten minutes at a time. "Jesus, Erika, this is all a lot to take in. I don't even know what to say about all of this. If you jump tomorrow, I'll be out there waiting for you when you land, but you better fucking land."

"Promise. Or I'll bounce at the very least. Have you seen my ass?" I tease her.

We laugh and head back out into the hangar to join the rest of the group. We spend the night around a campfire, and listen to adventures of skydivers from around the world. None of them talk about fear. They talk about living.

When I eventually sleep, I dream Matt and I are flying.

gypsy

Step One: *Keep the sperm in a warm and dark place until ready for insemination.*

Step Two: *Draw the semen up into a syringe, being careful not to push it out too quickly and damage the sperm any more than necessary.*

Step Three: *Lie on your back with your hips elevated on a pillow and relax your body. Listening to music might help. Once relaxed, insert the syringe as far as it will go without hitting your cervix. Depress the syringe slowly, "squirting" the semen towards the cervix.*

Step Four: *Remain on your back with your legs up in the air, hips still elevated on a pillow, for at least thirty minutes. Try to orgasm, the bigger the better, as this helps the cervix dip into the seminal fluid and increases your body's happy hormones. This is a great time to snuggle and imagine the formation of your child.*

Thank you, Google.

Who needs a $15,000 doctor's visit when you have a fabulous gay sperm donor, sample cup, and syringe? I follow steps one through four, minus the snuggling since I'm alone, then lie back and try to think happy, hormonal, sperm-swaddling thoughts, and ignore the absurd process I've just put myself through for the sake of creating a child.

A baby. At nineteen, I asked doctors to tie my tubes. Just wait, they said. You'll change your mind when you're older, they said. Just use birth control until you're ready, they advised.

I didn't want birth control, and I didn't want babies. I wanted to fuck with reckless abandon—to be free, independent, with a string of handsome and exotic lovers I kicked out of my bed at 2:00 AM. I read Anaïs Nin, Sylvia Plath, and Dorothy Parker, listened to Billie Holiday and Nina Simone. I wanted to be mysterious and smoke imported cigarettes, not spend afternoons at Gymboree with soccer moms wearing floral dresses.

If I'd known how to be truly honest with myself during those reckless years, I would have admitted how terrified I was at the prospect of becoming a mother. Deep down, I envied those little rosy-cheeked assholes sitting on their dad's shoulders, having their bellies tickled by adoring mothers, fingers and toes kissed by loving aunties.

And if I had stopped running from every feeling I had, I might have gotten to the root of my escapism—in the core of my being, I felt inherently unlovable.

Matt changed the course of my life. Loving him changed me, cracked me heart open and stripped away layers of protection. Losing him also had a profound impact on me, and was in some ways a huge gift. I would give everything I have for five more minutes with my friend. To hear his laugh. To rest my cheek against his chest, breathe him in, and feel his arms around me.

His death forced me to live, to walk through fear and be honest in ways I didn't know I could be. And now I'm thirty-eight with sperm inside of me, trying to make a baby *on purpose. If you'd had Matt's baby, there'd still be a piece of him here.*

Fuck! I should probably stop swearing so much.

Nah. The baby won't register it for a while. I've still got a couple years.

What if I screw them up and say things that damage their psyche, and fifteen years from now they stand in front of me, fists defiantly placed on either hip, professing their hatred for me? What if they're alcoholic like me? What if I am the worst mother ever and the baby is stuck with me?

Your baby will be loved, says the kind voice. *Trust. Breathe. Relax.*

Happy hormones. Happy thoughts. Happy, happy, happy.

I wiggle a little, stretch my legs up to the ceiling, and feel the moisture pooled between my legs.

I like my toenail polish. Bright turquoise is a good color.

Is the neighbor's dog ever going to stop barking? Geez, that is one yappy dog.

Not like my dogs. My dogs are cool.

My kid will be cool.

My kid will be cool and have cool dogs to play with.

The mind-numbing drone of a nearby leaf blower blares through the mental image of my very cool baby and puppies sleeping side-by-side.

I have to pee. *You can't pee, Erika. You'll pee the baby out.* I have a bladder the size of a walnut. Damn. Now I really have to pee.

I'm hungry. I should have eaten before I started all of this. When's the last time I ate? Mmm. Spicy peanut noodle bowl sounds perfect right now. I wonder what weird food I'll want when I'm preggo.

Oh my God, Erika. A zygote could be forming in your uterus this very second!

My fear is silenced by my hormones screaming *BABY, BABY, BABY!*

Is this really what I want, or am I just doing this because I'm at my scary age? This would be considered a geriatric pregnancy. *Geriatric.* What a thing to say to a woman over thirty-five. Do they tell men they have *geriatric* sperm? No.

I look at the clock. Seven minutes have passed.

I could end up a sad single mom like Toni Colette in *About a Boy* and my weird kid could be embarrassed to be seen with me. I could cease being me, and only talk about teething and potty training, and walk around with vomit in my hair and not know it. *And who would tell you if you did? You'll be alone, just like Mom.*

The baby might never understand why it doesn't have real dad. But this situation is different from my childhood. The baby will at least know Hiro, he just won't have a say on parental stuff. That's what we agreed to, at least. The process of baby creation started with forms and agreements. This baby would be mine and mine alone.

He could see the baby and change his mind, maybe fight for shared custody. *Crap.*

Focus on the task at hand. Calm baby thoughts.

Biology has turned me into a breeding pod person.

This might not even work. I might have blown my only chance to be a mom when I was twenty, when I thought there would always be time and second chances.

February 1990

I will never understand how I survived the last six months without relapsing. After Club Paradise, I lasted four days as a stripper, nine days as a phone sex operator, and finally hit bottom on selling myself.

I just turned twenty and have two years sober. I work as a reservationist at a swanky restaurant by day, and at night at an underground club run by a couple of sober guys. My friend, Melissa, and I wear black bustiers and serve watered-down liquor to underage metal kids.

Tonight, the club is extra crowded and smoky. *Sweet Child of Mine* pounds in perfect syncopated rhythm with blinding strobe lights. I feel woozy and like I'm going to vomit. I jostle my way through the long line to the ladies' bathroom, threatening to withhold drinks if the girls don't let me pass. I open the bathroom door and faint on the filthy tile floor.

I come-to and see a half-dozen, heavily painted faces hovered over me, framed by hair teased to heaven. "Oh my God, is that the bartender? What is she on? Do we still get drinks? I really have to pee."

With as much dignity as I can muster, I drag myself out to the parking lot. Dizzy, I lit a cigarette. I savor the first drag, and then throw up. There is no way I can finish my shift, so I tell Mel I'm going home.

"You okay, hun?" she asks in her southern drawl.

"Yeah. Too much smoke and too many assholes." I grin.

"Maybe you're pregnant," she quips back.

"Haha. You're funny. I'll talk to you later."

I go home to my studio apartment and sit in silence. My phone is disconnected for non-payment. I can't afford cable. I just borrowed money to pay my February rent three weeks late. My fridge is empty except for expired eggs, and half-eaten jar of pickles, and a moldy hunk of cheese. I survive on Top Ramen and cigarettes.

I have two years sober and feel more fucked up now than I did when I was new. How do people get their shit together? My rent is only $350 and a month and I can't even handle that. I want to act, but I'm so exhausted from working menial, shit jobs and driving in L.A. traffic, I never make time for auditions or classes. Chaos and failure follow me wherever I go. I curl into a ball of self-pity and hope sleep will make the nausea go away.

I wake up the next morning, exhausted and desperately in need of coffee and a new life. I sit on the toilet, eyes closed, with a cigarette hanging out of one side of my mouth, having my morning pee. I open my eyes and see a glaring red spot in the middle of my pajama bottoms. My mind searches my memory catalog, back to when my cousin was sixteen and pregnant. We were in the bathroom and she spotted. She told me it was common when you're pregnant. You don't get your periods anymore, just sometimes one spot of blood.

When was the last time I had my period? January? No. December.

Early December. It was now February 22nd. Fuck. *No way. My periods have always been irregular. No way in hell am I pregnant.*

Short the $12 for a pregnancy test, I drive to the free clinic. The disinterested receptionist tells me to leave my urine sample in the designated area and call after two the next day for my results.

I spend the next twenty-four hours trying to think about anything but the test. At 1:59 PM, I go down to the lobby of my apartment building and knock on my landlady's door.

Bernice opens the door. "Hi, Erika. What do you need?" She looks like Velma from Scooby Doo, only middle-aged, chubby, and with a droning nasal voice.

"Hi, Bernice. I was wondering if I could use your phone. Mine broke and I have to make an important work call," I lie.

"Uh, sure I guess." She eyes me suspiciously and retreats into her apartment. She returns and hands me a large, white, cordless phone.

"Thanks." I move a few feet across the lobby for privacy and dial the number.

"Planned Parenthood, please hold."

Bernice stands at her door, watching and waiting. I hold up a finger to indicate I'll only be a minute. Seconds dragged on. I pace back and forth. Fuzzy interference warns me when I drift too far away from the telephone's base.

"Planned Parenthood. Thank you for holding. How may I help you?"

I cup my hand over the mouthpiece and whisper, "Um, hi. I'm calling to get some test results."

"Name please?"

"Erika Worth. I took a pregnancy test yesterday."

"Hold please."

More holding and pacing. I look over at Bernice and see her partner, Michelle—who used to be Michael but is now transitioning—towering behind her, watching me interest.

"Just one more minute. Almost done," I say to them and smile.

"Hello, Miss Worth?"

"Yes. I'm here."

"Your test results are positive."

"What's wrong with her phone?" I hear the timber of Michelle's voice.

"I don't know. She said it's broken."

"Broken? Likely story."

"Um... you're sure about that?" I ask.

"Yes, Miss. Positive. Would you like to schedule a termination procedure?"

Positive. A nuclear bomb detonates in the middle of my brain. "Um...I don't know. I mean...yes, I think." *Pregnant, Erika. You're fucking pregnant.*

"We're scheduling appointments for two weeks from now. I have 8:00 AM on Saturday morning, March 10th available."

"And if I change my mind?"

"You can cancel at any time."

"How much does it cost?"

"Do you want local anesthesia or sedation?"

"What's the difference?"

"With local, you will be able to see and hear what is happening, and will feel some slight pressure from the procedure. With sedation, you will not see or feel any part of the procedure. You'll wake up afterwards with cramping and discomfort, which will subside in time. Local is $150. Sedation is $275."

Jesus. Almost a month's rent. I have no idea what exactly I'm going to do, but local is not an option. "Sedation, please," I mumble.

"Well get the phone *back* from her. I need to make a call," Michelle insists.

Numb. I give the receptionist my information and hang up. With tears in my eyes, I hand the phone back to Bernice. Michelle snatches the receiver and goes back into their apartment.

"You, uh, need to make any more calls?"

Who could I call? "No, I'm good. Thank you so much." I leave before I'm reduced to a pool of humiliation on the lobby floor.

Zombie-like, I return to my apartment and slump on my bed, my hands protectively cup my belly. *There's a person in there. A Little Bump.*

I light a cigarette and go over my options.

I can have the abortion. It seems like a fix, but I know it won't be that simple. This is a baby, and if I wasn't been so fucked none of this would have happened.

I can give it up for adoption. I flash back to little me, looking out a window, waiting. Not being wanted has scarred me. I can't knowingly do that to a kid. Not an option.

I can have the child. I can be a mom.

I look around at my world. A ten-by-thirteen room, second-hand clothes I pick up from vintage stores, a six-foot poster of Jim Morrison, a stack of records, and a case of chicken-flavored Top Ramen. I just used Bernice's phone to get my results. I can't take care of me, let alone another human being.

Termination is my only choice.

Little Bump's existence sparks a new flame of self-loathing. Acting out and hurting myself is one thing. Dragging a harmless kid through the mire of my shame is another.

And who is the dad? I was with David one time in December, and John once in January. I've seen them both in meetings, but avoid them, not that either of them are knocking down my door.

Had we used protection? John pulled out. David had been a painful, two-minute quickie on the hard tile floor of his shower. When he finished, he stood naked in front of the mirror, flexing his muscles.

In what world does that make a baby? *In mine, of course.* If I'm spotting, chances are I'm further along, which means it's David's. I hate the idea of talking to him again, but I need him to cough up half the money and give me a ride to the clinic.

I go to our regular Friday night meeting. He isn't there, so I take a seat facing the door. I look at the people sitting around me. *All of these people were babies, and their mothers didn't kill them.*

Half way through the meeting, David strolls in wearing a white

246

tank and baggy jeans. I shift in my seat, dreading the conversation I need to have with him. He looks around the room, glances past me as if I was invisible, and takes a seat by his buddies.

After the meeting, I find him talking to Giselle, a leggy model with a year of sobriety who looks like a brunette Marilyn Monroe. He whispers in her ear, touches a brown tendril draping her perfect cheekbone. She touches his arm, throws her head back, and laughs.

I walk up and interrupt them. "Hey David, can I talk to you? It's kind of important."

He looks back and forth at Giselle and me. "Uh, not right now, Erika. I'm kinda busy." He turns back to Giselle.

I stand my ground. "I just need a minute." *And $137.50.*

A vein pops at his temple, but he flashes Giselle a killer smile. He turns to me. "Yeah, sure." He grabs my elbow and pulls me ten feet away. "What do you want? I'm busy." He looks over at Giselle and winks.

"Yeah, well, I'm pregnant." I whisper.

For one moment, his slick façade slips and his jaw drops open. Giselle can't hear us, but watches us with interest. He sees it, too, and pulls me further away from her. "What do you mean, you're pregnant?" he hisses. His fingers tighten on my elbow.

I yank my arm out of his grip. "What do you think I mean, genius? I'm pregnant."

"And you think it's *mine?*"

Jesus. This was the same conversation my Mom had with my Dad. I know there's a possibility it isn't his. I know how wrong it is to lie about a baby. I know I'll never be able to come up with the money on my own. I am the same age my mother was when she got pregnant, and my father denied I was his. History is repeating itself. In this moment, all I want is for some man, somewhere, to step up and take responsibility for *something.*

So I lie. "Yes. It is. Can we go somewhere and talk about this? I was thinking of going to Canter's—"

"Um, hey, can we talk about this tomorrow?" He pauses and

looks back at Giselle. "I need to go home and do some writing and pray about this."

That's recovery-speak for *I have no desire to deal with this at the moment*, but what can I do but agree? "Sure. Tomorrow."

I leave without him. My loneliness is palpable. I don't give a shit about David, but Little Bump deserves better than either of us.

I go to Canter's Deli and see the usual gang of rowdy, sober alcoholics sitting at a big table in the back. I opt for a booth by myself, my journal, cigarettes, and a black cup of coffee. Writing is how I process my feelings, and I have suitcase-full to sort through.

Ten minutes later, David shows up, hand in hand with Giselle. They sit at the booth directly next to mine. The only thing between us is a thin glass partition. Incredulous, I stare at them from less than two feet away. They ignore me completely.

I knew David wasn't a good guy. I had stopped sleeping with good guys a long time ago. Lower companions are easier to stomach, and I don't end up with unmet expectations. I ask for nothing and receive it in abundance. But while my world and psyche crumble, this asshole acts like creating a baby means nothing. How could Little Bump be nothing?

"Oh, David, you're so funny!" Giselle giggles, throwing her head back again.

How does she not get whiplash from laughing like that?

"And you're so fucking beautiful." They lean into the middle of the table and start swallowing each other's tonsils.

Thoughts race through my head: Little Bump, abandonment, tossing cups of searing hot coffee over the partition and scalding their faces off. In my head, I scream *WHAT THE FUCK IS WRONG WITH YOU? I'M FUCKING PREGNANT! DOESN'T THAT MEAN ANYTHING?* But I stay mute and defeated, drowning in waves of shame.

Each moment I sit here, another piece of me vanishes. Before I disappear completely, I pay for my coffee and go home.

I wake up the next morning, and for one precious moment, forget how screwed up my life is. Then I remember. Emotionally hungover, I decide to call David.

In ripped jeans, a black tank top, and last night's makeup still caked on my face, I go down to the lobby and knock on Bernice's door.

Michelle answers the door wearing a long floral kimono. She eyes me up and down, then scrunches up her face like I'm human garbage. *She's got a point, Erika. Being a human train wreck tends to repel people.*

"Hi, Michelle. I hate to bother you, but is there any way I can borrow your phone again?"

"What's wrong with yours?"

"It's broken. Please, I'll only be a minute."

"Broken, or disconnected? And you know you were late on your rent *again.*"

I swallow each bite of humble pie she feeds me. "I know, I'm sorry. I'll have March rent on time, promise. I just really need to use the phone. *Please.*"

She gives me another once-over, then swings her front door open. "Oh, all right. Come on in."

"Um, can I stay out here to make the call? It's kinda private."

"Sure, honey." She disappears into their apartment and returns with the cordless.

"Thank you." I retreat to a corner of the lobby and dial David's number.

"Speak to me," he says when he answers the phone.

"Hey David. It's Erika."

"Oh...yeah. What's up?" Irritation tightens his voice.

"I made an appointment for an abortion at eight in the morning, March tenth. I need $137.50 for your half, and a ride because I'll be sedated and can't drive."

"Phew! That's a lot of cash."

"Tell me about it. The whole thing is almost a month's rent."

"Well, I'll see what I can do."

"David, come back to bed," coos a female voice in the background.

Giselle. I imagine her, all leggy and gorgeous, wrapped up in a white sheet, nibbling on one finger as she woos him back to bed. She can have him. I only need money and a ride.

"Um, hey, I gotta go. Can we talk later?"

"We don't need to talk later. I just need to know you'll be there."

"Yeah. Sure. A ride."

"And it's Saturday morning, March tenth. Pick me up by seven, okay?"

"Yeah, yeah. Ride at seven. Gotta go." He hangs up.

I drift through my week in a haze of depression. I tell no one what's happening. Morning sickness has kicked in with a vengeance, and my uppity boss at the restaurant, Manfred, is putting two and two together.

"Are we having issues?" he snarks after watching me run to the bathroom for the third time in the last hour.

"No. No issues. Just the flu." I blot my face with the wet paper towel I brought back from my last bathroom trip.

"Hmm. That's an interesting *flu* you've got there." He raises one dark, perfectly tweezed brow at me.

"Yeah. It's a bad one, Manfred."

'Well, there's no one to cover for you. You're needed on the phones, not in the bathroom. If your *flu* doesn't get better soon, perhaps we need to find someone who—"

"I got it, Manfred. Handle the phones. I'm your girl." I smile and pray he will go find someone else to torment.

The restaurant is closed for lunch, but the staff eat a big meal together daily at noon. Normally, I love pasta. Now, the smell of it makes me gag, as do pork and peppers. I also feel a slight pressure building in my lower abdomen, and my boobs ache so much I can no longer sleep on my stomach. Little Bump is taking over my insides whether I like it or not.

The next week, Melissa moves in with me. With her contribution, I'm able to pay rent on time and restore my phone service. The ring of my telephone is music to my ears.

"OH MY GOD, ERIKA! HE CHEATED ON ME WITH MY *BEST FRIEND!* I THOUGHT HE *LOVED* ME!" a female voice wails on the other end of the line.

"Who is this?"

"It's Gisellllle," she moans.

I envision her biting a knuckle. "Giselle? How did you get my number?"

More uncontrollable sobbing from the other end of the line. "I went through David's phone book," she mewls.

"And you thought to call *me*? Do you have any idea what's going on with us?"

"I didn't know who else to call. I know you're, like, pregnant, and you have an abortion scheduled for next week. And I just want you to know we will *totally* be there for you. It's already on our calendar."

"Giselle, how long have you known David?"

"Since last week, when you guys were talking after the meeting."

One week, and they are already a "we" with a calendar. She's giving me a headache. "That's the night I told him I was pregnant. I asked if he wanted to talk, and he said he couldn't because he was going to go home and write and pray about it. Then he shows up at Canter's, *with you,* instead."

"Like, oh my God, Erika. I had no idea. That was the first night we were together." *Sniffle. Sniffle.*

"Did you use birth control?"

"No. He said he needed to, like, feel being inside of me, and the pill makes me fat so..."

A fresh wave of nausea gurgles up my esophagus. "And now a week later, he's slept with your best friend, you love him, and decided to call the pregnant girl for comfort? Infuckingcredible."

Sobbing, "Erika, I'm soooo sorry. I didn't know who else to call." Nose blowing.

"Like, oh my god, how about someone who actually gives a shit. Bye, Giselle." I hang up the phone. I will not shed one single tear over David the Douche. Good riddance.

But I am raw hamburger meat inside over Little Bump.

A few more days pass and, no surprise, David stops returning my calls. With no one else to turn to, I call Mom. I need help.

I anticipate her disapproval—yelling, screaming, followed by a litany of I-told-you-sos—but she is incredible and tells me she'll support me no matter what I choose. At night, I curl on my side, my hand resting protectively on my stomach. Despite my decision to terminate, maternal instincts are kicking in. Every cell in my body wants me to protect Little Bump. My heart is heavy with indecision. I want to keep Little Bump, but can't see a way to do it. I am nothing and have nothing to give.

I stay at Mom's the night before the appointment. I bury my face in my old pillow and cry until I run out of tears.

My sponsor suggests I write a letter to the baby. I cry so hard when I write the letter, I can barely put words on paper.

Dear Little Bump-

I want so much to have you, love you, and give you the life you deserve. Childhood should be filled with joy, unconditional love, and encouragement. I can't give you anything but anger, fear, and resentment. None of those qualify me to be your parent. Not bringing you into this world is the only act of love I have for you.

I hope one day, if I'm worthy enough, you'll come back to me. I hope you can somehow forgive me. I'm certain I will never forgive myself.

I will always love you.

mom

Spent, I lay on my bed, face-up, arms spread wide, and beg HP for guidance and courage.

Mom comes into the room, takes me in her arms, and hugs me. "It's going to be okay, Erika. I promise. Whatever you do, it will be okay."

"But Mom, you didn't abort me. I know you regret that but—"

"No, Erika. I don't regret having you. I haven't always been the best Mom, and I haven't always said the right things, but I don't regret having you. I regret the mistakes I've made. Not giving you a father. George..."

"Forget about him, and Dad. You did it, and without help from anyone."

"And it was incredibly hard, Erika. I'm not telling you what to do, but you were there. You know how difficult it was. How tight money was. How miserable I was all the time."

I remember all of it.

"Whatever you choose to do, I love you, Erika."

Exhausted, I pass out until the next morning. Mom wakes me at 6:30 AM. I stand in a hot shower, tilt my head up, and let the water wash over me. There are no tears left, only resigned sadness.

Mom drives me to the clinic in silence. I wonder what her decision would have been twenty years ago, if she'd legally been allowed to make one. I have never been as grateful for my mother as I am in this moment.

We arrived at 7:45 AM and checked in at the reception desk. After paying the fee and filling out the paperwork, I am handed a stack of blue paper garments and told to change in the next room. Mom stays in the reception area and I walk through the doors alone.

I am instructed to remove everything but my socks and put on the blue paper gown, cap, and booties. Once dressed, I am escorted to an exam room where I am greeted by a formal female doctor.

"Verify your name for me," she dictates while looking down at a clipboard with paperwork.

"Erika Worth."

"And how far along are you?"

"I'm not actually sure."

She looks up from her clipboard and peers down her nose at me. "I'll be able to tell from the pelvic. Are you on any form of birth control?"

"Condoms," I lie.

"Would you like to leave here with the pill today?"

"Yes, please. That would be great."

"Well, you smoke, so I won't give you the pill. Stick to condoms," she scoffs.

If you weren't going to give me the pill in the first place, why the hell did you ask if I wanted it? I am too numb to fight.

The doctor briskly performs a painful and impersonal pelvic exam. "You're ten to twelve weeks pregnant."

Little Bump is David's.

The doctor removes her latex gloves, deposits them into the waste bin, and exits the room. A few minutes later, a nurse escorts me to the waiting area. The room is set up with a dozen plastic chairs along three walls. On the fourth wall, Saturday morning cartoons blare from a television.

Like wallflowers at a school dance, six of us girls sit in matching blue paper attire. We stare quietly at the television or the floor. *Shame sisters.* Between each cartoon, baby commercials flash across the screen, bombarding us with images of healthy, happy babies. I try to make eye contact with each of my companions, desperate to connect with anything other than the television. Nothing. We remain mute strangers drowning in the gravity of whatever brought us to this decision.

One by one at ten minute intervals, a nurse summons each girl.

"Erika Worth?"

I stand and follow her into the procedure room.

The room is cold and sterile. Various medical staff dressed in green paper caps, gowns, and surgical masks bustle around the room. I can't see anyone's faces. The nurse assists me up into what looks like a dentist's chair. She positions my feet in the stirrups. Spread open and naked in a room full of strangers, and blinded by a surgical floodlight directly above me, I feel like an alien experiment.

"Hi, Erika. My name is Dr. Johnson and I'm going to be performing your procedure today."

"Hi."

A different person holds an anesthesia mask over my face while Dr. Johnson continues talking to me. "Now Erika, I want you to count back from one hundred with me."

"One hundred... ninety-nine... ninety-eight..."

I wake up on a row of gurneys, my mind a complete blank.

"PULL UP YOUR PAD," commands a loud voice.

I look at my blue gown, and fuzzy remnants of memory surface.

"PULL UP YOUR PAD," commands the voice again.

Groggy and cramping, I realize the voice might be talking to me. "Huh?" I ask.

"REACH DOWN AND PULL UP YOUR PAD," the voice instructs again, piercing the veil of anesthesia.

I look down and see a jumbo-sized maxi pad attached to an elastic belt—the kind they give girls in elementary school to teach them about their periods—and finally realize what she is asking of me. When I try to sit up, pain rips through my abdomen. Still, I manage to cinch the maxi pad up and secure the elastic belt around my waist.

"SLIDE DOWN."

"Huh? I pulled it up."

"SLIDE DOWN. MOVE DOWN A BED."

I look to my left and see my shame sisters lined up on several gurneys in a row. When we come out of the procedure, we're put on the far-right gurney. Each time the voice yells at us, we move one gurney to the left. By the time I get to the last gurney, I am lucid enough to dress and leave.

I reach down to touch Little Bump as I have done so many times during the past two weeks. I am empty. Little Bump is gone.

I shuffle out to the reception area. Mom comes over to help me walk.

"You okay?" she asks.

"I think so. It feels like an alien creature is trying to claw its way out of my uterus."

"Ouch."

"Yeah," I whisper. *Ouch.* The pain in my womb is nothing compared to the one in my heart.

"Let's go home," Mom says.

They instruct me at the clinic to wear pads for the next two weeks, since tissue and blood can continue to shed for that long. Every day, I'm reminded of my choice. I know in my heart I made the right one, but the lingering evidence is depressing. I vow whatever happens down the road, I will never go through this again.

A text alert from my phone brings me back to the present.

HIRO: *Does someone feel pregnant yet?* ;-)

ME: *Lol. Possibly. Say a little prayer.*

HIRO: *You don't need prayers, honey. My sperm are excellent swimmers. They've just never been in the right pool.*

ME: *Lol. Well, your sperm and I are having a blast over here*

HIRO: *I'm off to meet Hot Jorge from the gym. Have fun making a beautiful little Irish/Japanese baby!*

ME: *Love you xxx*

HIRO: *Love you too Mama*

Little Bump would have been eighteen this year. Have I come far enough to deserve a child? I look around my bedroom, at my adult life filled with abundance. I have everything but a partner and a child. I do well without a partner, but what about the baby?

I look at the clock. Thirty minutes have passed. I send a silent prayer out to the universe.

If I get to be a mom, I'll give it everything I've got. And Little Bump, if you come back to me, I will love you with all my might.

trouble me

I know her before we speak. Black leather jacket over a ripped, black Green Day T-shirt. Last night's smokey-eye makeup smudged under caked-on mascara. Bleached-blonde hair with black roots, limp and stringy as if it hasn't been washed in a couple of weeks. She smokes and leans against a brick wall outside of the meeting, tries to look cool and immune to the world around her. She plucks at the fraying gashes of her skinny jeans, ashes on the sidewalk, and glares at the cliques of people standing in front of the meeting.

She's me—me and a million other angry newcomer girls who got sober in Hollywood. The clothes and hairstyles might be different, but the feelings are always the same. *What the fuck just happened to my life?*

I smile at her as I walk by and resentfully hold my breath as I make my way through the haze of smoke. *I can't believe I ever smoked. Nasty fucking habit.* I reach into my purse for my keys.

"Hey. You're that lady that led the meeting, right?" she asks.

"Yes. I'm Erika." I reach my hand out to shake hers.

She eyes me suspiciously. Instead of shaking my hand, she gives me a head nod. "Hey. I'm Simone."

"Nice to meet you, Simone. How much time do you have?"

"Why? You gonna report it to someone or something?"

I laugh and her eyes narrow even more. "Um, no. That's not how we do things around here. It's just a question. Feel free to answer it, or not. You can pretty much do whatever you'd like around here."

She pauses for a moment and takes the last drag off her cigarette before squashing it out under her black, scuffed, well-worn Doc Martin. "I have seventeen days."

"Wow. That's a lot of fucking days of not drinking or using. You ever had seventeen days before?"

"Not since I was ten or so." Her face is frozen in fear as we stare at each other in silence. She breaks eye contact and reaches into her jacket, lights another cigarette.

I want to hug her and tell her it's all going to be okay, but I know better. It'll freak her out, and I'm not interested in scaring people out of recovery.

"How much time do you have again? Twenty years or some shit like that?"

Before I answer, I realize I've probably been sober longer than she's been alive. Damn. I was just seventeen, like, a minute ago. Now I'm forty, and old enough to be this girl's mother.

"I have twenty-two years. How old are you?"

"Eighteen. I'll be nineteen next month."

"I got sober at seventeen. It can be done, but it takes work."

"Like, what kind of work?"

"That's a great question, but I'm starving and need to eat. You hungry? Wanna join me for dinner at Café 101?"

She looks sheepishly at her cigarette. "Nah. I'm not really hungry."

"Hmm. You look kinda hungry. And dinner's on me. You sure you don't want to join me? I'm down here visiting from Portland, Oregon. You'll be doing me a favor by saving me from eating at a shitty Hollywood diner alone. You in?"

"What are you doing down here?"

"I lived here for twenty-seven years. I moved up to Portland a couple of years ago. I come down here to see my friends. My history is here. It's good to remember where I come from, and hang out with people who've known me since I had really big eighties hair, wore black lipstick, and smoked like a chimney."

She inspects me from head-to-toe: black cardigan sweater over a black tank top, grey pencil skirt, my favorite red patent-leather pumps and matching purse. "You? You look like some fancy business lady."

I chuckle to myself. *If she only knew.* "I am a fancy business lady...at forty. You should have seen me at fifteen. We'd have hung out and gotten into trouble together. Come on. We can talk about it over bad coffee and French fries."

"I guess I could eat. But I don't have a car."

"Lucky for us, I have an amazing Chevy Aveo rental. It's the tiniest car on the planet but it'll get us where we need to go. Let's hit it."

We park underneath the Best Western on Hollywood Boulevard and the 101 and walk up the stairs to the iconic diner. We nestle into a diarrhea-brown pleather booth in the back and order two coffees to start.

I drink my coffee black. She adds ridiculous amounts of cream and sugar to hers, and bangs the spoon as she stirs. She sets the spoon down and slurps coffee through charcoal-painted lips.

"So, Simone, where are you from?"

She sets the cup down, then traces the rim with fingers coated in chipped-black nail polish. "Oh, you know. Here and there. You?"

"Originally, I'm from Washington, D.C. My mom fell in love when I was eleven and we moved to L.A. I lived here from 1981 until 2008, when I moved up to Portland."

Our waiter, Buster, sidles up to our table. "You kids decide what you want?"

Simone glances over the menu, her brows furrow. "I'm not really hungry."

"Simone, are you vegan or vegetarian?"

"No."

"Buster, can we please have two cheeseburgers and fries. Sides of ranch dressing. A chocolate shake for me and, Simone? Chocolate shake?"

Simone sinks lower into the booth. "Um, sure. Yeah."

"Perfect. Two shakes. Thanks, Buster."

"I don't think I can eat all that."

"Eat what you want. Leave the rest. There's plenty."

Simone takes off her jacket, revealing skeletal arms adorned with chunky, studded bracelets and arms spattered with tattoos.

"Nice ink," I say to her.

"Lady, what do you know about ink?"

I take off my cardigan, displaying two arms adorned with ink from elbows to shoulders. "Quite a bit, actually."

"Whoa, I didn't see that coming."

"People aren't always what they seem, Simone."

She goes quiet and traces the rim of her coffee cup again. Then mumbles, "Don't I know it?"

"Care to elaborate?"

She slumps back into the booth and tilts her head to one side. "Look, lady, what are you? A shrink or something?"

I pause for a moment, letting her tantrum settle. "No. I'm a private detective."

Her eyes grow wide and she perks up. "No shit! For real?"

"Yep. A real-life private dicktress. I started my own agency nine years ago."

"So, you follow cheating assholes around and stuff?"

"No, only if a child is in danger. We do background checks, deal with stalkers, do corporate investigations for embezzlement and workplace violence. Stuff like that."

I break the ice by telling her some of my crazy detective stories. She relaxes, leans into the conversation, and even smiles a few times. At one point, she extends her left forearm out onto the table in front of her. Angry, red gashes slash through much of the skin. She sees me looking at her arm and quickly hides it under the table.

Her spine stiffens, her body goes rigid, and she scowls at me from across the table. "What the fuck are you looking at?"

She's infuriating. And broken. And lost. And I get it so much I want to scream at her to stop being such a brat. But I know better. How many years did I try the tough girl act? I can still get a little ghetto with the best of them, but now is not the time.

I take a swig of coffee, cross my hands with my crimson manicured nails on the table in front of me, and respond. "I'm looking at pain."

She huffs at me from across the table. If she was a hedgehog, this would be the time she curled herself into a ball and disappeared behind prickly stingers meant to keep the world at bay. But all she's got is a leather jacket, a foul mouth, and a shitty glare, none of which scare me nor shield her from much. "What the fuck do you know about pain? What, did you break a fucking nail shopping for that designer bag, or those fucking shoes? I bet you're one of those bitches with Louis Vuitton luggage, too. Just like my mother. All you care about is yourself."

Hurt people hurt people. I repeat this in my mind as she lashes out, throwing verbal barbs at me seeing which ones might stick. None of them do. She has zero idea who I actually am, and is not the first girl to project mom stuff onto me. I've pulled that one more times than I can count. I was just as impossible, probably more so. I give a silent shout-out to the patient souls who listened and guided me through my first couple of years of sobriety.

"Here you go, ladies. Two cheeseburgers, fries, ranch, and ketchup. Need anything else?" asks Buster.

He looks at Simone, who shoots him a death glare.

I beam a huge smile at him. "No, thanks Buster. This is perfect."

After he walks away, I focus my attention back to Simone. I then do what I've done countless times before, with hundreds of young women just like her, and at thousands of meetings. I cut open an emotional vein and bleed openly, in the hope that by baring my pain and shame, it will give her license to feel and survive her own.

I tell her about my childhood, addiction, sexual assaults, and abusive boyfriends. While I talk, she stares at me and digs into the gashes on her left arm with the fingernails of her right hand. When I pause, she stops picking at her skin and shoves a French fry into her mouth. She looks around at the people around us, then whispers, "Aren't you afraid of people hearing this shit?"

I don't break eye-contact with her. "Not one bit."

"Jesus, you've got balls," she says, with a tone close to admiration.

I laugh and slurp the dregs of my milkshake. "Yes. That I do."

She leans in over the table and whispers. "So, guys have hit you?"

"Let's just say I used to have a very bad picker."

"So, guys don't fuck with you anymore? Like, *ever*?" Her tone is one of disbelief.

My chest tightens. When will we stop annihilating our girls? "A man will never lay hands on me again. I don't live that life anymore. Haven't for a very long time."

Her chin drops down to her chest. "I'm so tired of being fucked with. My dad did all sorts of shit to me before he bailed when I was ten. Then I was left with my asshole mother, who blamed me for everything that's ever been fucked in her life. She looks perfect on the outside, but inside, she's vile."

"My grandmother was exactly like that. She passed away a couple of months ago. My family used to jokingly call her Satan."

"That's fucked up."

"Yeah, well. She earned it."

"Is everyone an asshole?"

"Not in the least. There are just a bunch of hurt people walking around who find each other. As you change and heal your damage, you attract different levels of people. There amazing souls in this world, people whose love will take your breath away. Love won't always hurt, Simone."

She clenches her fingers through the top of her hair. "Gah! So, like, what does that even mean? How is life magically not going to be fucked up? What happened to make you change? I mean, why aren't you a puddle on the floor with all the shit you told me? That's crazy."

"I spent years of my life as a puddle, Simone. I eventually got tired of the floor. I didn't know it at the time, but I loved being a victim. I wore it like a cape or a badge of honor. I had three feelings before I got sober: being pissed, being depressed, or being suicidal. Getting loaded as much and as often as possible was how I was able to breathe. Then, when I got sober, I couldn't turn my brain off. My head screamed at me all the time. You're nothing but a piece of shit worthless whore pile of crap who deserves to die."

"I have that voice, too, man. Like on a constant loop. It never goes away."

"We call that K-FUK, the radio station that greets you every morning with nothing but shitty things to say. *Good Morning, loser. I don't even know why you're getting up this morning. It's going to be a miserable day. You might as well just go back to sleep. Or, better yet, why don't you go get loaded then kill yourself?*"

Simone's jaw drops open and her eyebrows raise. "Yes! That's it! I thought I was the only one with that shit in my head."

"No way. We all have that. I gave mine a persona. The asshole in my brain is this lumpy, troll-looking dude with huge bulging eyes, Don King hair, one snaggletooth jutting out from his bulbous purple lips, and he smokes cigars. When he talks, a green, noxious stench billows out of his mouth. When I do stupid stuff, he gets me on all fours on the ground and rides me like a rodeo bull. When I'm in balance, I tell him to fuck off and go about my day."

"So, how did you get sober?"

"I was thrown into a mental institution two days before Christmas. I had this funny drug counselor. Dave. He would tell me, 'Erika, you can't get rid of your problemth by drinking and doing drugth. You have to get thober.' I'd say horrible things to him every chance I got. I was terrified of my feelings, so I lashed out at him to make myself feel better."

"How long were you there for?"

"Three and a half months. I don't know if I could have gotten sober on my own. I needed to be safely removed from my choices. Plus, I had a ton of issues besides alcoholism. I needed extra help.

"I never thought I'd get sober. I didn't even know I wanted to. I couldn't imagine being alive past eighteen. Then one day, when I least expected it, I felt a baby spark of hope that wanted to live. It was enough to keep me moving forward."

"What happened when you got out?"

"I still had to finish high school. Rumors had run rampant about where I'd been. I was dead. I was in prison. I'd run off with a drug dealer and was having his baby. Talk about awkward. And I couldn't hang out with any of my old friends. All we ever did was get loaded together."

"So who did you hang out with? Who did you talk to?"

"I had a few phone numbers and a meeting directory. I went to a ton of meetings because I didn't have anywhere else to go. At each meeting, I heard something that I related to, or met someone who inspired me. I also got a lot of attention from guys, which kept me coming back. Not a great reason to be at meetings, but at least I was there. The pain from my behavior with men made me willing to do the steps."

"But weren't you better by then? I mean, you had over three months clean."

"Getting sober didn't fix me. Alcohol and drugs are just a symptom. I am and will always be my biggest problem, and harshest critic. There's a reason I drank. I *needed* obliteration. Without drugs and alcohol, I felt like a raw, gaping wound."

"And you never relapsed?"

I knock three times on the Formica table. "Not yet."

"Did you ever want to? I mean, do you ever think about it?"

I laugh. "If I had a nickel for every time I've thought about relapsing, I could retire. It hardly occurs to me anymore. I know it won't fix it. The only way to deal with pain and life is go directly through it."

"How do you not get loaded?"

"Initially, I played tricks with my head. I'd tell myself I could get loaded tomorrow, but not today. The urge to get loaded always passes. So much of staying sober is just riding the wave. That's why they say one day at a time. Sometimes an hour. Or a minute. Look at a clock. You can stay sober for sixty seconds. Just breathe.

"Another thing I did was tell someone when I was thinking about it. I had a sponsor who told me I was as sick as my secrets, and anything I didn't share I got to keep. She said if I walked around smiling all the time and telling everyone I was fine, the festering stuff inside me would get worse."

"And that's it?"

"I watched people who relapsed. Listened to them when they came crawling back in. They always said the same stuff. They kept secrets, didn't share, didn't do the work. I paid very close attention. I've never seen anyone skip back into a meeting after a relapse. They always look hollow, and it gets harder every time to make it back. A lot of them never do."

"You've seen people, like, die and stuff?"

I get quiet. The list of lost souls is endless. "My first year, twenty people I knew died. Suicide. OD. Drunk driving. AIDS. That part of recovery is never easy."

She takes a huge bite of cheeseburger and chews slowly, looking at me with skepticism. "And even through all of that, you've never had a single sip or a puff of anything? Nothing?"

I laugh. "Nope. Nada."

"And you just go to meetings, talk, and here you are?"

"It's a combination of things. Meetings are important. They're where I learned there are other people like me, that I'm not an alien. Service changed my life—not thinking about myself all the time. But I also needed to work with a sponsor. I needed to tell one person everything, no matter what. They took me through the steps. Each facet of recovery is okay on its own, but when you put them all together, magic."

She eats another fry, a contemplative look on her face.

"There's one other trick that kept me sober when I was really fucked and ready to kill myself."

"What?"

"I'd picture the little-girl version of me sitting in the middle of a room, naked, with my knees pulled up to my chest. In a circle around me were all the men who took my innocence and trust. Hungry eyes watched me as they touched themselves, moved in closer. Their taunts overlapped in whispers. *Haha, Erika. We got you. You're our good little girl.* I knew if I gave up, they'd win. They'd own me. Not only would they have stolen my childhood, but my future as well.

"In that moment, it didn't matter how awful or hopeless I felt, I knew I couldn't give up, no matter what."

"And it was that easy?"

"I don't know from easy, Simone, in or out of sobriety. What does easy even look like? Every good thing I have in life is something I busted my ass for. That's what makes it worthwhile. Having someone hand everything to me would be boring."

Simone takes her right hand and traces her lips with her fingertips. "Hmm."

"My first two years were insane. I stayed sober by the skin of my teeth. I bounced from one terrible mistake to the next. When I needed them most, these incredible teachers showed up."

"What kind of teachers?"

"People who gave me enough faith to take one more step, stay sober one more day. Some of them kicked my ass into a state of willingness. Not all teachers gave me gold stars and tickles. Some of them kicked my teeth in, figuratively speaking."

"I don't fucking know if I can do this. I mean, stay sober and feel all this shit. I'm not even sure I want to."

"Why do you have seventeen days?"

Simone furrows her eyebrows and scrunches up her lips. "Hmm. Well, partly to get my mom off my back. She told me I had to get clean or she'd kick me out. I don't have a job. Money. Friends. I didn't know what else to do."

"So, are you only staying clean for your mom, or is there a part of you that wants to stop getting loaded just for you?"

Simone doesn't scowl, fidget, or look away. After a long moment of silence, she responds, "I've wanted to stop for a long time, but I don't know how. I hate my life. I hate who I've become. I feel lost all the fucking time."

"I know exactly how you feel."

"And I'm tired. The stuff I do to get what I need...it's not right."

"What we do is not who we are."

"Easy for you to say."

"Simone, I've lied, cheated, and stolen. I've sold myself. I've hurt so many people, including myself. You are going to fuck up countless times in your life. That's what you're here for. Life's messy. Get dirty. Roll around in it. *Learn.* This isn't about *not* making mistakes. It's about owning them, trying to clean up your mess as best you can, and moving along to make new ones. If you're making the same mistakes every year, you're missing it."

Her tough girl veneer cracks like a porcelain doll. Tears perch on rims of kohl eyeliner, ready to dive into the pasty sea of her cheeks. "You swear it gets better?"

"I promise you on everything I hold dear, yes. Life is worth living, worth fighting for. I can also promise you that shame will corrode the best parts of you if you let it. What happened to us as kids is not our fault. What we do with it as adults is entirely up to us."

"Damn, Erika, I have no idea what to say to all of that."

"You don't have to say anything. Just do something, preferably something different. If you keep doing what you've always done, you'll keep getting what you've always gotten. You have nothing to lose by doing the work. Try it. See how it goes. If everything is still the same after, go back out. Drugs and alcohol certainly aren't going anywhere.

"But maybe, just maybe, something will change. I never expected to still be here, yet here I am. If this weren't better at least most of the time, I wouldn't still be here. I'd have given up long ago."

Buster strolls up to the table. "Can I get you ladies anything else?"

"Simone, you want anything else?"

Simone shakes her head.

"Nope, just the check please. Thanks."

Buster walks away, and I throw a fresh napkin at Simone. "You might want to wipe your face there, softie. You look like Blondie having a very bad day."

Simone looks at me blankly.

"Blondie. The singer."

"Who?"

"*Heart of Glass? Call Me? Atomic?*"

"Nuh uh."

"Oh my God. She's one of the greatest rock n' roll female icons ever. How about The Cure? Bauhaus? Depeche Mode?"

Simone shakes her head at all of them.

I can feel at least one ovary wilting, possibly both. "YouTube them. Eighties music is life. David Bowie?"

"The old guy?"

"Oof. Them's fightin' words. Bowie holds the fabric of the universe together. Remember that."

She laughs. "You gotta pen so I can make a note of that?"

I chuckle. "Okay, smartass. One day, when Green Day and Radiohead are playing on oldies radio, and you start singing about being an American idiot, and some youngster doesn't know what you're singing and probably wasn't born when that song came out, I want you to remember this exact moment."

Simone laughs at me. "Must be rough getting old."

"Keep it up, funny girl." I throw a fry across the table at her.

She catches it and eats it.

"Come on. Let's hit it. I'll drive you home."

Simone puts on her leather jacket, reaches into an inside pocket, and retrieves her cigarettes and lighter. "I'm going to pop out for a smoke. Meet you by the car." She slips out of the booth and walks outside.

I watch her slight frame amble across the restaurant. Fierce. Frail. Beautiful. *Please watch over her, and give her the courage she needs.*

I pay the check, then meet Simone at the car. During the short drive to her house, she stays quiet in the passenger seat and looks out the window. By the time I park in front of her mother's Hollywood Hills bungalow, she's a storm cloud.

"How are you feeling?" I ask her.

"Sad. Fucked up. Scared. I don't know." She plays with the six piercings in her left ear.

"Okay. Look around us. Is anyone physically attacking us?"

Simone looks around the quiet street lined with palm trees and luxury vehicles. "No."

"Have you eaten? Do you have cigarettes in your pocket?"

"Yes."

"A place to sleep tonight?"

"Yeah. I mean my mom's a total bitch, but yeah. I have a place to sleep."

"So, in this actual moment, you're okay, yes?"

"Well, if you put it like that, yeah."

"And look. Here's another new moment. How about this one? You still okay?"

"Obviously, yes." I can hear the inner *duh* as she rolls her eyes.

"This moment is perfect. It's when we take our shame and regret from yesterday, and mix it with terror of tomorrow, that we destroy these perfect moments. When you're overwhelmed and have no idea what to do, look at your feet, count to ten, and breathe. This is where you are. This is the only moment you need to be in. Just breath."

She looks over at me, then down at her hands folded in her lap. "Thanks for spending so much time with me tonight, and for dinner and stuff. I really had you pegged all wrong."

"People will surprise the hell out of you if you let them. That's part of the fun." I scribble my number on a piece of paper and hand it to her. "I'm in Portland, but I come down here at least every other month. Text. Call. Skype. Whatever. I'm always here if you need me."

"Thanks." She gets out of the car and disappears into the house.

I feel spent, raw, and eternally grateful. This was not what I imagined as a good time when I first got sober. *Thank you, HP, for every glorious moment of this life.*

A couple of weeks go by and I don't hear from her. I wonder. I worry. I send a silent prayer out to the universe. Then one day, my phone rings.

"This is Erika." I answer.

There's a long pause. Breathing. "Hey, Erika. It's Simone."

"I'm so glad you called." I smile.

til the end of time

October 21, 2016

Back in Barcelona, my spiritual home. One day, I'll sell my company and buy a villa in the countryside ripe with bougainvillea and lemon trees. I'll write, cook, and paint, surrounded by music and animals.

Once a week, I'll take a train into town. I'll shop in open-air markets, visit museums, wriggle my toes in the Mediterranean Sea. I'll wear loose linen garments accented with brightly-colored scarves.

Perhaps I'll take a lover, and we'll bask in the afternoon heat, tracing each other's bodies with our fingertips. We'll feed each other warm figs. I'll cook paella. Make olive bread from scratch. Drink strong espresso.

Today, I'm in a rented flat in El Born, my favorite neighborhood. It's ten in the morning. I sit at a table and chair on a second-floor balcony and sip from a giant cup of tea. I should be writing, but I'm distracted by the church bells from Santa Marie del Mar.

The city beckons me to leave the isolation of my writing and join the bustle of Barcelona. I throw on jeans, a cream sweater, and black sandals. It's brisk out, so I wrap my oversized crimson scarf around my neck and put on matching lipstick. Now I'm ready for a date with my beloved city.

I exit the flat and turn left, walk past the church, and head towards the Barcelona Cathedral. I pass gypsies shaking cups of Euros at passing tourists. Shrunken old women, hunched over with age, are accompanied by loving companions. Children laugh and chase each other through the narrow alleyways. Shop owners lift metal doors and ready their stores to open, each one a mini museum for its wares. Groups of old Spanish men sit at outdoor cafes, dressed in black, cheeks flushed with alcohol and humor. They talk, laugh, and debate in Catalan.

An old man with bloodshot eyes and blotchy red cheeks sits on a bench. He takes swigs from a green bottle wrapped in a brown-paper bag, and tosses pieces of a baguette to dozens of small green parrots and pigeons flocking around him. He yells at me in Catalan as I walk by. I smile and keep walking.

I arrive at the cathedral, one of my favorite buildings anywhere. I must have been a devout Catholic in another life. Gothic shrines of devotion never cease to move me. I walk down to the crypt of Saint Eulalia, a thirteen-year-old girl murdered by the Romans. Although they subjected her to thirteen forms of torture, one for each year of her life, her faith never wavered. The spirit of children astounds me.

I leave the church and stop at a local café. I eat a croissant, enjoying every buttery, carb-filled bite.

A reminder pops up on my phone. Today is the three-year anniversary of my father's death. My life has come full-circle.

I reconnected with him shortly before he died. I interviewed him, recorded his stories. I was amazed at our similarities. We both barely slept, we devoured books, we traveled the world alone, flew private planes, were entrepreneurs. We both smoked four packs of cigarettes a day, and both quit cold turkey at the same age. Both intensely stubborn.

From the power of genetics alone, I am so much like him—minus the fascism. I left him in peace. He died less than two months later. I knew my father for nine days.

As I stood over his ashes, I realized he'd been right all those years ago. I didn't need him. I had Pop-Pop, who was the best father I could have asked for. I sent out a silent prayer of thanks to Dad for being exactly the father I needed him to be—absent.

When I returned home from his funeral, I looked through old journals, poems, and stories I'd written. My writing stopped abruptly after I met him. For eighteen years, I'd silenced the voice inside of me. It was time to let her out.

Three years ago, I wrote one chapter. Then another. Digging through the mire of memory, I unburied pieces of my history. Like a mummy unraveling layers of decrepit, dusty bandages, today I stand nearly naked in the center of my life. With clean eyes and an open heart, I can now see the valuablue lessons I've learned along the way.

His abandonment taught me loyalty. Being abused as a child taught me resilience. Making huge mistakes, and living with their consequences, has taught me compassion. I am who I am because of where I come from. I have to embrace all parts of me, not just the pretty ones.

Life is beautiful. I thank all my teachers.

I am forty-six, single, with no children. I have not found a partner, and perhaps I never will. But I found myself, and that's everything.

A look up and see this sign on the wall next to where I sit.

"Puedo cambiarme a mí mismo. A los demás solo puedo amarles."

I can change myself. Others I can only love. ~ Unknown

r o a r

January 20, 2017—Washington, D.C.

The idea for ROAR came to me in a dream last September before I left for Spain. I woke up to a nagging poke between my eyes. *Do this. Do this now.* I started my detective agency the same way. I accepted an idea from the universe, then honored, cradled, and nurtured it.

Excited, I ran the idea for ROAR by a friend. She was less than enthusiastic. *ROAR. Eww. Something about that word just offends me. And do you really think you can start your own show? And seriously, what would be the point? There are so many other storytelling shows. Why would anyone want to come to yours?*

Critical women are home to me. I recognize them as family and invite them in to my dearest spaces. I made her opinion more valuable than my own and somberly tucked ROAR away into my hope chest, right next to the idea of finishing this book.

I don't blame her in the slightest. Her doubts fed my own internal critic, and gave me permission to give up before I could fail. After the crash of 2009, and the loss of much of what I'd built professionally, my confidence was shaken. I had forgotten what I'm made of.

I spent most of October in Barcelona, visiting friends and working on a book I was convinced I could not finish.

A week after I came home, a schism ripped through this country—dividing husbands and wives, parents and children, siblings, neighbors, and friends. Like countless others, I felt powerless, hopeless, furious, and devastated.

With pink hat in hand, I return home to D.C., where my passion for life and justice began. My friend and I make our way through throngs of people. Indigenous People. Black Lives Matter. The Water Protectors. The older activists, still in the fight after decades of dedication. Young friends on their first protest together. LGBTQ. Muslims, Christians, Jews, and Secularists standing together. Men holding their small daughters on their shoulders. Sons standing with their mothers. I am moved to tears by the unity of this country. These big beautiful voices infuse me with hope.

I pass countless inspirational signs. One sign stops me in my tracks.

WE ARE THE ONES WE'VE BEEN WAITING FOR. A quote from June Jordan, it demands my immediate courage. I can't wait for someone else to show up and do the work I am here to do. I must honor the drive inside of me, despite my fear.

The power of one sentence, and millions of people coming together worldwide, reminds me who I am and what I'm doing here. The future is female, and I am hungry for the loving, fierce, compassionate, and courageous sounds of women's voices.

We will not stay silent. We do not whisper. We ROAR.

about the author

If you've made it this far, thank you! I appreciate you coming on this journey with me. You can find out more about me through the following links:

www.erikaworth.com
www.facebook.com/erikalworth/
https://twitter.com/spygal

You can find out more about ROAR at:

www.roarvoices.com

If you feel so inclined, please add a short review on Amazon and/or Goodreads.

acknowledgments

First and foremost, thank you Momma. I burst into your life unexpected, and upended your whole world. Thank you for the endless sacrifices you made raising me on your own. I know this process has been challenging for you. Thank you for loving me anyway, and for holding me together when I got lost along the way.

To Carol Horwath Fischbach, there is no way I would have completed this without you. Your love, wisdom, insight, and talent were my guiding light. A million thanks. It's your turn now. ;)

To Jonna Ivin, for years of friendship, and for showing me this was even possible. Thank you for always telling me like it is.

To my writing groups, thank you for countless hours of reading, critiquing, and editing these stories. I'm so grateful to have found my people. A very special thank you to my ladies: Andi, Jessie, and Kim (alphabetical, FYI – I love you each to pieces). You're some of the greatest people I've ever known, and it means so much to be on this journey with you.

To Linda Stirling, for telling me I could actually do this, and for all of your help and support.

To Shawna, Jeff, and Stacey—my friends of 30+ years and counting. Your love means more to me today than ever before. Thank you for trudging this road with me.

To Dr. B for hearing me. You saved my life.

To Drewski (aka the Van God), thank you for being such a decent man and incredible friend.

To Kelly, your honesty saved my life. Thank you for inviting me into the league of kickass women.

To Melissa, for loving me through some of the worst years of my life. Thank you, and Riccola. ;)

To Java, they just don't make them better than you. xoxo

To Leslie (ESSL), for your spirit, your belief in me, and decades of friendship. I love you.

To Scott Clarke, for being my ride or die friend and helping me bring my visions to life. Thank you.

To Espere, I carry your heart with me. I carry it in my heart. Esperika for life.

To Deb, I will never be able to put into words how much I love you and how much your support means to me. You fill my heart, and I'm lucky to know you.

To Zoe (Little Petal), you are an eternal gift in my life.

To Reema, for your friendship and guidance, and for being a voice I can hear above the din in my brain.

To Bill, Bob, and mutual friends too many to mention, I love you. You make life worth living.

To Cheri—my midnight writing buddy and endless source of support. Thank you for everything. You're the bomb dot com.

To Dawn, for clearing the dust and chaos and bringing the sunshine. I love you.

To Tom Koos, thank you for the use of the greatest writing cabin ever. And many thanks for the unwavering support (and goodie deliveries). You are a gem!

To all the Ladies of ROAR, it is an honor to know each of you. Thank you for your courage, vulnerability, and your beautiful voices. You are a constant source of inspiration. I couldn't do any of this without you.

To Oprah, I only believed I could do anything because I saw you do it first. Thank you for the light.

To the many angels who are no longer with me, thank you for inspiring me, loving me, and reminding me how precious this life is. I promise to always do my best.